What a Long Strange It's Been

BY

Dr. Jeffrey W. Neal

D1412327

DORRANCE PUBLISHING CO
EST. 1920
PITTSBURGH, PENNSYLVANIA 15238

Dorrance Publishing Co
585 Alpha Drive
Suite 103
Pittsburgh, PA 15238
Visit our website at *www.dorrancebookstore.com*

ISBN: 978-1-6853-7170-8
eISBN: 978-1-6853-7713-7

CONTENTS

INTRODUCTION

After fifty years in classroom and winning numerous district and state instructional awards, I have arrived at a didactic conclusion. Great teachers are not born. They are created by a series of events, some good, some bad, and a few qualify as sad. These occurrences present themselves along the path to educational excellence or destruction if that be the case. Analogous to a pedagogical maze, these incidents that display themselves during an instructor's formative years either help to mold the teacher into a fine-tuned instructional machine or break the person in but a matter of three years. Sadly, the teaching profession loses one of every three instructors within the first three years. Those who survive this engaging period of employment rise to navigate the maze, meeting challenges at every corner and continue to grow exponentially as each obstacle is overcome.

This memoir exemplifies the successful maneuvers one has to accomplish as he or she works through the obstructions met along the educational career path. As you read this extremely interesting saga, you will experience precisely what it takes to become a great teacher. You will laugh with the author and you will cry as well, but you will emerge from having read it with a feeling of joy, for the book is a celebration of a life in education written by one of the coolest persons whom I have ever met, Dr. Jeff Neal.

Thomas Tufts

Teacher/Educational Consultant/Author of *The Night Before Middle School* and *Fruit and VegeFables*. Tom is still teaching English after fifty years at Conniston Middle School in Palm Beach County, Florida.

PREFACE

When you really want to understand something, one should write about it. Writing forces you to grapple with the subject and allows you to come to terms with whatever is on your mind. I spent thirty-four years at Lake Worth Community Middle School (LWCMS). It is located in Lake Worth Beach, Florida. As for that city, the locals call it L-Dub. This school was my one and only site as an educator. I earned a doctorate, just before retirement, with plans of being an adjunct professor. Then this respiratory virus, named after a Mexican beer, surfaced just as I was leaving my life's work. Instead of boldly going where I haven't gone before, I was quarantined in lockdown. All of my former colleagues were going off to battle on a new frontier in education, teaching in a pandemic.

I wanted to make sense of what happened during the last three decades, and so I began to write. I believe there is a story to tell when looking back at my career. Teacher, coach, counselor, and administrator were the hats I wore at LWCMS. There was a critical incident at our school in 2000. That's a technical name for a school shooting. As hard as it was to put that part of the odyssey on paper, it did help me to write about it. It was a catharsis on some level. It's hard to take the time when you're working to examine what you were thinking and feeling at a time that has passed. I finally interviewed myself, asking questions that were unuttered at the time. To remember the journey that was not just a job but an adventure was a crucial mental exercise. To remember the names, events, and conversations was challenging. The dialogues are as close as I can get through recall. As for students in certain cases, the names were changed to protect the innocent. These are my recollections of a life spent in school. When I was hired that summer of 1985, a good friend of mine, a brother from another mother, named Troy Durand congratulated me and said, "I hope that school's your ticket." I bought the ticket and took the ride.

CHAPTER ONE
"THE POWER OF A MILKSHAKE"

To be the son of a principal and a student at his school is never easy. To further compound this misfortune, I was the lucky recipient of attention deficit hyperactivity disorder (ADHD). This was in the days before they labeled this affliction. My dad, M. Wayne Neal, was the principal of Central Elementary. The school was in Hampton Township outside of Pittsburgh. My teachers would never have dreamed that I would become an educator. Looking back, I marvel at my journey as a student and then as an educator. What a long strange it's been. Those of you of a certain age may think I omitted the word "trip" from a Grateful Dead song. I will explain that later when I tell you about a gift I received from a rather drug-addled student. In 1972, I was in the throes of (ADHD) with my left leg furiously pumping in a fourth-grade English class of a former nun, Miss Carroll. For some reason she thought it necessary to march me down to my dad's office for a reprimand. This led Dad to ash out his cigarette and get the large set of keys from the wall. "Let's make sure this never happens again," he said. He opened the locker behind his desk that concealed a work of art in the form of a wooden paddle. It was complete with aerodynamic air holes to allow the highest degree of pain for the sting. This punitive practice all Baby Boomers remember was known as Corporal Punishment.

The sound of air whistling through the tiny holes in the instant just before contact is unmistakable. At impact it can best be described as a crack. An entire class would jump in their seats, simultaneously, if the "swats" occurred outside of the door. That day as the wood made contact, I quickly put my hand back to avert the next whack. Dad bellowed, "Move that hand or I'll hit it and you don't want that, young man!" I didn't want any of it. I moved my hand as the second one hit with even more pain. This time I decided to keep my hand back there. Surely, some inkling of paternal love would stop this. The warning to move my hand was repeated. I stood my ground. Not a recommended practice as the wood, like a ball of fire, created a throbbing red beet out of my small palm.

This is no diatribe against M. Wayne for child abuse. On the contrary, my cantankerous behavior caused me to have many swats. I deserved most of them. As my fifth-grade year ended, Dad and my mom, Kathryn, decided to move twenty-five miles north of Hampton to Penn Township outside of the steel town of Butler. It was a bucolic, Norman Rockwell-like community. In their infinite wisdom they decided to retain me to give me a year to mature. They mistakenly thought, without the pressure of being the principal's son, I might start to behave. They didn't factor in the undiagnosed ADHD and the astrological influences of being a Cancer born with the Moon in Aries. A dangerous cocktail both physiologically and astrologically.

Perhaps, my opus of deviant behavior occurred at Penn Elementary. I detested being in Ms. Beikert's math class and took any opportunity to get out of that numerical hell. One day I raised my hand to go to the restroom. This act had benefits that were two-fold. For one, I was free from arithmetic, and for another, I was able to walk around. It was impossible to sit still. I am not sure what spirit leapt into my soul and caused me to perform those recalcitrant acts that day. I made my way to the bathroom. The urinals were the tall porcelain type that stood four feet high. It seemed like a good idea to take out a roll of paper towels and jam then around the bottom of the drains. Once I had them properly blocked, I pumped each one to overflow. Not content with just the urinals, I packed each toilet in the stalls stuffing them with paper. I proceeded to flush until the water filled like huge porcelain goblets about to overflow. I realized I'd gone too far as the flood of water gathered together on the floor and proceeded to enter the hallway like a tsunami.

You would think this act of vandalism would have been enough to satisfy my desire for insolence. I was just getting warmed up. Gazing into the cafeteria, I saw the sixth-grade chorus singing to their parents. This was a ceremony held each year for the sixth-grade class who was moving on to junior high. For all intents and purposes, it was a mini-graduation.

My devious mind began to work. I knew there were no windows in the cafeteria. There was a huge switch to shut off all power leaving the room in total darkness. What a perfect way to put the entire class, along with parents and teachers, in a moment of panic and chaos. As water spewed from the bathroom, I pulled the switch down. Immediately, high-pitched screams emanated from the cafeteria. The following day I was summoned to the principal's office to see Mr. Molloy. He had gotten to know me and had used his paddle several times in an attempt to get me to conform to the rules. As I walked into his office, I put forth my best effort to look confused.

"Sit down, Jeff."

"Okay," I answered.

"I know you flooded the bathroom yesterday. I also know that you cut the power off in the cafeteria during the sixth-grade graduation." I shrugged and began removing the papers from my back pocket, anticipating my rendezvous with his thick paddle.

"What are you doing?' he asked.

"You got me, Mr. Molloy."

"Sit down. I'm not going to paddle you."

"Okay," I said, relieved that the sting wasn't coming.

"If you can manage to behave yourself for two weeks and I don't hear your name from one teacher, I will take you to the Dairy Queen for a milkshake. What do you say?"

"Will you take me out of Ms. Beikert's class?"

"Yes," he smiled. "I will take you out of her class if you are able to hold up your end of the deal." We shook hands, and he didn't let go right away. "Behave yourself!" he commanded in an authoritative tone. Somehow, I found the inner strength to resist getting into trouble. After the two-week probation, Mr. Molloy's tanned, lived-in face appeared in Ms. Beikert's class. He whispered something to her and she smiled. On the way to the Dairy Queen, I felt elated. The whistling sound from the holes of the paddle were familiar to my ears every now and again, but not nearly as BM (Before Milkshake). This intervention from Mr. Molloy combined with a love of basketball was a recipe to keep me on the straight and narrow path to graduation.

I did keep up with some antics in school, enough to be in the running for the dubious honor of Class Clown my senior year in 1981 at Knoch High School in Saxonburg, Pennsylvania. It was a good thing not to be the class clown as I thought it was akin to being the "village idiot." Saxonburg was originally a farming colony founded by Joseph A. Roebling. He invented the wire cable, first used to raise canal boats over the Allegheny Mountains, and furthermore, conjured up the Brooklyn Bridge in the 1880s. My senior year I was having a pretty good season on the basketball team averaging 14 points per game when I broke my arm. Both the radius and ulna snapped in half. If you ever experience that type of pain, your brain will do a wonderful job of protecting you from the agony. You can actually feel it pump endorphins. I looked in amazement at my arm dangling with no real sense of discomfort. Suddenly, as the pumping stopped, pain reared its ugly head. Only morphine in my shoulder and Demerol in my thigh alleviated the suffering. I woke up later with a huge cast while still in my uniform.

The handful of Division 2 colleges that had expressed interest sent me a handful of what can only be described as break-up letters. M. Wayne suggested that I go to a community college, being that no colleges were banging on my door and I had a meager "C" average academically. My fellow classmates were going to four-year institutions while I reported I was attending Butler County Community College (BC3). It was a fortuitous decision. Pursuing my Associates Degree in Liberal Arts and playing basketball, I was not exposed to the party scene of a four-year institution. With my Scotch-Irish heritage, I had more than an inclination to enjoy the early '80s party scene. In the second year at BC3, a coach contacted me from the State University of New York, at Fredonia. I enrolled. This school is located on Lake Erie about 50 miles southwest of Buffalo. I unwisely thought I could withstand the cold of upstate New York. What I didn't factor was the arctic blasts coming out of Canada across the lake with bitter winds. One morning I had the imprudent idea to walk to class in -67 degrees. It wasn't that far, I rationalized. The cold literally seared into my bones. I couldn't get my fingers apart until I placed them on a heater.

I had to choose a major. The courses that interested me were philosophy and psychology. I ran it by M. Wayne that I was contemplating being a philosophy major. "Really," he scoffed, "I bet there is a large job market for that. Perhaps, you can put on a white robe and get up in a tree and have them pay you for telling what the meaning of life is." He had a point.

Many people encouraged me to go into sales. I probably could sell ice to Eskimos, but the dog-eat-dog world of business held little appeal. A counselor mentioned education. There's no way I could be a teacher. M. Wayne and all my teachers couldn't fathom it. Any teachers who were deceased would be spinning in their graves. I recalled a teacher in high school, Mr. D'Antonio, telling me that I would become a teacher and get my payback.

For some reason, I started to think seriously about majoring in education. In the mid-80s, teaching was still a revered profession. Unlike, today in 2020, where it is hard to get students to enter education and the ones that do come into the fold often are disenchanted and usually stay two or three years at the most. At that time there was real competition to get a teaching job. I was encouraged to go the elementary route because there would be a better chance of landing employment. So, I opted to major in elementary and the state of New York offered a junior high endorsement. This meant that you could specialize in a subject area and teach up to eighth grade. I took an immense number of credits in English at BC3. I could take three classes and have my concentration in English, or I could take seven courses and have one in history. I naturally chose the path of least resistance.

The basketball experience didn't work out. I rarely played my junior year, so I opted to just enjoy my senior year. It was a fun college town that was in the *Guinness Book of World Records* for having the most bars per capita than any town in America. I passed my courses and began to student teach. I preferred the junior high experience. It takes a special person to teach elementary. I always correct an elementary teacher who says, "I only teach elementary." It's the foundation, and without good teachers in those formative years, education is in trouble. It is a serendipitous tale how I ended up in sunny South Florida. One Saturday I received a call from Jeryl whom I carpooled with during student teaching. That particular morning, I was nursing the aftermath of a party. A tiny miner was tapping methodically on my brain with a sharp pickaxe. Jeryl was excited about a teacher recruitment day at Buffalo State University that morning. State University of New York schools have an excellent reputation for education majors, and it was a recruiting hotbed. School districts from across the nation were present.

"I will pick you up in an hour," Jeryl said.

"No thanks. I'm going to sleep 'til noon," I said with that miner still chiseling the pickaxe on my brain. As I hung up the phone, I crawled into the fetal position. My conscience started to prick me. Whenever I would sleep in as a kid, Dad would appear in the doorway of my room, particularly, if he knew I was out carousing the night before. "Productive people are out of bed by this hour," he would bellow. If I was really slow to move, he would quip. "You are the laziest person that God ever put breath into." That one was always uplifting.

Thinking of Dad's words, I found myself calling Jeryl back. As I showered and shaved, I was unaware of a chance meeting that would transpire in the men's room that would alter the path of my life for the next thirty-four years. Every education major in the SUNY school system must have been there. They looked nervous as they made their way into the vast auditorium looking for employment. Over seven hundred school districts from all over the country were in search of high-quality teachers. After my trek in the negative sixty-seven degrees. I was going to interview somewhere that didn't have winter. I started to look at school districts in California and Hawaii. The prospect of moving that far away felt dismaying. Florida! I had never been to the Sunshine State. I got in line for the Polk County School District. Providence had a stranger come up to me who said, "Do you want to work in Florida?"

"Yes," I replied, "like to be near a beach."

"You don't want to live in Polk County. Where you want to interview is Palm Beach County." He pointed to a line that had at least fifty people waiting their turn. Three tables were set up with recruiters. I thanked the stranger. Conversations in line centered around how nice it would be to live in West Palm Beach. Spending winter in the sun by the ocean and not enduring arctic blasts out of Canada sounded good to me. Finally, a tan guy with dark hair motioned me to the table. I heard the words I didn't want to hear.

"Do you teach Math or Science?" he asked.

"No, English," I replied.

"Sorry. We're only taking Math and Science teachers." This was something I feared. All I kept hearing from my professors was that there is a shortage of teachers in those two subject areas. I walked away. I dropped a couple of resumes at some New York school districts in Syracuse and Utica. I needed to piss. In walks the tan guy from Palm Beach. I glanced over not wanting to turn my head too much, which is standard behavior in a men's room. Thinking this might be my last chance, I decided to break protocol and speak to someone next to you with a penis in his hand.

"I was wondering if you had any opportunities in Palm Beach County for someone who can coach?" He raised an eyebrow and looked my way as he zipped his pants up. I was probably one of a thousand faces he'd seen that day.

"What would you coach?' he asked with the faintest hint of a smile as he moved to the sink and washed his hands.

"Basketball," I said emphatically.

"Basketball, huh? I used to coach round ball. Let's go to the table and see what we might have for you." My heart leapt as I followed him. Most districts were packing up their materials and exiting for chicken wings, the staple of Buffalo cuisine. "Did you play college ball?" he asked. I told him my history with BC3 and the one year at Fredonia. He seemed more interested in basketball than he did teaching. He had coached at a junior high. Finally, he asked, "What subject area do you teach?"

"English," I said. "It has to be junior high, though?"

"Hey, do we have any openings for an English teacher in junior high?" he asked one of the attractive ladies that flanked him that day. She looked through a stack of papers before replying, "Only one is Lake Worth Junior High."

"Well, I'll be," he replied, "good ole Lake Worth Junior. Do you want an interview?"

"Yes!" I said exuberantly.

"I do have one question," he said, leaning forward. "Are you ready to pull up stakes and move to another state? It's a big decision." I thought for a moment at what he asked. The memory of that freezing weather in my bones came back, and I answered, "Absolutely."

"Good luck in your interview. My name is Randy Stewart," he said, shaking my hand. I graduated shortly thereafter with a Bachelor of Science in Education.

CHAPTER TWO
"WHERE THE TROPICS BEGIN"

That summer I purchased my first car, a Green 1977 Mercury Monarch for a whopping $3,000. Dad gave his friend, Gerry Goga, all of the cash up front with the stipulation that I would pay him in monthly installments. "Nothing in this world comes for free," he told me as he handed me the keys. "You'll pay me back when you get a job."

"Yes," I replied, thinking he could have offered the car as a graduation present. I started the drive to Florida. I was so wired on adrenaline, excitement, and coffee that I drove the entire 1,200 miles straight through. A quarter pounder and one of McDonald's good cups of black coffee fueled me the entire trip. At the city limits the sign read, "Lake Worth, Where the Tropics Begin." That sounded pretty nice. It was getting dark when I checked into the Howard Johnson's, across the Robert A. Harris Bridge, that leads to A1A and Lake Worth Beach. That night I barely slept. I got out of bed a little before 7:00 a.m. and walked to the beach. The sun was just over the horizon and the water had a salmon hue that danced like orange diamonds. The salt water tasted good on my lips. I waded out just past where the waves were breaking and said a prayer for help to get the job. The pastor of the church I grew up in, Ken Hall, once told me, "Be careful what you pray for, you just might get it."

I found my way to Lake Worth Junior High. The school, originally Lake Worth High, was built in the 1955. It was open air with pods. In the main office, I had that familiar, discomforting feeling when the secretary said that the "principal will see you now." Waiting inside was the principal, an English teacher, and a bear of a man with a full beard who had this countenance of wisdom. His name was Charles "Coach" Owen. The principal, Mr. Jenkins, asked most of the questions. The English teacher, Ms. Ricketts, asked a literary-focused question. "If you were going to have your students read literature, what book would you choose?" She had a tough school-maid energy.

"Without a doubt I would have them read "The Outsiders" by S.E. Hinton. It touches on the very heart of the differences in our society in the experience of youth. The fact that the author wrote the book when she was sixteen enabled her to translate the feelings of universal angst adolescents experience out of the human condition. It's one book that once a kid picks up, they will read it front to back." Not really sure where I pulled that answer from, but I was feeling confident. Throughout the whole interview Coach Owen said nothing. He just lit one cigarette after another and drank coffee out of a bowl-sized mug. I looked over at his scrutinizing eyes behind that blue smoke, with the thick, bushy eyebrows that gave him the look of an Old Testament prophet.

"Would you say you have a sense of humor?" he asked, finally breaking his silence with a rough and gravelly voice. I thought for a moment. Should I tell them I was up for the accolade of village idiot? I decided to go for it. "I was in the running for class clown in high school," I said hesitantly. They smiled and relief swept over me.

Coach took a drag on his cigarette, "Do you like kids?"

"I like kids a lot," I said.

"Good, because if you get hired you better like kids and you damn sure better have a sense of humor. Being a teacher here is like joining the Peace Corps."

"Do you have any more interviews?" the principal asked as he stood up. For some unknown reason my instinct was to palter that I had another interview. I had noticed another local junior high that had the controversial name of Jefferson Davis.

"Yes, I have an interview at Jefferson Davis," I said.

"Well good luck to you, young man," Jenkins said. "We'll call you in a few days when we make our decision. Thank you for coming." I shook hands with all three and walked out of the office. The Monarch sat in the morning sun. It felt like a sauna as I opened the door. When I touched the blistering steering wheel, I decided to step out of the car to disperse the heat. As I pondered if I made a foolish decision to say I had another interview, around the corner came the principal.

"Jeff, hold on," he said as he came to my car. "I'm glad I caught you. We are going to offer you the position."

"Really!" I exclaimed.

"Absolutely, we think you would be a wonderful addition to the Warrior Family." Mr. Jenkins was the first person to make reference to the Warrior Family as it is known.

"Thank you so much!" I said, being unable to stop my smile. I followed him back to the office and got my first taste of the bureaucracy of education. I spent the afternoon filling out forms and trying to find the District Office that was on Belvedere Road near the Palm Beach Airport. I was told to report to work in August for pre-school. I stopped at a phone booth and called my parents. Cell phones were nonexistent.

"That's so wonderful, Jeff. We are so proud of you!" Mom exclaimed before handing the phone to M. Wayne. "Well, even a blind squirrel finds a nut once in a while," he quipped. Even with his dour comment, I knew deep inside he was proud. A man born in America in 1928 wasn't taught the lessons of Dr. Spock. There was none of that building my self-esteem in his game plan. In those days a man showed his affection for his son by cracking the window and letting the smoke out of the car while he was driving you home from the hospital.

On the way home, I stopped in St. Augustine, the oldest city in the United States. While walking on the cobblestone streets and marveling at the Castillo de San Marcos, seventeenth century Spanish stone fortress, I was transported back in time. As I drove north on I-95, I thought of Coach Owen's words that taking a job at Lake Worth Junior High was like joining the Peace Corps. Kennedy created the Peace Corps, whose mission was to promote world peace and help people in third world countries. I had no idea of the demographics of Lake Worth Junior High. I was about to be exposed to cultures, countries, and languages that weren't in my experiential background.

I found a condominium for rent in Palm Springs, a town near to Lake Worth. I rented the unit from an older couple for $350 a month. I didn't realize I would be the only WASP there under age seventy. The entire complex was made up of Jewish people from New York. I could have found a better place to meet people my age, but the price was right. M. Wayne and Kathryn were avid antique collectors and gifted a wooden rain barrel, copper kettle, and an old wooden school desk. "The Fashion Desk" was invented by John Loughlin of Ohio and when in use attached to one another and had the ubiquitous inkwell. A mattress rounded off my first apartment's furnishings. The night before I was going to make my departure for Florida, Mom had a summer meal outside on the patio. She was sad to say the least. We feasted on grilled hamburgers and corn on the cob that was picked that day. Mom said, "I just wish you didn't have to move so far away."

"Don't you do that to him. He made a choice and Florida is where he's moving. At least he has a job," M. Wayne interjected in that firm voice that he had. "I just wish you had found a job in an elementary school."

"Why's that, Dad?"

"Elementary is such a better environment. For the life of me I don't understand why you want to begin a career with those ulcer-breeding monsters in junior high." After dinner I walked around the yard that he kept manicured as if it were Augusta and contemplated his description of ulcer-breeding monsters. I stood amongst the lightening bugs flickering in the night. The next morning, I hit the road bursting with the exuberance of a young man embarking on a journey. As I weaved through the mountains of West Virginia, I thought about how I was going to be a different kind of teacher. My class would be fun and the kids would relate to me. Little did I know that I was going into a gonzo land known as the classroom. No education professor or student teaching experience will give you the ammunition you need to navigate the quagmire ahead behind that closed door. I drove on thinking I was going to change the world.

CHAPTER THREE

"FLYING ERASERS"

My class numbers were: 34, 36, 38, 35, 33, and 42. That's a voluminous class load of 218. There was no classroom size amendment. "Where is my room key?" I asked Regina, a secretary that reminded me of Peggy of the *Mannix* detective series. She pointed to the wall on my right. I saw a large chart with about fifty paper flaps arranged in perfect rows. In walks a tanned teacher in gym shorts and a white tennis shirt. He had thick, white billowing shoulder length hair and was sporting Ray Ban sunglasses. The epitome of tropical cool.

"Hey, Holly and Regina," he said in a suave manner.

"Good morning, B," they replied.

"Okay, let's see what we have this year," he said.

"What's the deal with this chart?" I asked him.

"Every year Coach Owen comes up with a clever idea to give us our keys. This year each teacher has a clue on a flap and underneath is your room key. Let's see," he said as he scanned the chart looking for a clue. "A carousing fellow." That could be me." He lifted the flap. His name, Dave

Bingeman, was there with his key taped to it. I started looking and couldn't seem to find a clue that fit me. Just when I was about to give up, I came across the phrase, "Position for prayer." You kneel when you pray. My last name is Neal. Sure enough, there was Jeff Neal and my key. My room was on the right just down the hall from the office. I opened the door to find an antiquated room with a water-stained ceiling. Desks were filled with graffiti and some were chipped on the writing surface. The only books on the wooden shelves were a set of dictionaries. They looked like they'd been used in the fifties. Nothing was on the wall and the chalkboard was a faded green.

As I surveyed my new academic home, one of M. Wayne's phrases came to mind. "There's a lot to be desired here." The library was the site of the faculty meeting. Most of the staff were over forty. One guy with a beard came over and said, "Welcome to the Warrior Family, man." His name was Jose Garcia and he looked like he was right out of a *Miami Vice* episode. There were only a few new teachers. I happened to sit by David Youngman who was from the Finger Lakes region of New York. We decided to go out to lunch and found out we had some things in common. Both of his parents were in education as were mine. This was his first teaching job. He was living in his parent's winter house on the southeast side of Lake Worth. We both wondered just what we'd gotten ourselves into.

That first week passed with some departmental meetings and an in-service training at a school in Boca Raton called Loggers Run Middle. All of the secondary English teachers in the county attended this training. It was ominous for me as I didn't understand just how huge the Palm Beach County School District actually was. I was used to three elementary schools, a junior high, and one high school being a school district. At that time there were around 10,000 teachers in Palm Beach County. The first workshop was being conducted by a veteran teacher named Tom Tufts. He published books specifically designed for teaching writing at the secondary level. He was articulate and was doing an excellent job of presenting. The topic was choosing literature for your classes. In addition to *The Outsiders*, I was contemplating teaching *The Adventures of Huckleberry Finn*. I did have a question regarding the term "nigger" as it was splashed across the pages of Mark Twain's classic novel. I raised my hand and Tom called on me.

"What if we want to read *Huck Finn* with our students and the "N" word is in the text?" I asked. Tom paused as he looked like he was thinking.

"I don't see why we feel the need to shove down the throats of our students supposed 'classics' when they aren't that relevant to our students today," a female teacher put forth.

"I'd like to respond to that," I said.

"Go for it, man," Tom said.

"I believe it was Ernest Hemingway who said, 'All modern American literature comes from one book by Mark Twain, called *Huckleberry Finn*. There has been nothing better'. Maybe Hemingway thinks it wouldn't be a bad thing to share one of our greatest works of literature with our students," I added. Tom interjected and we moved on to something else. As we were leaving, a tall guy with a beard and a full head of hair came over and said, "I liked what you said about Hemingway. Cool." He was about my height and he had these clear eyes and I judged him to be about my age. He was teaching English at Logger's Run. Years later I would come to know his name, Barry Grunow.

The week passed and on Friday, I was invited by someone on the staff to go to a happy hour at a place not too far from my apartment called Mulligan's. There were about ten or more teachers seated around a table. Those were times when you could eat pretty well for free at a happy hour with free hors d'oeuvres. Chicken wings, potato skins, fresh raw veggies with ranch dip, and pitchers of cold beer were the fare. Dave Youngman was there and we took stock of the cast of characters surrounding us. Some of the veteran teachers that sat around that table at the inception of the first happy hour were Tom Long, Kenneth Long, Peggy Cook, Dave Bingeman, Jose Garcia, Frieda Proctor, and Jim Sanders. Each of those teachers were giving pearls of wisdom to Dave and me that were much needed for novice teachers.

The weekend passed by with the highlight being my going to Lake Worth Beach. The sun and saltwater was all that I hoped it would be, and the hamburger at "Benny's on the Beach" was out of this world. That Sunday before my first day of teaching, I didn't sleep a wink. The day arrived and I went into the main office to the sign-in sheet. Each teacher put their initials to show they were present. Coach walked by in the morning while I stood outside my door. "Don't forget to take your attendance," he said. "Have a good first day. It's the beginning of a great adventure."

The halls were abuzz with students trying to find their classrooms. At that time the entire population of the seventh and eighth grades was 860. I began to notice how diverse the student body was as there were many different races. One Hispanic boy who looked like he should have been in high school came by and said, "Fuck you, cracker." He turned to see my reaction. I decided not to engage. I nodded slowly without a smile and kept looking at him. He turned and kept walking. The cracker comment was a new one on me. I asked Peggy Cook, science teacher and athletic director, about that term.

"They called you 'cracka,' huh?" she said, laughing. "It's a slur. What'd ya say back?"

"Nothing," I added. "Just stayed quiet."

"That's okay, the first time. Next one you better come back with something or they'll think you're soft." About the only thing I got done in those six periods on that first day was the taking of the roll. Even that was challenging as some of them either weren't there or refused to answer. Many refused to sit down or stop talking. Adding to the challenge was the fact that four or five students stood in the back because I didn't have enough desks. The final bell rang, and I sat slumped in my chair exhausted. I looked at the empty classroom after the last student filed out and couldn't believe how much paper was on the floor. I went to my mailbox in the main office and Coach saw me. "How was the first day?"

"It went okay," I lied.

"Good," he answered. "See you tomorrow."

"Coach?" I asked.

"Yes."

"I don't have enough desks."

"We are fresh out of desks, but we can come up with a way to rectify your dilemma." Coach led me out of his office and I followed him through the hallway. He stood 6'2" and had quite a lot of weight. As large as he was, I could tell he was an athlete. He was bowlegged and yet his stride was graceful. Later I was to find that he had been a linebacker for Ohio State. He was in his sixties and his eyes had a twinkle, like Santa Claus. He opened my door. "Let's see what we have here," he said as he moved some desks that were in the back row. He started to stack the dictionaries on the top shelf. After clearing them out he put chairs facing the empty shelf.

"You have three chairs. That's three makeshift desks," he said as he grabbed his walkie-talkie and called to Willie Grimes, the head custodian.

"Go ahead, Coach," said Willie.

"Bring four chairs to Room 2-103."

"On my way," Willie's voice answered. The kids would have to lean under and write on the shelf. This was an old school remedy for a lack of desks.

"Really, how was the first day?" Coach asked.

"To be honest they didn't listen to me or my instructions," I said, thinking of the boy Leon who refused to sit down.

"That's why teaching is an art. You have to be smarter than a CIA operative to coerce these kids to listen. You have to have more charisma than a stand-up comic to get them to pay attention. Then you have to deliver instruction. It's an art, my young friend. It usually takes a teacher a good three years to get ahold of it all."

"Three years!" I exclaimed.

"That's about right. Go home and get some rest tonight," he said. "You're going to need it." The ancient air-conditioner was steadily dripping water in a small puddle on the floor. No one told me that teaching was like a minefield on an academic obstacle course. That night my body seemed to sink into the mattress. All I kept seeing were those faces staring back at me from the desks. Day two brought some drama as I had a situation with Leon.

"Leon!" I yelled.

He waved me off like he was flicking a fly away. Leon was tall and big, a man-child. I asked one more time for him to sit down to no avail. He ignored me and kept up his one-way conversation. The rest of the class was talking, but they were taking note of this impasse. Immediately, I started to think of my teachers and what they would do in this situation. I thought of my favorite teacher, Mr. Bowers. He was a brawny man who taught English, coached football, and was nobody's fool. If a student in his class dared to take a nap, he would fire an eraser at their head. I decided this might be a good tactic with Leon.

I turned to the chalkboard and saw my weapon, the eraser. I slowly walked to the board and grabbed the instrument usually reserved for removing chalk markings. I slid my fingers around the strips on the ergonomically designed handle, like a quarterback who finds the laces on a football. I eyed my target. Leon was still talking and unsuspecting as I leaned back and fired the eraser. It smacked him right on the side of his head leaving an indelible yellow square after the initial dust from the impact settled.

"You crazy fucking, cracker!" he yelled.

"That's right I'm crazy," I said loudly. "I needed you to sit down!" He turned at the front of the row and ran out of the classroom. I panicked as he exited the room with the yellow square still fresh on his head. I just threw an eraser at a student! I ran after him yelling his name. Just then I saw Coach Owen coming out of his office with his trademark big, red bowl of coffee.

"What are you doing, Jeff?" he asked.

"I hit Leon with an eraser," I muttered nervously.

"You just left a room full of students unsupervised. Let him go and get back in there!" His forehead was wrinkled with concern. As I came to my door an oriental boy was standing outside. "What are you doing, Ralph? I asked.

"It's too loud in there. Your students are off the chain."

I wasn't familiar with that phrase in 1985. When I reentered the room, I saw just what "off the chain" meant. Paper was flying, desks had been turned over, and my yelling for them to sit down and be quiet went unheeded. Mercifully, the bell rang and it was time for Period 2. The day was just beginning. The other five periods passed, and although there weren't any objects thrown by the teacher, it was nothing to write home about. On the way home, I wondered if I was going to survive.

CHAPTER FOUR

"WELCOME TO THE JUNGLE"

Coach said as I signed in the next day, "Come see me on your planning period."

"Okay, Coach," I said nervously. Later I went to his office.

"Sit down, Jeff," he said, lighting one of his seemingly ever-present cigarettes.

"Coach, about yesterday I—"

"Let me tell you something," he interrupted," I just got a call from Leon's grandmother. She told me in no uncertain terms that she wants Leon out of that crazy White man's class. Jeff, if bull shit were snow it would be a blizzard right now. I told her you were the best thing to hit Lake Worth Junior High since sliced bread. I also said that Leon would be missing out on a great learning experience by being taken out of your class."

"What did she say?"

"She agreed to leave him in your class providing you don't throw erasers at him," Coach replied.

"Sorry about that. He wouldn't sit down."

"Listen, I should be serving ten consecutive life sentences at San Quentin for all of the things I did over my career that could be construed as abuse," Coach said in a paternal voice. "I feel sorry for you young teachers. We can't even paddle kids anymore. We used to put them up against the wall, grab them by the collar and let them know who's in charge. It's different today. You have to try not touch them at all. Definitely, don't throw anything at them. It's a whole new ball game."

"You mean we aren't able to paddle the kids?" I asked.

"No, some little guy out in Belle Glade put his hand behind him when getting swatted and it broke his wrist. The higher ups say no more paddling."

"What is Belle Glade?" I asked.

"It's a town about 50 miles west of here, sugar country."

"So, what do we do when students are acting up?"

"That's the million-dollar question," Coach said, "The board was our equalizer. A suspension is hardly punishment; it's a reward. Detention? What if they don't show up, then what? I'm really scared about what's going to happen."

"What do you mean?" I asked.

"We're going to lose control. It's a numbers game. There are a lot more of them than there are of us. The kids will have no fear. This generation of parents doesn't help either. They want to be their child's friend. Hell, they'll be shooting teachers someday." Coach uttered those words to me in August of 1985. I wasn't quite ready for what was waiting in my desk on my fourth day. After taking roll, I gave a few examples for the grammar lesson. I'm sure it was something scintillating like subjects and predicates. After checking for understanding, I let the students work on their own. To my astonishment they were working. The majority of them were engaged. Eureka! I stood beside my desk and gave a small sigh of satisfaction, triumph if you will, that they were working.

My old, wooden desk creaked when I opened the middle drawer. I looked twice to see if what I saw was really there. It was a large Tampax soaked in a brilliant red. Once I grasped this hideosity was real, I slammed the drawer. My first inclination was to yell and demand to know who put this plug of cotton with bodily fluids in my desk. I prayed it was food coloring. The class kept working. Maybe they were all in on it? Perhaps that is why they are working? I scanned the room. Two boys in the back seemed to be smirking. Their heads were down. They were both White with shoulder-length hair that wasn't unlike what my peers in the 1970s had as a hairstyle. The main giveaway that they could be guilty was they were working. The bell rang and I asked them to stay back.

"This was very creative," I said, holding up the Tampax with my index finger and thumb making sure not to touch the red. They vehemently denied any wrongdoing on their part. I stood up and my height of 6'5" caused their necks to crane back. I moved closer. "I can appreciate a practical joke, but this one went too far. You can deny all you want, but I know you two did this." My voice was rising. I could see one's heart palpitating. "Go!" I yelled and pointed to the door. They moved at full tilt. I smiled after the door closed. Carefully, I placed the red item in the paper bag that once held my morning doughnut.

That first week was full of challenges. Erasers thrown, a bloody Tampax, and then came my first time breaking up a fight. How well one fights is most important in my students' world. My first experience with this pugilistic phenomenon was outside my classroom door. It is expected that a teacher goes out in the hallway during the class change to supervise and greet the students. This day I noticed a couple of boys in an argument. It was strange what I witnessed. Their voices were raised and then became softer as they moved slowly toward each other. They drew close and touched their shoulders together. Right shoulder to right shoulder. They circled slowly. It was like a ritual dance. All of the sudden they were throwing punches and the crowd began to gather. Peggy Cook was walking down the hallway. She yelled, "You got to do something!" She moved kids making a pathway for me.

I surmised my best bet was to run between them and push one away. I sprinted into the melee, ducking my head, hoping not to catch a stray fist. The school policeman arrived and grabbed the other. I did my best to wedge myself and blocked him from passing like an offensive lineman. To my surprise he didn't push me. He just kept yelling at the other boy. "Keep jawin', motherfucker. I got 'chu," he said. Coach Owen arrived. "I have this," he said as he grabbed the boy and escorted him away holding firmly to his triceps.

"You did good, White boy," Peggy said with her deep belly laugh. I realized that a lot of adrenaline was running through me. It was the first of many fights that I would see between students. Aside from the lessons I was learning in the classroom, the one thing that I did that helped me adjust to this strange new world was to find my way into coaching. Jose Garcia was the basketball coach. He was in his early thirties and sported a dark beard on his tanned Cuban face. His voice was raspy from years of yelling out on the PE field. There was no gymnasium at the old Junior High. He also coached track. He was ready to turn in his whistle. Garcia came down the hallway during a class change. He had a sixties generation vibe about him. "Hey, man, a little birdie told me that you may be interested in coaching basketball. Is that true?" The cigarettes he smoked in the teachers' lounge no doubt added to his discordant vocal chords.

"I'm interested," I said. "I thought you were the coach."

"No, I'm burned out, man. I'm ready for a change. Come out to see me sometime in the PE world and I'll tell you some things you need to know if you are going to coach." The next day, on planning, I made my way to the athletic field. As I rounded the corner, I saw close to eighty students in T-shirts and shorts milling about the outdoor basketball courts. There was a baseball diamond and a soccer field that led to the boundary of Lake Worth High.

"Hey, Jose," I said.

"Good morning, man. Welcome to my world," he said with a broad grin like a Cheshire cat. I noticed that B was way down at the other end of the field. He was leaning back on the chain-link fence and had one knee propped up and his arms outstretched in a T formation. His head was down.

"What's up with B?" I asked.

"Oh, he's hungover today," Jose said. "I can't help myself. I fuck with him. Today he was asleep at his desk in our office. I came in and as soon as I saw he was sleeping I blew my whistle near his ear and started to sweep our office. "We have to keep a tidy office, B." He told me to fuck off and walked down there. Check this out. This is going to be a classic." He blew the whistle and to my amazement all of the students herded around him in a large semicircle like bees drawn to honey. "Everyone we have a new game today. Do you see Coach B down there?" The class turned and looked. Does everyone see his baseball hat?"

"Yes," they answered in unison.

"The baseball hat on his head says Quasar. Whoever gets that hat off his head and brings it back to me gets extra credit. We have to be organized. Let's form a straight line." Garcia spread them out just off of the basketball courts, like a general in an ancient war preparing his troops for battle. B put his one leg down and wasn't holding to the fence. He was looking at the spectacle of this massive line of kids facing him. Garcia placed the whistle an inch or so from his mouth and raised his other arm straight above his head. "I am going to count to three and blow the whistle," he said as the students assumed a crouching position. They were in starting blocks.

"All right," Garcia growled. "One. Two. Three!" As the whistle blew and his arm came down, they broke out of their crouch and began the sprint across the field yelling at the top of their lungs. Garcia was holding his stomach staggering with laughter. "This is going to be a classic," he said once again. By this time B had moved away from the fence observing the stampede coming his way. In seconds Jose's smile vanished as he said, "Oh, shit!" The students were circling B trying to grab his hat. He thought the kids had gone crazy and were trying to attack him. B started swinging his fists wildly, like a windmill, in the punch known as a haymaker. The students approached dodging his punches thinking this was part of the game. Jose was in a full sprint to the end of the field. I was running beside him. It would be hard to explain why a PE teacher punched a student in the face who was trying to get his hat. Jose got closer and blew his whistle over and over, and was able to stop the onslaught. Jose was coughing up a lung when he said, "Damn B, I thought you were going to kill one of those kids."

"I'm tired of your bullshit," he answered as he adjusted his Quasar baseball hat and walked away. Jose reminded me of why I went out there in the first place.

"You want to coach, right?"

"Yes," I answered.

"Tryouts are starting next week. You'll get maybe 300 kids. Do a tryout for seventh one day and a tryout for eighth the next. Then put them together and start cutting. Get it done in three days. Just know you're going to break a lot of hearts. At this age they all think they should make the team. Once you get a list of potential players, ask Ms. Laureano, the Guidance Counselor, to check on their grades. The majority of your team will be from the hood."

"What's the hood?" I asked earnestly.

"Man, you are green. That's the Black section of town. It's over by Twelfth Avenue on the other side of the tracks. These are street kids and you're White. If they smell that you're soft, they'll never respect you. Understand?"

"Yes," I answered, realizing what a tremendous learning curve I had. As I got to know the diverse student body, I became aware of the existence of battles amongst people of color. It wasn't all black and white. An example was the Black and Haitian phenomenon. There was a massive influx of Haitians in the1980s. They were met with resistance from American Blacks, perhaps, more than any other subgroup. There was a true ethnic conflict going on between these two groups. One day I was helping a student edit a book report about Haiti. This student was dark as were many Haitian students. The head of the English Department, Mr. Kenneth Long, who is a Black man described very dark people as being "jet black blue." This student was jet black blue.

"Are you, Haitian?" I asked.

"Hell no, Mr. Neal!" he replied emphatically.

"What's so bad about being Haitian?"

"They different."

"Wouldn't it be a boring world if we were all the same?"

"My grandma told me they nasty," he replied.

"Yeah, well my grandmother told me because I had a mole on my arm I'd own a large farm," I added. "I don't own a farm." The animosity directed toward the Haitian population by Black Americans, was in turn reciprocated by the Haitians. One Haitian teacher spoke condescendingly about Black Americans. "We Haitians believe in the American Dream of hard work can get you anywhere. American Blacks do not." The chasm of resentment was not limited to these two subgroups. One day I asked a student named Nancy if she were Cuban?

"Hell no, Mr. Neal. Cubans think they all that."

"Really?' I asked.

"Yeah, ask anyone. Cubans think they better than anyone."

So, I decided to ask my Cuban connection, Jose, what he thought about that. Jose replied, "No, man that's not true. We don't think we're better than anyone. We know we are. We are the Jews of the Caribbean." The issue of racial divide was one thing to process, but I also needed to acquaint myself with generational poverty. A working definition of this term is when a family has been in poverty for two or more generations. Taking a part-time job with a non-profit called "Cities in Schools" afforded me an opportunity to comprehend where my students were coming from, literally.

My role was called parent liaison. I was to visit homes of students who were having difficulties in school either behaviorally or academically. If you want to have a practical understanding of your students, visit their homes.

Think of a childhood friend who suffered abuse either physically or verbally. Usually, you cut them slack because you know what they're dealing with at home. The same holds true with students. Once you see what they are faced with in the supposed sanctuary of home, you develop patience, tolerance, and compassion. My first home visit left an ineradicable mark on my psyche.

There were a pair of brothers who were hell on wheels. One of them went up to a young male teacher in front of the whole class and got behind him, grabbed the guy's waist and simulated buggery. Students who witness something like that never let you forget. He never recovered as the students referred to him as "Butt-fuck." He resigned shortly thereafter. I found the address of the brothers and the structure was condemned. A neighbor, an elderly Black woman, saw me snooping around. "What do you want?" she asked.

"I work for the school and I'm doing a home visit."

"Better pray because those boys are filled with evil. Satan got his paws on them. Their new place is down two blocks."

I found the house and a woman with gray, dirty-blond hair answered who introduced herself as the boy's aunt. She looked like she'd been through a lot, an addiction, perhaps. She reminded me of a biker girl, and the years weren't kind to her. The two brothers weren't around. She pointed to a couch for me to sit. I leaned forward and we began a discussion that opened my eyes to horror.

"Where is their mother?" I asked earnestly.

"You don't know, do you?"

"What do you mean?" I asked.

"Both of them saw their mom get raped and murdered in the kitchen while they were at the dinner table. They were probably five or six." The words stayed in the air and hit me forcibly. I was at a loss for a reply. The emotionally detached way this woman shared this event was chilling as well. I shifted my weight on the couch. I placed my hand on a blanket that was covering a huge hole in the couch. Immediately, my arm disappeared into a hole and I cut myself on a spring.

"I'm sorry," she said, "I shoulda' told you 'bout that."

"That's okay," I said, looking at the scratch and hoping my tetanus shot was still viable. "No wonder those two are acting up in school."

"No shit," she replied. "Listen, I need to get going."

I thanked her for her time and on the way home I couldn't get the visual out of my head of two little fragile kids watching that unspeakable act, helplessly. Who recovers from that? That was my initiation into the home environment and background that exists for all too many students. The week of tryouts came. It is no easy task to cut hundreds to get to fifteen. You can see in their eyes how badly each kid wants to play. The third day of practice I watched on the three courts as they played full court man-to-man. It was time for them to shine. I blew the whistle and told them I had hard decisions to make and thanked them for trying out. A list would be put up the next day with the fifteen members of the team. Just as I was walking to my car a smaller student, who was nicknamed Butter, came up to me. He had these big, sleepy eyes. He asked softly, "Did I make your team?" I stood there looking at his bashful face. In fact, he hadn't made it. He was slight and I didn't think he would be physical enough so I scratched him. I told him that I would be thinking about it and make my decision tonight. He nodded and walked away with his head down. I added his name. I didn't have it in my heart to cut him. Life takes strange twists. If he hadn't come up to me, I never would have kept him on the team. Later he would show his skill and become an integral part of my first team. He went on to be a standout at Lake Worth High.

As I taped the list to the wall, I noticed an old wooden plaque that read, "Palm Beach County Boy's Junior High Champions." I read the names of the players and to my amazement the coach was someone I knew. It was the recruiter in the bathroom in Buffalo, Randy Stewart. What are the chances that the guy who got me the interview was a teacher and basketball coach at Lake Worth Junior High? I asked Coach about Randy. "Randy's a good ole boy," said Coach. "He won the championship, which isn't an easy feat." Just as he said that a fight broke out right around the corner from where Coach and I were conversing. This one was a different scenario. The two combatants were a boy and a girl. It was Nancy, the Puerto Rican girl, who had the distaste for Cubans and a boy named Dwayne. Nancy was giving him all he could handle as she wailed on him. He was covering up like Muhammad Ali, doing the rope a dope. Coach got behind Dwayne and pulled him away.

"Get a hold of her," Coach said as he started to walk Dwayne away from the fray. I grabbed Nancy's arms and she tried to break free. I held on tight and leveraged my weight to stop her. She let out this ungodly scream that hurt my ears. She seemed to be settling down.

"Are you calm now?" I asked, still holding on to her arms. She took a deep breath and nodded in the affirmative. Then I made the mistake of releasing my grasp. Immediately, she darted to the unsuspecting Coach and Dwayne. She leapt over Coach's shoulders and continued her assault. Coach made eye contact with me. "Get her," he said with frustration in his voice. I grabbed her from behind and began pulling away. It was all I could do to remove her from the scene.

"Never let go!" Coach admonished me as he ushered Dwayne inside the office. They disappeared as I held onto Nancy. Later Coach gave me sage advice. "You can't trust these kids to stop. Hold on while the fire cools and the other combatant gets out of sight."

"She was out of control," I said.

"That's girls for you. I would rather break up a hundred guy fights than one with girls. God forbid if they get a hold of each other's hair." I walked away. Jose who had seen the exchange walked by and said, "Welcome to the Jungle, dude."

CHAPTER FIVE

"FIRST VISIT TO THE HOOD"

The first day of practice was as advertised. The athletes clearly had an attitude with me. They wanted to play for Garcia, and not this cracker. They moved listlessly as I gave directions. The straw that broke the camel's back was when I was trying to show them an intricate zone offense and I looked around for Gary, who I was looking to be the point guard. I called out his name and there was no answer. Upon further inspection, he had meandered over to a chair and was leaning on the chain-link fence. He was watching the girls practice on the neighboring court. As I looked at him, stunned at his audacity, the team smiled and snickered. I remembered Peggy's admonition to not be soft. For the second time, it seemed like a good idea to throw an object at a student. The first, the eraser, was not as formidable a missile as a basketball full of air.

Never in my wildest dreams would I walk away from a coach who is explaining an offense, let alone sit down on a chair and watch girls practice. Every bit of frustration at these students who seemed to respect no one, especially me, reached its crescendo. I could easily palm the ball as I pressed it firmly into my right hand. I eyed my target. He was oblivious, in a daydream, looking at the girls. My plan was to throw it to the fence and have it narrowly miss his head. Just something to catch his attention. I wound up like a pitcher and took three steps and fired.

As soon as I let go of this orange, speeding meteorite, I knew it wouldn't hit the fence. The ball collided with his temple and caused his head to bobble side to side before he hit the ground, face first. Coach's words rang in my ears for me not to touch them, or throw anything. I held my breath, steeped in anxiety, as Gary lay motionless. My career flashed before my eyes. The girl's team stopped practicing. My players were frozen in place, jaws dropped with eyes wide as saucers. The girl's coach, Hester Taylor, who laughed at first, now had a look of panic.

Then it was as if a divine presence came and breathed life into his body. He sat up for a moment. One of the players started to move to him. "Don't move," I growled. The boy froze in his tracks. "All of you, get on the baseline," I commanded. The boys jumped to attention and sprinted to the baseline under the basket. This one act, potentially career ending, had transformed this disrespectful group of athletes into being compliant and eager to please. They moved like their lives depended on it. Just as I had done when I'd thrown the eraser at Leon, I surmised that I'd already screwed up, and I might as well play it off like Gary was the one who did something wrong.

"Get over here!" I ordered as he stood, stumbling like a barroom drunk getting his equilibrium. I continued with my tirade. "I am explaining an offense and you, who could be the point guard, the quarterback of our team, are sitting down!" The term "suicide" is a conditioning exercise where the athletes line up on one end of the court and sprint in quarters to the foul line and back, half-court and back, opposite foul line and back, and finally from end to end. The boys lined up and Gary tried to join them. I told him to stay by the fence.

I blew the whistle and the boys bolted like colts being set free. This decision had a two-fold purpose in that I wanted Gary to feel bad about checking out of practice and I was conditioning the athletes. The boy's speed was impressive. I yelled, "Better be under thirty seconds or we go again." All fourteen boys were bent over their chests heaving looking for air. I made them stand up and fold their hands behind their heads to open up their passageways allowing for more oxygen. As they stood there, hands clasped behind their heads, I began, "Gentlemen, we have two weeks to get ready for your first game. We have no offenses, defenses, out of bounds plays, presses, press breakers, we've got nothing."

The words carried in the air. They stared at me without flinching. The act of violence with Gary was the vehicle I needed to gain their respect.

"We have nothing except each other," I said. I saw their heads rise a little and I could tell this hit a chord. "We have to be a team. I will do my best to help you be ready, but I need you to keep your grades up, stay out of trouble, and most importantly, don't sit on a damned chair and watch the girls practice." They laughed in unison, and to my relief, Gary smiled. NBA coach, Phil Jackson had a theory that basketball was like a jazz band where each player knows the strengths and weaknesses of the other and they build on that. The key is for the team to become a pack. The strength of the pack is the wolf. The strength of wolf is the pack. That old Indian proverb has worlds of meaning. Something as simple as a team huddle can build this invisible net amongst a team that leads to the promised land—teamwork. As we stood there, in a circle, all hands together I had to think of a mantra. I told them to bring their hands in and on the count of three we'd yell Warriors. Hands went up, and as all hands went down, they yelled, "Warriors!" It emanated from the fifteen boys as they broke from the huddle.

A coach can touch the lives of kids in a way that one can't in the classroom. Students see you differently. You're not just another teacher. You're a coach. Being that I knocked Gary out, I thought it was time for me to incorporate one of the most important tools to reach kids. If you do something that tears them down, you've got to build them back up. Anyone can put a kid down, and sometimes they need it, but the tricky part is building them back up. It is imperative to construct what you took down. My high school basketball coach was named Terry Thompson. He would have players, one by one, stay after practice and feed them jump shots from five different spots on the floor. He would count until you made 100. After shooting he built a rapport with each player through conversation. I decided this might be a good night to keep Gary after practice. "Gary," I said.

"Yeah, Coach," he replied, coming over to me. It was the first time I was called Coach. I explained the process of the drill and began to feed him. He had a smooth shot with a fluid follow through. This was a time when there were no activity busses. If an athlete couldn't get picked up, walking was the only option. I offered to take him home. That wasn't a big deal in 1985, but not a recommended practice today in our litigious country.

"It's getting dark. How about I give you a ride?" I asked.

"Ah, Coach, you don't have to do that."

"No problem," I added.

"Yeah, Coach there might be a problem. You don't want to come to my neighborhood."

"Sure, I do."

"Okay," he said. He tilted his head, examining me. We drove south on Dixie Highway. Gary pointed to turn on Twelfth Avenue. We went over the railroad tracks. "Turn here," he said as he pointed to a long white wall that ran along the street. The wall was a mural with the images of Martin Luther King, Jr., Malcom X, Rosa Parks, and Maya Angelou. The artwork was colorful and intricate. The sun was going down.

"Nice mural," I said.

"Coach, you better be ready up here."

"For what?"

Before he could answer, I pulled up to the stop sign. Then like ninjas in the night, twenty or so Black males ranging from teenagers to men in their twenties surrounded my car. A muscular guy with gold teeth who was wearing a red bandana pounded on my window. I noticed that he had a thick gold chain that Mr. T. would be proud to wear. I looked at Gary as he pounded on the window. At this time, I thought he was right about it not being a good idea for me to be in the neighborhood. "You'll have to talk, Coach. They think you're here to buy crack. Once they see me, it'll be okay," Gary put forth. I put the window down about four inches.

"What you need? I got 5s, 10s, 20s," the man said quickly as his head darted back and forth. "C'mon hurry up."

"Hey, Brick. It's me Gary."

"Gary, what the fuck you doin?"

"He my coach. Givin' me a lift home."

"Aaight," he said, leaning toward the window. "Coach, we won't approach you no more. Sorry for the misunderstanding. Nigga got to make a livin' out on these streets." I nodded and drove forward. We pulled up to a small house that was kept up very well. There was a chain-link fence and an old Plymouth Duster in the drive.

"Is it always like that?" I asked.

"Yeah, but it's gotten worse this last year. Everybody be hittin' the rock. Normal people go crazy when they start smoking that shit. People ride down the street with refrigerators on their roof, headin' to the pawn shop."

"Really?" I said, thinking how outlandish that sounded.

"No, it's true, Coach. People lose their minds. Most of the customers they sell to be White like you."

"Yeah?"

"Once they get a taste, they come back," he said. "Thanks for the ride, Coach. You'll be all right on the way out."

"Gary, I'd like to meet your family. Is that okay?" He thought for a moment and scratched his head. The same head that had received a blow from a basketball earlier.

"Well, you come this far, might as well come in," he said without a lot of enthusiasm. "Only one home is my mom and the little ones."

"Is your dad working?" I asked.

"No, he lives in Jamaica."

"Are you Jamaican?"

"Yes," he said as he put the key in the door. Once the door was opened there was an enticing aroma that wafted through the house so pungent that it made my mouth water. "Mom," Gary said as she was in the kitchen not knowing there was a stranger in their midst.

"Why you late, boy?"

"Mom, Coach Neal is here."

"What!" she exclaimed as she came around the corner fixing her hair. She looked to be in her late thirties or early forties. There were two toddlers crawling around looking at me as if I were an alien from another planet.

"I just wanted to introduce myself," I said.

"Nice to meet you," she said with her thick Jamaican accent. It was the first time I'd heard the musical cadence of the English-based creole language with the West African influence. She began to pick up some toys that were strewn on the floor.

"I should be going now. It was nice to meet you."

"Is Gary in any trouble?"

"No, he's not. He's on the team and I think he's going to be a good player. All of his teachers had good reports about him." Gary beamed as his mom looked at him.

"I'm glad he has a sport. Keep him off that street out there. Did you see them? Sellin' the devils dandruff is what they doin'," she said emphatically. "Will you stay for dinner?"

"No, thank you."

"Nonsense," she replied. "You sit down and try my specialty, Jerk Chicken." The next thing I know I'm seated at their wooden table awaiting my first taste of the marinated hot-spice mixture. Gary said grace and I helped myself to a large thigh. There were also beans and rice. It was the first home-cooked meal I had in a while. I asked Gary's mom what exactly is Jerk chicken? It was like an episode from Anthony Bourdain as she described how she uses Scotch Bonnet chili peppers, All Spice, and healthy dollops of Jamaican rum with molasses. Whatever she did with that marinade was magical. She even told me the history of the dish as it originally developed from Maroons, African slaves who escaped into the wilds of Jamaica, when the British captured the island from Spain. The door opened and a huge man with the same distinguishable accent asked, "Who dis' man at our table?"

"This is Gary's basketball coach, Coach Neal."

"Okay there, Coach Neal. You need a Red Stripe with my sister's Jerk Chicken," he said, shaking my hand with a vicelike grip. He disappeared into the kitchen and brought out my first taste of Red Stripe beer brewed in Jamaica. The cold beer perfectly enhanced the spicy chicken. To this day I think of that meal. Over the course of dinner, I learned a lot about Gary and his family. His mother came to America when the heat of political unrest in the capital, Kingston, became too dangerous. I didn't linger too long after we finished eating. On the way out of the neighborhood, the ninjas were still hard at work. I saw three exchanges as I passed. The window went down money comes out and another satisfied customer. This was my first introduction to the crack epidemic that surged through America's inner cities in the early 1980s.

CHAPTER SIX

"JOURNEY TO THE MUCK"

I was learning a lot about the cultures that were on my team. One word of advice, if eating Haitian food, don't mistake Pikliz for coleslaw. The spicy mixture of cabbage, carrot, and Chile-laced pickle will blow your doors off. Two weeks went by and we had our first away game. Peggy brought out the tattered, rag-tag uniforms with the faded "Warriors" across the chest. "You drew a tough one for your first game, away at Lake Shore Middle," she said with a wry smile.

"Where is Lake Shore Middle?" I asked.

"You are going to the muck."

"What's the muck?" I asked earnestly.

"Belle Glade," she said, laughing. "They're from the muck, and they don't give a fuck." Belle Glade has large quantities of muck, the name given to soil out there. It is fed from the Everglades and is ideal to grow sugar cane. Some of the best sweet corn I've tasted in Florida comes from Muck City.

"Where's the sports bus?" I asked.

DR. JEFFREY W. NEAL

"We drive them. Coach Taylor and I have the girls covered. You need at least one driver."

"For fifteen kids?" I asked, freaking out.

"Only take ten. That's what Garcia did."

So, I had to decide which five athletes would be left behind. Dave Youngman agreed to drive. We set off with four vehicles jammed with twenty athletes to Belle Glade. At that time, I had never ventured west of I-95. There were less and less signs of civilization, and eventually there was nothing but sugar cane fields on either side of the road. There was smoke in the distance. Finally, I saw a prison with barbed wire fences with hundreds of Black men in blue prison uniforms. My athletes looked on expressionless. We came into the city limits of Belle Glade. Lake Shore Junior High was an old school that looked about as aged and dilapidated as Lake Worth Junior High. There was a thick, pungent smell in the air as we walked toward the gym. "Something's on fire," I said to Peggy.

"That's the cane burning," she replied. Being the science teacher that she was, she gave me a quick lesson regarding this strange new place. "From October to April sugar companies light massive fires in their fields to remove the outer leaves around the cane stalks before harvesting. That's the nasty odor you're smelling." Just as I was digesting this information a burly, White man with a gray beard walked out to meet us. He was the athletic director. He knew Peggy and they exchanged a barbed conversation. Apparently, Lake Shore and Lake Worth were old rivals.

"Where's Garcia?" he asked.

"He gave it up, and my man Jeffrey has the team this year."

"Good luck, Jeffrey. We are ready for you with an early release today," the man said, smiling, "a packed house."

"You didn't do that to my man," Peggy said.

"What's an early release?" I asked earnestly.

"You don't want to know," Peggy said, shaking her head.

She was right. An early release entails the entire student body being released early so that they can go to the game. Charge the students a buck and it's a fundraiser for the athletic department, and you have an enhanced home court advantage. The sound emanating from that tiny gymnasium was deafening. A sea of students was standing up clapping their hands once and stomping their feet twice, yelling in unison, "Lake Shore!"

One of my players named Linwood, with a smile, said, "You and the refs be the only White people here, Coach." I had already surmised that fact. Gary was warming up and was knocking down his jump shots consistently. Little did I know that he would do something that would make me want to fire another basketball at his head. We were evenly matched with Lake Shore. It was the type of game that's fun to watch. One team would rebound a ball, throw an outlet pass and it was off to the races. I couldn't believe my eyes when I saw one of their players, on a fast break, take two steps and rise in the air to dunk. As he slammed the ball through the hoop with authority, the place went into pandemonium. We hit a shot with eighteen seconds on the clock to go up by two points. The other coach called a time-out. I told my team that we would come out of our zone defense and pick them up man-to-man.

Peggy, who was keeping the books, nodded at me from the table. Gary, guarding their point guard brilliantly, with his catlike quickness, stripped the ball from the player in a clean steal. In his momentum, he spun around twice. How he didn't lose control of the ball I'll never know. Regaining his balance, he was facing the other team's basket and was dribbling under control now. I glanced at the clock to see ten seconds remaining and was thinking Gary was demonstrating excellent court sense as he was seemingly winding down the clock.

Then for whatever reason, perhaps a side effect from his blow to the head, Gary pulls up and shoots a jump shot at their basket. He executes a textbook jumper with a perfect follow through. The ball swishes through their net. Two points for Lake Shore and the game is tied. I tried to call a time-out, but with the clamorous, earsplitting roar of the crowd the referees didn't hear me. We were in overtime.

Once in the huddle I looked at Gary. He was rubbing his head over and over so hard that I thought he'd remove his hair. One of the players, Shawn, began to criticize him and I put an end to that. "Shut your mouth. Gary made a mistake. You might be the next one to blow it. I patted Gary on his knee and said, "It's okay, do something to make up for it." The three-minute overtime began. We were tied when one of their players shot the ball at the buzzer. It was rolling around the rim and the crowd waited breathlessly. It fell out. A second overtime was imminent. In the second overtime we were up by two with a few seconds remaining. My center named Pat, a strapping redhead, fouled one of their players at the buzzer. The player calmly made two foul shots all by his lonesome and a third overtime ensued. I remember admiring the boy as that was a lot of pressure in front of his whole school.

In the huddle the Warriors chugged Gatorade as the sweat formed puddles on the old wooden floor beneath them. Again, back and forth scoring and we had the ball with seven seconds to go on the side by our basket. The score was tied once again. Ishmael, one of my best shooters, with five seconds left took a shot from the corner. As the ball careened off the rim it bounced high above the heads of the players milling about under the basket. It was heading out of bounds when I saw Gary and an opposing player race for it. Two seconds remained when Gary grabbed the ball and in an amazing athletic feat spun around and shot a fade away jump shot as he fell to the ground. The ball arched in the air spinning backward on its descent to the rim. The buzzer sounded and, whoosh, the ball went through the net. This game was finally over. Gary was beaming ecstatically.

He came over and grabbed me saying, "I had to make that shot, Coach!"

"You sure made up for scoring for them," I said, smiling. The athletic director tapped me on the shoulder and in an urgent voice said, "Get your players and follow me, now!" His tone was demanding and of consequence.

I didn't understand the weighty situation we were in at that moment. The school policeman on duty had been summoned to defuse a fight at Pahokee High School. We were in the midst of 1,000 hostile fans without security. We were outnumbered. They hated Lake Worth to begin with, let alone after a triple overtime loss. It never occurred to me how dangerous a crowd could be.

He led us out a side door and we arrived to our cars safely.

On the trek home along that desolate highway with the sugar cane on either side, I looked in the rearview mirror at Gary. He stared dreamily into the fields with the black smoke still hovering in the distance. The winning shot was, undoubtedly, replaying in his mind. The sun was going down with a glow coming through the remaining clouds. The students asked if they could put on "their" music. I said as long as you win. I silently regretted this as Run-DMC and The Fat Boys filled the airwaves.

Two days later, I ended up in the hospital for an emergency appendectomy. It was excruciatingly painful and a Dr. Chong, who did my surgery, said that out of the hundreds of appendixes he had removed, that mine was the largest he'd ever seen. He said it was embedded in my colon and had it burst with all of that poison puss, well, perhaps I wouldn't be writing this. The next day, I opened my eyes to hear a voice. "How are you feeling, Mr. Neal?" a blond student named David asked with his raspy voice.

"Pretty good, David. How did you know I was here?"

"They had a hard time getting a sub for you yesterday and Coach Owen covered the class until they got one. He told us you were in the hospital. Are you going to be okay?"

"I am a little sore. They took out my appendix."

"That must hurt," he said. "I hope you come back soon. It's not the same with a substitute. You make us laugh." It didn't seem like I was talking to a thirteen-year-old boy. He was like a little man. A nurse came in to check on something and David said, "I've got to go, Mr. Neal. I had to hide my bike in the bushes because I don't have a lock."

"Thanks for coming, David. I really appreciate it." He left and the nurse took my temperature and gave me some antibiotics. I was tired and drifted off to sleep. Probably an hour or so passed when another David arrived. It was B. He sauntered in the room wearing an old T-shirt, gym shorts, Ray Bans, and was carrying a huge Puma bag.

"I need to use your restroom," he said and disappeared. I remember thinking what a nice guy he was for coming to the hospital. In less than a minute he walks out of the bathroom transformed. He had on a white jacket and a blue Versace T-shirt and tan loafers with no socks, not unlike Detective Sonny Crockett played by Don Johnson.

"Wow, that's a change," I said.

"Yeah, I have a date for lunch with an old flame from St. Augustine. She's a fox. I couldn't go out of the house looking like this. My girlfriend would lose her mind," he said, combing his hair in the mirror and seemingly falling in love with his reflection. "Yeah, I still got it," he said. "You look like you're going to live. Later," he murmured and was gone. No more than ten minutes went by and Coach Owen and one of the secretaries from Student Services, Holly arrived. Coach then pulled a yellow fruit out of his bag.

"Here take some of this. I grew it in my backyard."

"What is it?" I asked grabbing what he offered.

"Starfruit."

"I've never heard of it," I said, smelling the yellow fruit.

"It comes from the Philippines. It has amazing healing properties. Get some rest and come back whenever you are strong enough."

"Thanks, Coach." They were about to leave when I remembered the student's visit. "Hey, Coach."

"Yeah," he said.

"I had a student visit today."

"Oh yeah, who was that?"

"Dave Meader."

"Dave Meader!" he exclaimed. "Really?"

"Yeah, he rode his bike."

"Now that tells me something."

"What do you mean?" I asked.

"Dave comes from one of the worst home situations you can imagine. Both parents are raging alcoholics and his older brothers are in and out of jail. He's seen a lot. For him to make the effort to see you is remarkable. Hell, he lives on the south side of Lake Worth a good ten miles from here. You created a relationship with him. You must be doing something right. Maybe there's some hope for you," he said, winking as he left the room. When I returned to school, the students did seem glad to see me. Dave Meader was pleased when I handed him a bicycle lock.

CHAPTER SEVEN
"Parental Involvement with an Airborne Ranger"

Parent conferences are something that should occur for a parent to be informed of their child's progress. This one went awry. Jerome never gave me much in the way of behavioral problems, nor did he give me much in the way of work. Jerome's dad was tall and large like an offensive lineman. He had dreadlocks. Each teacher gave the same story that Jerome did little or no work and was failing for the year. Jerome's dad, in a loud voice, questioned our teaching skills and kept asking for extra credit or make-up work. He turned his nose up and showed his annoyance by sucking air with pursed lips while moving his tongue over his teeth after each comment. Then it came time for Tom Long to share. Tom was an Airborne Ranger in Vietnam. He was part American Indian and had a lived-in face with a grimace that was almost a death stare. It said don't fuck with me. The students never challenged him in the classroom. He began to speak. "You know what annoys me?" Tom said. Coach shifted in his chair nervously.

"What?" the dad said, leaning forward aggressively.

"It's when a parent comes in close to the last week of school, in a last-ditch effort, to coerce teachers to pass a student who hasn't done a lick of work all year."

"You talkin' to me," the dad replied, puffing out his chest.

"Yeah, I'm talking to you. I also don't appreciate you cleaning your teeth every time a teachers say something about your son. It's disrespectful."

"You better watch your fuckin' mouth," the dad said, standing.

Tom stood with alacrity and no fear ready for it all, saying, "You need to watch your profanity. There are ladies present." Coach stood up between them. The dad moved forward. Tom dropped his grade book rolling up his sleeves revealing his Airborne Ranger tattoo. I watched wide-eyed my heart pounding. Coach gently touched the dad, providing a buffer. I think the dad who saw Tom's horn-mad face might actually have been glad that Coach was intervening. Coach asked the dad to step outside. As he was walking out the door, he turned to Tom and said, "Better never show that face by the wall."

"You better hope I don't," said Tom. "I've offed more people than anyone by your damned wall." Tom's voice was loud and strong. Coach got the dad out the door. Dave Youngman turned to me and said, "They can never say we don't have parent involvement at Lake Worth Junior High."

The last five days of school before summer vacation are crazy. I think teachers look forward to the break more than the kids. The last day arrived and I learned how sentimental kids that age are. The girls cry and hug like they are leaving and will never see each other again. A couple students ran up to me giving big, heartfelt hugs. They were my first group of students. A few thoughtful students gave me some presents like drawings or something they made. A few even wrote letters designed to instruct me on how to be a better teacher. More than one said I needed to be stricter with them.

There was an announcement over the PA system that there was an important meeting after school at Mulligan's. It was the chosen tavern for the happy hour to kick off summer vacation. On the way out, I asked Coach if he was attending the festivities. We had an important conversation that I truly needed at that time. He started off by telling me that he didn't drink anymore. I had heard tales that he was a heavy consumer back in the day. He told me to go enjoy with the staff. He put his hand on my shoulder and said, "You did a pretty damned good job in the Peace Corps this year. I know our kids aren't easy."

"Thanks, Coach," I said, my back straightening.

"I mean it, you'll get better as you go. Do me a favor."

"What's that, Coach?"

"I have been at this school for twenty-seven years. Our school community, the Warrior Family, has become my family. You remind me of a young guy we had a few years back. He coached like you and did a great job. But, like a lot of the young ones, he left us for greener pastures."

"Another school?" I asked.

"No greener pastures as in more money. I think he went into real estate. What was your beginning salary this year?"

"$17,500," I answered.

"You see," Coach said with a slight irritation in his voice. "That's probably nowhere near what some of your peers with college degrees make, right?"

"That's true," I said as I thought about my friend Lance who just started with Pittsburgh Plate Glass (PPG) as a Computer Analyst in Pittsburgh. He made about $20,000 more than me.

"I just hope you give us some more time, Jeff."

"I plan on it," I answered. Dave Youngman was getting into his 1980 Diesel Oldsmobile. When starting it sent more black smoke in the air than a locomotive. As we walked together into Mulligan's we both had that feeling like we survived. Not everyone makes it through their first year of teaching. Dave and I unwittingly joined the Peace Corps that 1985–1986 school year. For two guys to move from upstate New York and Pennsylvania, landing in Lake Worth, where the tropics begin was fate.

Mulligan's was almost all wood and was a combination of an Irish Pub with connotations of the nautical with pictures of anglers with huge fish caught locally. A plate of chicken wings complete with blue cheese and carrot/celery sides was just the ticket. Cold pitchers of beer spread around the table as each teacher washed a little of the residue off from a year with junior high kids. Tom Long who was at the head of the table, raised his glass and said," To the best three reasons to be an educator: June, July, and August." Everyone was happy. B and Jose were holding court with another staff from a local elementary school, Barton. Little did they know that amongst them was seated a person who was going to come into our lives. I was bitten with the bug of curiosity about Tom, which stemmed from him being a Vietnam veteran who served with the elite Airborne Rangers. There was this shaman, warrior-like presence to him. The cold beers removed my inhibitions about going near him. It was time to engage him in conversation.

"I'm glad you had a chance to work with me this year," I stated. I informed Mr. Tom Long that he was fortunate to have worked with me. He looked at me for a second and a huge grin spread across his face. I'd never seen him smile.

"Sit down," Tom said as he pulled a chair out next to him. We began to talk. He really wasn't the tyrant that his countenance put forth. He poured himself another, saying, "The nectar of the Gods. Hey, you did all right this year."

"Really?" I answered, skeptical of this statement.

"Yeah, no matter how well you know your subject matter, it is not until you have to teach it to others that the information becomes embedded in your mind." I thought of me reviewing what a gerund was so that I could do a lesson on it. Tom continued, "I've had some deep conversations with Coach Owen and we both fear that schools, quite soon, are going to lose the discipline battle. Without structure in the classroom true learning will be dead. It's going to be a slow capitulation where gradually the students will have more rights while the educator will have less and less leverage."

"Is it because they took corporal punishment away?"

"No, it's more complex than that. It's the last day of school. Let's have this discussion another time." He went back to drinking his beer. I was disappointed as I was hungry for knowledge. Colleges by nature, in their assembly line-degree systems, don't take enough time to really give education majors the crucial information they need. You study educational philosophies and learn to write lesson plans. Student teaching will truly make or break your chances of being prepared for the task, and this all hinges on whom your cooperating teacher is that you are assigned. "More nectar of the Gods?" Tom said, tilting the pitcher toward my empty mug.

"Sure," I said. He poured the golden liquid.

"Have you ever been to the Keys?" he asked.

"Key West, no," I answered, my senses perking.

"I am going to Marathon this summer for mini-lobster season."

"What's mini-lobster season?"

"The regular eight-month lobster season is August through March. The mini-lobster season is when your allowed to catch the little guys. It's toward the end of July. If you want to go, you are welcome."

"I would love to," I exclaimed. "What should I bring?"

"A couple pairs of swimming trunks, T-shirts, boat shoes, and a big appetite. A bottle of rum wouldn't be a bad idea either. Give me your number and I'll call you," Tom said.

It felt good to be invited by this larger-than-life character. I always had a curiosity and respect for someone who saw combat. They have an education in life that no one else can know unless they step into that fire. I had some time before this lobster diving excursion, so I decided to make the drive to Pennsylvania in the Monarch. This time I stopped in Savannah. It was a nice stop with the manicured parks and a long walk around the historic district. The old southern houses with the antebellum architecture took me back in time to the Civil War. It felt strange to be pulling into the driveway in Butler. Something was different. Florida had taken ahold of me. It was good to see my family. My sister, Kitty, received an education degree in elementary education, though her passion would have been to be an anchorwoman reporting the news. She fooled everyone and took to the skies with Delta. M. Wayne was still the headmaster of Central Elementary and Mom was teaching Home Economics at Hampton Middle.

I have five friends that I've known since elementary school and we are still tight to this day, fifty some odd years later. Back then we were young and strong and thought nothing of staying out to two or three in the morning. M. Wayne still liked to knock on my door, particularly, if he heard me coming in during the wee hours of the morning. My first morning home I heard, "Get some breakfast, I could use some help with the lawn." Some things never change. My friends referred to his lawn as Augusta. While we were planting Pachysandra, we talked education. I admitted that my classroom management needed tweaking to say the least and I elaborated on the challenges of working with kids from generational poverty.

Dad said something that stuck with me. "I know that I encouraged you to teach elementary instead of junior high. I just thought it would be easier on you. Still, the middle grades are a crucial time in a student's life. There's a huge responsibility to prepare students for high school. You could be their last chance." I never thought of it like that. Mark Monteleone, one of my close friends, was fixing computers at hospitals in Pittsburgh. They were just beginning to enter education. July rolled around and I returned to Florida. As I got out of the Monarch, my sunglasses steamed from the transformation from the air-conditioning to the tropical heat. Tom Long called telling me we were leaving for Marathon Key in two days. I tried not to sound excited.

CHAPTER EIGHT

"ADVENTURE IN THE KEYS"

I heard the beep of Tom's horn from his red Dodge Ram. His boat was in tow. I purchased a rum called Brugal because I liked the net on the bottle. Tom had more bottles stashed in the cab. We were meeting his good friend, Gary Weed for breakfast. He taught with Tom at Lake Worth Junior High and jumped ship to teach History at John I. Leonard High School. While we made the three-and-a-half-hour drive from Lake Worth to Marathon, Gary's infectious laughter filled the truck as they relived their days together at the junior high. We arrived to a little spot in Marathon. It's about an hour away from Key West. We docked Tom's boat and spoke to Captain Dan, a local fisherman. He reported that there are a lot of lobster near Grassy Key, one of the islands that comprises the City of Marathon. Once the boat was docked and secured, we popped around town enjoying the mom-and-pop-type resorts around Sombrero Beach.

Gary knew his Florida history. He informed me, "Marathon is comprised of thirteen islands that were originally inhabited by Calusa Indians. Ponce de Leon in 1513 arrived in his quest for the fountain of youth and gold. They enslaved the Indians and logged out the mahogany trees. Then they mapped the Keys to use Florida as a route for their ships journeying between Central America, the "New World," and Spain. The Spanish were the ones who gave the chain of islands the name "Keys," from the Spanish word "cayos," meaning small islands. It was inhabited by hard-working fishermen and farmers, until Henry Flagler began—"

"I came down here to get lobster, not have a history lesson," Tom said, interrupting the plethora of thoughts emanating from Gary. We had huge hamburgers as the sun was going down. We went back to the boat at the marina where Tom had rented the slip. There was a good-size mid-cabin beneath the aft where the three of us fit to sleep. The moon was almost full and the water was gentle. Tom turned in early after a couple of beers and a stiff rum drink.

Gary and I sat up on the front of the boat sipping rum. He spoke endlessly about all things Floridian. Later I went down below. Tom was snoring and I was extra quiet not to awaken him. I remember thinking he might get up in a flashback and attack me. The next morning, I awakened to the smell of eggs and bacon drifting through the cabin. Gary was cooking on a grill by the stern. Tom was attaching two thick lines right behind Gary. He had them folded in a perfect circle.

"Lobster diving is a lot like spearfishing. Those little sea critters are hard to find," Tom said as he grabbed a plate.

"Yeah, but we're going to find them. This is the life. Warm clean water, good exercise, and, of course, the feast of lobster we are going to have," Gary said.

"Are you guys using dive tanks?" I asked.

"Don't need 'em," said Tom.

"How do we find them?" I asked.

"All in good time, son," Tom said. We untied the boat as Tom fired up his twin Evinrude Outboard engines. Gary said, "Divers call lobsters bugs because the crustaceans and insects come from the same phylum,

Arthropoda. They are the tastiest cockroaches of the ocean. They share a lot of the same traits such as jointed appendages, legs, antennae and—"

"I don't want to listen to your yap spewing facts all day. Let's just catch some lobster," Tom said while trolling the boat slowly. Gary laughed and yelled, "Who wants a beer?"

"I do," said Tom and he opened it one handed and took a long draw. "If you don't start drinking in the morning you can't drink all day," he said with a grin.

Gary picked up the lines and threw them behind the boat on either side of the engines. "There's your gear," he said, pointing to an Army duffel bag, which contained a snorkel mask and fins. The mask fit tightly and there was a thin wetsuit shirt. I watched as Gary put on his gear. He was sitting on the back of the boat when he said, "We are going to jump in and grab the rope. Tom is going to pull us. On the sea floor you look for four long, thin antennas. If you see them, drop off and go down for 'em." He fell backwards into the water. I did the same. I grabbed the line and started to drag.

The water was clear. I could see the bottom easily. All the sea life looked magical. Gary saw an antenna and dropped the line. I observed him diving straight down. He immediately came up with a huge lobster. He swam toward the boat and tossed it to Tom. A huge sea turtle swam by, followed by a manatee. A family of dolphins seemed to watch us curiously. We trolled on and then I saw a set of antennas. I dove down and my ears hurt slightly as I grabbed the lobster. It wasn't as big as Gary's, but it felt good to get my first lobster. Tom circled the boat and made a motion that he wanted to get in for the fun. I saw some other fish and asked Gary, "What are those?"

"Nurse sharks," he replied nonchalantly. The one I was asking about looked to be about seven feet long. Tom was in the water with his spear gun and I thought these sharks don't know who's in town. The noon sun was directly overhead when we stopped. Wherever we anchored, I don't know, but I couldn't see land. We had peanut butter and jelly sandwiches. I was starving from the sun, saltwater, and exercise. I wolfed down three sandwiches. I drank a cold bottle of water and could feel it going down the whole way. Tom and I jumped back in and we hit a spot that Gary had planned on going. There was a city of lobsters on the sea floor.

At the end of this diving frenzy, we had eleven lobsters in the cooler. Gary made a rum that was his favorite from Trinidad, called "Zaya." Tom, reddened from the sun, was seemingly pleased. Dolphins were swimming on the north side of the boat, coming up out of the water as if to say hello as we trolled back to the marina. I could see a man standing at the dock with white hair. It was B. "Oh shit he did come down," Tom said. "Hide the rum, or it'll be gone by the end of the night." I thought Tom was kidding, but Gary handed me two bottles and told me to stow them away in the cabin. Tom tossed Dave a thick rope. He tied us to the dock, weaving rope over and under quickly like a sailor who had done this before.

"You could be a good first mate with that skill," said Gary.

"That comes from my days in the Bahamas," Dave said as he grabbed his red rumrunner off the wooden pole by the pier. There was a bar with a tiki roof giving off the feel of the tropics. Dave had booked a room on A1A not more than a mile from our boat. There was an outdoor shower by our slip, and we jumped under the cold water. A little soap and shampoo and I felt great. Dave was driving his old Jeep that the students had named, the "Green Puke." He scouted out a rustic restaurant with a huge wooden horseshoe beam running across the bar. We all sat down. Dave ordered a Seafood Tower. It consisted of a pound of Key West Pink Peel-and-Eat Shrimp and a half a dozen Gulf Oysters and Indian River clams on the half shell. Tom sneered at Dave.

"Is there something wrong?" asked Dave.

"Yeah, I think there is," answered Tom.

"What?"

"You are not going to come down here and freeload! You're not going to dive for lobster and drink all of the rum. I want money for gas too."

"No problem," said Dave.

"There better not be," Tom said, his glare in full force now.

Gary winked at me as he ordered some Conch Fritters and a pitcher of beer. I ordered Mango Crab Cakes loaded with blue crabmeat, diced mangoes, peppers, and onion. It was pan seared and was served with key lime mustard sauce. Gary couldn't resist poking the angry bear.

"What exactly did happen when you were roommates?"

"I'll tell you what happened," Tom said. "He never cleaned the kitchen. He ate onions with everything."

"I did clean up," Dave protested.

"You did not. One day I had to carry all of the dishes into the front yard to hose them off. They were coated with butter and onion. You ate my food too when you were drunk."

"Well at least I didn't attack you," said Dave.

"You're lucky I didn't kill you. I warned you." There was a silence. Gary couldn't let a sleeping dog lie, enjoying the gas he was putting on the fire. "You attacked Dave?'"

"He had it coming," Tom said agitatedly. "I was on the phone in my room talking to a gal. Dave kept knocking on the door. I told him I was on the phone. He kept on knocking."

"I needed to use the only phone we had," Dave added.

"I told you to wait. Do you remember when I opened the door and said if you knock one more time, I will hurt you?"

"Yes," Dave answered, sounding like a little kid.

"What did you do?"

"I knocked again."

"That's when you got what was coming to you," Tom said as he exited to the men's room. Gary started to laugh.

"Did he hit you?" I asked.

"Hit me," Dave said animatedly. "He attacked me like a wild animal. He was scratching at my eyes and tried to bite my jugular vein." Gary was in hysterics as he added to this anecdote explaining, "Dave came to school with scratches all over his face and his shirt was ripped. The odd couple only lived together for four months, right?"

"Four of the longest months of my life," Dave uttered.

In a few minutes, Tom was back. Fresh seafood is like nothing else. When the bill arrived, Dave threw a hundred-dollar bill on the table. Tom thanked him and collected some money from Gary and I. Once back at the marina, a similar scenario as the night before unfolded. Tom went below to sleep. Dave, Gary, and I were up. Gary, like a juvenile delinquent, opened a bottle without Tom knowing. This bottle was Ron Zacapa out of Guatemala. The conversation that ensued was illuminating.

"So how was your first year teaching?" Gary asked.

"It was quite a year. I didn't have much discipline in my classroom. I had an appendectomy. It's a lot harder than I thought it would be."

"He did all right," Dave interjected, "especially with the basketball team."

"You know what, Jeff," Gary said as he sipped his rum, "it's probably one of the hardest jobs in the world. If you made it through a year at that school that says a lot. You need to think like Frank Sinatra who used to say in New York, New York... if I can make it there, I'm gonna make it anywhere."

"Amen," said Dave, adding ice and a generous dollop of rum to his glass. The moon was full. I felt good to be in the company of these older men. I knew I was lucky to be privy to their wisdom as each of them were decades older than me. Gary was from Arkansas and mentioned that William Jefferson Clinton was his student and that he was intelligent but was a real smartass.

"You had quite a journey, Dave. You were in the Bahamas, right?" Gary asked.

"Yeah, I spent three years in Nassau," Dave said.

"I have never been to the Bahamas; how was it?" I asked.

"It was beautiful. Paradise."

"Why did you leave?" Gary inquired.

"To survive. I was going to drink myself to death. I was working at a school and didn't have to do shit. A typical day was showing up at the school around 11:00 and taking these cute little Bahamian kids to the clinic for shots. While they were there, I would walk over to a tiki bar and have a rum and Coke or three. No one gave a shit. Their schools were ass backward at that time."

"What years were you there, Dave?" Gary asked.

"The early 1970s. I met my second wife, Anita, there."

"How many times were you married?" I asked.

"Three times. Twice for love and once to get back in the country," he added nonchalantly.

"Back in the country?" Gary asked with a laugh.

"Yeah, I was born and raised in Canada."

"Did you work in Florida before the Bahamas?" I asked.

"I got a baseball scholarship to Ball State. I was playing pretty good and the Yankees drafted me to a farm club my senior year."

"Really? Did you go?" I asked, impressed.

"No, something happened that derailed my chance."

"An injury?" Gary asked.

"No, I got my college sweetheart, Coleen, pregnant. She was beautiful, drop-dead gorgeous. She was in education. Her major was teaching deaf and dumb kids. We both were working at a high school in Indiana after graduation. While I was teaching PE, I got my master's in counseling."

"You were a counselor?" I asked with surprise in my voice.

"Yep," Dave said, pouring another glass of rum. "Anyway, one of the best schools for the deaf and dumb is in St. Augustine. It was Ray Charles's alma mater. Coleen interviewed and got the job. I interviewed for a guidance spot at St. Augustine High School."

"This was in the mid-1960s, right?" Gary asked.

"Yeah, I was put in charge of desegregating the schools."

"Whoa, you must have a story there," said Gary.

"Oh yeah, there were death threats on me and my family. You see St. Augustine has a racist underbelly that is strong until this day. The KKK is big there. Hell, when Martin Luther King was staying in downtown St. Augustine, they put an alligator in the pool of the hotel where he was staying."

"Tell me about the Civil Rights thing?" asked Gary.

"I remember the night vividly when I had to go up in front of everyone in the high school auditorium and address the whole town. The Blacks were on one side and the Whites were on the other. Desegregation was scary for all stakeholders. You could have heard a pin drop when I stepped up to that podium. I told 'em we have to grasp that this is the law, and it's our duty, as Americans, to follow the law of the land. I laid it out right there, bussing, the whole nine yards. In the days following I had to do what is known as a Charette. It worked."

While I was digesting this and trying to picture the hard-drinking PE teacher with his Quasar hat, as a young man, in charge of desegregating a school system, Gary broke my reverie.

"You know what's amazing about that story?" Gary said.

"Go ahead," Dave stated, gesticulating with his glass like he was a blue blood.

"It's that you were up lecturing the entire community about their patriotic duty and you weren't even a citizen."

Tom awakened and yelled from below, "Shut up! I'm trying to sleep!" We looked at each other like kids at a sleepover getting scolded. Dave slept on the boat that night in the captain's chair. It was our last day in the Keys when I noticed a roadrunner tattoo on Tom's left thigh. The twin Evinrude engines spilled blue smoke as we embarked on a final outing. Dave opened up his cooler, pulled a can out and bellowed, "Got up in the morning and grabbed myself a beer!" Jim Morrison would have been proud. I looked out over the water and in the distance, the sky was a dark purple mixed with royal blue. You could see the rain coming down under a veil of darkness. Tom steered his vessel as we had blue sky above us.

We were trolling along at about seven knots. I spied an antenna and dropped, like an old pro, to extract him from the ocean floor. After about an hour, Tom anchored and we ate lunch. Dave and Tom fell back in the water and grabbed the lines. Gary grabbed a machete and promptly began cracking some coconuts that we found near the slip. He was like a surgeon pouring out the water and once filled with ice, was a perfect tropical glass for rum. Tom and Dave were dragging on the lines. The sun felt good and the storm seemed far off in the distance. Gary was telling me a story of a time he'd stolen a golf cart from a marina in Marathon with another inebriated debauchee. They drove up A1A not knowing they were blocking traffic behind them. Gary was immobile with laughter when he recalled the golf cart caper. I turned around. There was one empty line in the water. I squinted and thought maybe Tom went under. Dave was waving his arm side to side frantically and pointing behind him.

"Gary, I don't see Tom," I uttered.

"What?" Gary said, turning around killing the engine. Dave was swimming up to the boat. He sat on the seat on the small ladder aside the engine, took off his mask, and said breathlessly, "Tom dropped off a while ago."

"Oh shit," Gary said. "He's going to be pissed." He turned the boat around and pushed full throttle against the wind. I climbed up to the front of the boat to look for signs of Tom. Gary was panic-stricken. "There he is," said Dave who'd found some binoculars. He pointed to the east and Gary didn't let up on our speed. Gradually, Tom's tiny head appeared. As we got up closer and eased off the throttle Gary pulled the boat beside Tom. The wake covered Tom's head. He choked on the water. He came up slowly doing the side stroke to the ladder.

The Tasmanian Devil had nothing on Tom as he climbed on the boat, struggling to remove his flipper with this menacing howl. He looked at the coconuts on the floor of the boat. He promptly began to fire them at Gary. "You motherfuckers almost drowned me!" he blurted out as he fired one green missile after another at Gary. He ducked and caught one on his shoulder and started to laugh. This infuriated Tom more. Gary's laughing and Tom in his shorts with the roadrunner tattoo made me laugh as well. Upon seeing me snickering, he picked up the last two coconuts and fired them at me. One caught me square in the middle of my back. Dave calmly stood behind Tom drinking his beer. Tom grabbed the spear gun. That led Gary to stop laughing.

"I came here to get lobster and by God I'm going to do it," Tom said as he put back on his flippers and snorkel gear and dropped off backward into the water, this time with the speargun.

"I knew he was going to be pissed," Gary said, his smile returning. "Dave, you going to get back in with him?"

"Hell no," said Dave as he picked up my half shell of the coconut and made himself a rum and coconut water.

"Jeff, don't let him drag alone," said Gary who by now was gathering himself after the onslaught of coconut missiles. I reluctantly put on my gear and fell backwards in the water.

I felt the tension on the line and we began to drag slowly. A crazed Vietnam Veteran with a speargun was eight yards to my right. I looked over at his face scanning the ocean floor with his flippers rhythmically pumping like pistons. He looked over at me and with our eye contact he sneered and looked back at the ocean floor. The whole time we were dragging, I fully expected the spear to pierce my side.

Fortunately, the biggest lobster we'd seen appeared and he dove down. This capture seemed to cool Tom as his snarl faded away. Shortly thereafter the rain came. It was surreal underwater as the rain pelted the sea. There was peace and quiet just under the surface. Lightening filled the sky. Tom nodded for me to get in the boat. I went down below and dried off. We had a good mile or more to get back to the marina. Once there we put the lines away and locked the cooler. We decided to seek shelter at the tiki bar. The monsoon raged and we were under the natural canopy of a thatched roof. I had my first rumrunner. We placed about seven lobsters on the grill, which we devoured with clarified butter. The meat was firm yet sweet and soft, delicious.

Awakening in the morning, I found a lemonade jug and gulped right from the container in an effort to cool the fire in my throat. It was a beautiful day with clear blue skies and stratus clouds, like white mountains, sporadically floating in the distance. Dave offered Gary a ride back. He accepted right away, still leery of Tom, with realistic concerns of his retaliation. It was just before noon when we pulled onto A1A. We drove a few miles in silence. I decided to break the ice.

"Tom, thanks for taking me to the Keys."

"You're welcome," he replied. I looked out at the Atlantic to the south and the Gulf of Mexico to the north. Tom looked over and said, "We never finished our conversation from the happy hour."

"About discipline?" I asked.

"Education in general."

"No, we didn't."

"Do you think you want to stay in teaching?"

"I think so," I said.

"Well, sit back and I'll tell you a few things. "Two years ago, Reagan commissioned Bill Bennett, Secretary of Education, to prepare a report about the state of education. This was an 'Open Letter to the American People.' It had military analogies calling the nation to arms and apocalyptic references that a rising tide of mediocrity threatens the future of our nation because of education. There's no doubt about it; we are in decline."

"Why do you think that is?" I asked.

"Well, this report will tell you that the US is going down the tubes because of the poor job we're doing in the classroom. Reading and math scores have been going down for years; this is nothing new."

"Why is that?"

"Most of the problem is the home. White upper-middle parents are the worst. They do nothing but run interference for their kids. Instead of challenging kids, they want lower expectations. One parent told me that I was giving too much homework and that her little Johnny didn't have time to be a kid. They also think their child's gifted. It's like we don't have any dumb kids now! Can you imagine that?"

"Actually, I can," I answered. This was years before "helicopter parents" became a catchphrase, but Tom was on to something in 1987.

"I started to teach in 1974. Those kids wanted to learn. Right now, these kids could give two shits about learning. There may be an achievement gap, but I say there is an ambition gap."

"What's the answer?"

Tom continued, "There is no simple answer. Preschool would equalize the playing field with students such as ours. The government will never pay for that. Education has to become a priority again instead of missiles. We spend more money on alcohol and tobacco than we do on education. We made the transition from an agriculture-based society to one that is industry-based. Now a new frontier is upon us and it's going to involve technology."

"Computers?"

"Yes, that's where the future lies. Not just computers, other technology that hasn't been born yet. We are going to compete with China and India. Most of the developed world is doing better than us. We are going to have to have the basic skills first. The television is going to need to go off and books need to open. Parents have to help with that and I don't have a lot of confidence in the one's I'm seeing now. If you're going to stay in this education career path, just know it's going to be a salt-dust trail."

"This has been inspiring," I said with sarcasm.

Tom cracked a rare smile and said, "There's two books you should *read. The Closing of the American Mind by Allan Bloom, and Cultural Literacy* by E.D. Hirsch. They explain what's happening today in education. Speaking of books, I'm watching you. You study people and are an observer. That's what writers do; they observe. Maybe you have a book or two in you?"

"I never thought about it." A seed was planted. We drove north on A1A. Tom, with his roadrunner tattoo, and the meanest face known to mankind was looking at the road ahead. I bought and read both of the books he recommended for my own edification.

CHAPTER NINE

"THERE'S A NEW SHERIFF IN TOWN"

Preschool week arrived. I ascended the stairs to the library for the first faculty meeting. That morning the cast of characters had changed. Larry Jenkins, one of the first Black principals in Palm Beach County, was gone. There was a woman with two young men in suits and ties that flanked her. Along with them was a large man, a Deputy Superintendent, named Berryman. He wore no socks and had leather shoes from Italy. There was rumbling amongst the faculty. Teachers don't like change. They detest it with a passion. It is an egregious shock to a teacher's system to introduce a new administration.

At that time Palm Beach County School District had a true good old boys club at the helm of leadership. "Good morning, teachers," began the sizable Deputy Superintendent. "I'd like to welcome everyone back to a new school year. I hope your summer was filled with relaxing activities with family and friends. This morning, it is my pleasure, to announce some exciting new changes to your school. Mr. Jenkins is retiring for health reasons. I would like to introduce your new principal, Sharon Walker." The two guys in suits were introduced as new assistant principals. The only members of last year's administration that were present was Coach Owen and Virginia Smith. Coach looked stoically upon the faculty, leaning on a bookshelf as we absorbed this news. I tried to read how he was feeling. His gaze was expressionless. Tom was seated across the room. His hand went up. The big man called on him.

"What's going to happen with Coach?" Tom asked.

"That's an administrative decision," Berryman answered.

"What does that mean?" Tom asked curtly.

"Exactly what I said, an administrative decision."

Just like that after twenty-seven years of dedication to one school, he had to pack his bags. "Do you have any idea what he means to us, and to the kids for that matter?" Tom asked. Coach watched silently. His back seemed to straighten as Tom spoke positive affirmations about the beloved man of Lake Worth Junior High.

"That question was answered," he said. "Mrs. Walker, please greet your faculty." Sharon thanked Mr. Berryman and took the microphone. She began to speak. Her voice was friendly and professional, but she had a look like you didn't want to cross her. She said, "I come from a family of educators. My daddy was a principal and my mother was a librarian. My sister is a teacher and so is my husband, Dan." The way she said Daddy reminded me of a southern woman. I wasn't too far off as I found later that she was raised in Fernandina Beach, the northernmost city on Florida's Atlantic coast. The meeting concluded with an argument over how the money generated from the soda machine would be distributed departmentally.

When I walked out of the library, the news of Coach being transferred hit me with blunt force. He was such a treasured figure to the community of Lake Worth. There was a legacy. Tom was not happy that he had been let go. We were standing there discussing the changes when Coach appeared. He thanked him for speaking up. "Tom, you were always a man's man. Good luck, Jeff," Coach said, smiling, "I hope you remain a Warrior for a while." As he walked away with that bow-legged gait, he lit a cigarette. I'd never seen him smoke in the hallway. I guess he figured he deserved it. Only a handful of people I've met mastered the art of living in the altruistic way that Coach did.

There were two new computers in my classroom. Tom's words reverberated as I saw we were at the dawning of a new age, computer-aided instruction. I didn't even know how to turn one on. These new-age technology monsters sat in the back of my room and I did my best not to touch them. Dave Youngman was asked to teach the newly added computer class. My classroom switched to the second floor and my new neighbor was Tom Long. The new wave of students came in and my numbers soared. At that time Palm Beach County had the fastest growing population in the state of Florida. I remember seeing more Haitian students on campus. The boys would look like they were dressed for church and the girls would be in colorful dresses with tiny white socks and shiny black shoes. I remember watching a couple of neatly dressed Haitian students passing my room and I remarked to Tom, "They dress sharp."

"Yeah, wait a few months and they'll be Americanized" was his retort. He had his own way of doing things. There were two little munchkins who sprinted down the hall each day. I kept telling them to slow down. "I'll handle this," Tom said. The next day as the sprinters were flying down the hall, Tom unhooked the large wooden door. Just as they were passing, he flung it open and, bam, both students collided with it and fell to the ground. One was moaning and the other was rubbing his head.

"I'm so sorry," Tom said, picking one up by his wrist. "If you hadn't been running that never would have happened." They walked the rest of the year. Something inside of me wanted to change the way I was teaching. I knew I needed to provide some instruction that was going to grab them. I began to ruminate about lessons I gleaned from that challenging first year. Journal writing was something that students liked. Some of the things that came from their pens to the paper made my brain do backflips. The one event that stood out in my mind, of that first year, was the space flight of The Challenger.

It was a crisp, beautiful day with the sky a brilliant blue, not a cloud to be seen. Students are notorious for being unaware of current events, but they were surprisingly cognizant of this flight. It took place on January 28, 1986. I was probing them the day before the flight and they knew a lot. One boy named Toby knew this NASA flight would be the first to go into space with a teacher aboard. Her name was Christa McAuliffe.

I ventured outside with my class to the PE field to see if we could get a view of the flight. It was a clear day and NASA was a mere 137 miles northwest from Lake Worth. It was cold that morning. We made our way out to the basketball courts. The students brought their yellow legal pads to jot down their observations. The flight went off around 11:30. We were watching white exhaust smoke created by the millions of gallons of water evaporating from the back of the space ship. The kids were pointing at the white trail when out of the blue, literally, there was an explosion. We couldn't hear it, but we sure could see it. The white cloud of smoke created from the explosion stood out in the blue sky.

"Wow!" the kids bantered back and forth.

"What happened, Mr. Neal?" a girl named Terry asked.

"I am not sure," I answered honestly. I was hoping that it was part of the shuttle breaking off like the old Apollo 11 missions I watched on TV as a kid. On the way back to the classroom with the students chatting incessantly about what they witnessed, the principal, Larry Jenkins, was walking by and delivered the news. He watched from a TV in his office. "Seventy-three seconds into the flight and the whole thing blew up," he said. "I can't see how there were any survivors."

"Oh my, God" was all I could muster as I looked at my students. They had a vague realization about what just happened. I waited until we got back into the room to tell them. Their reaction was quite surprising when I revealed to them that all members on board were probably dead. A boy named Pancho asked if we could have a moment of silence in remembrance of the crew. I agreed and we stayed quiet for one minute. I remember being able to hear the ticktock of the antiquated black clock on the wall. I decided to incorporate a language arts activity in this moment by asking them to write about their reaction to what just happened.

Once again their cooperation and maturity took me by surprise as they started to write their feelings experienced in response to this event. So much for the ulcer-breeding monsters that day as I read with amazement at the heartfelt and astute essays. I had to laugh at one boy's thought that it was "Saton." This taught me the power of bringing current events into the curriculum. After I came out of this reverie from a year ago, I knew I wanted to engage this new batch of kids with more than grammar or spelling. What could be that hook?

CHAPTER TEN

"HIP-HOP IN THE CLASSROOM"

That next morning as I walked by the cafeteria, I heard a boom box. I remembered in 1975 when this portable sound system came on the scene. Ten years later with hip-hop culture on the rise, everywhere you went, one could hear the bass pounding sound as the rap music flowed on our campus. There were four or five boys nodding their heads to the rhythm that morning as I stopped and put my briefcase down. They were oblivious to my eavesdropping until one of the boys tapped the other and pointed at me. He turned the music down.

"You need somethin'?"

"No, I was just checking out the sound."

"You like hip-hop?" one asked.

"Can't say. I haven't heard enough of it," I replied.

"Play something for the man," the biggest of the crew said.

"What should I play?" the boy asked.

"Play him Grand Master Flash and The Furious Five," the boy calling the shots said. He rifled through a gym bag full of cassette tapes. The music started. They sang every lyric without missing a beat:

"It's like a jungle sometimes
It makes me wonder how I keep from going under
Broken glass everywhere
People pissin' on the stairs, you know they just don't care
I can't take the smell, can't take the noise
Got no money to move out, I guess I got no choice
Rats in the front room roaches in the back
Junkies in the alley with the baseball bat
I tried to get away, but I couldn't get far
'Cause a man with a tow truck repossessed my car
Don't push me 'cause I'm close to the edge
I'm trying not to lose my head
It's like a jungle sometimes
It makes me wonder how I keep from going under...."

The boys finished my private concert. The words explained the desperation of living in the "hood." They knew each word and every inflection. Later after the Pledge of Allegiance my students sat down with all of the enthusiasm of someone going to a dentist's office. "Good morning," I said. A few students murmured unintelligibly.

"I was going to ask you to get out your grammar book, but I decided to alter my plan." A few faces brightened. "Instead, I wanted to talk to you about something that I've been thinking about." I stayed quiet for a few seconds. Then I repeated the verse from the rap that the boys sang to me just fifteen minutes ago, "It's like a jungle sometimes it makes me wonder how I keep from going under."

In unison, the class roared, "Ah, heh, heh, heh." This was the sound the rapper made after certain stanzas. There was a transformation and the entire class was engaged.

"You are going to teach me about rap music," I said.

"Whooo!" Todd said. "You are off the chain, Mr. Neal." I'd already spoken and there was no turning back. I decided to speak to them about some pretty highbrow concepts. I put forth how our brain or memory is still a mystery, even to scientists. Encoding was mentioned and how information in the brain is stored, either in short term or long term.

"Our ancestors remembered stories if they were told in a song. Just like you remember the Grandmaster Flash song and every other one I hear you singing."

"It's not singing, it's rapping," said Jeffrey.

"Name some of the other rappers," I said. A first for me occurred as all hands were raised. I compiled a list on the board: RUN-DMC, Rob Base and DJ EZ Rock, Grandmaster Flash & The Furious Five, Vanilla Ice, Beastie Boys, and 2 Live Crew. There were only ten minutes left. I gave a homework assignment to write the lyrics to their favorite rap song. The next day my hip-hop class had their favorite rap on their desks. We began a concept known as peer editing. Once they were in pairs, I asked them to take turns reading their raps with their partner.

In moments they were reading aloud and the cacophony was circulating around the room. A quiet classroom doesn't necessarily equate learning. There was an enthusiasm for learning I hadn't seen in my classroom until that day. Out of the corner of my eye, I saw a face in the window of the door. It was one of the new assistant principals. Sure enough, Sharon was right behind him. She was very hands-on and walked through classrooms daily. I was supposed to be teaching the standards that the county had put forth that were mandatory. How would I explain that they were reading raps? "I don't see your objective for today's lesson on the board, Neal," the assistant principal, Mr. Williams, said in a no-nonsense tone.

"This class is a day ahead of the others, so I am having them analyze some poetry," I answered as I watched Sharon go up and down the aisles, hands behind her back, inspecting the pairs in action. She nodded to the assistant principal and they left. I asked if someone would volunteer to share their favorite rap. I called on Trevor who was shaking his arm so hard I thought it might come out of socket. He came to the front of the room and performed "Raising Hell" by Run-DMC. Despite the title there wasn't a lot of profanity in the rap. I learned my lesson when Linwood came up and started to do a rap from 2 Live Crew titled, "We want some Pussy."

After that I proofread anything that was going to be read in front of the class. Without exception each day they requested that we rap. I used it as a carrot to get them to finish their grammar and vocabulary lessons. The students came up with all kinds of ideas to incorporate rap into lessons. We had twenty vocabulary words to learn each week and they asked if they could use the words in a rap and make a contest out of it. It was amazing the way they weaved words.

The Libyan dictator, Muammar Gaddafi, bombed a West Berlin nightclub, killing three people, including a US Service man. It was all over the news. Ronald Reagan launched a series of air strikes. I asked my students to bring in articles from the paper and write a reaction paper to the US bombing of Libya. The Hip-Hop class wanted to do raps regarding this current event. They were in groups of three reading the articles and writing rhymes about this dictator 6,000 miles away. When you're really teaching and students are engaged, there is little to be done by the teacher. I sat at my desk, in amazement, as they scrambled to get organized for their performances. Each group came up with their own beat and their rhymes were in sync. They grasped the nuances of the bombing. Gaddafi was the villain and a patriotic theme emerged.

In the middle of the fourth performance, another assistant principal, whose name was Mr. Leach, appeared in the window. The students were so engrossed, I don't think they even noticed his presence. I sat up a little and studied his expression wondering what he was thinking. The smile on his face caused my concern to abate. When the students finished their rap, he began to clap and the other students joined him. "Very innovative, Mr. Neal. Getting your students to use their music to be abreast of current events, I'm impressed. I want you to pick out a group and they are going to deliver their rap on the morning announcements tomorrow."

"Okay," I stammered, thinking that picking out one of the groups of students would be a difficult task not unlike cutting basketball players. The last group to strive to be selected was Todd, Jimmie (a girl), Jeffrey, and Ralph. Ralph almost blind, wasn't much on the rhythm, but the lyrics were definitely influenced by him. He captured the essence of what happened with a US Servicemen being killed and our retaliation with the term "extreme prejudice." Keeping them after class, I asked if they'd be willing to go on the announcements. They acted as if they'd hit the Powerball.

The next morning the four boys and Jimmie were nervous. Students at that age are self-conscious and to know that their voices would be blasted into each room via the PA system weighed heavily. I left them sitting in the main office. They looked as if they were facing a firing squad. Just after the Pledge and morning announcements there was silence. At first, I thought they decided not to put them on. Then Mr. Leach got back on the system, "Today, we have a special treat from Mr. Neal's class." (He named them.) "His students will be performing a rap that they wrote about a current event that is going on right now with our country and Libya."

We heard them getting the mic settled. They began and no fear was discernible. When they finished, Mr. Leach said, "That was a fantastic job, students, and an example of stepping out of the box by Mr. Neal to choose a creative way of teaching. Have a wonderful day in Warrior Country." When the four rappers came back after their performance, they were greeted with a round of applause. I was glad the students got some accolades, but I wished that Leach hadn't complimented me publicly.

Teachers are by nature competitive with one another. They're always seeking praise from administrators. Sure enough, snide remarks headed my way in the faculty lounge. About this time Sharon announced we were making a transition to be a middle school. The term *junior high* was antiquated and now Lake Worth Community Middle School would be on our letterhead. There was a conference near one of the Jackie Gleason Theaters in Miami. The Head of the English Department, Mr. G. Kenneth Long and I were chosen from that department to attend.

Kenneth is one of the most unique individuals that I've met. Born in Bradenton, Florida, home of Tropicana Orange Juice, he attended Kentucky University which was a bold move for a Black Floridian in the early 1970s. He and Tom Long may have had the best discipline of all teachers. They would tell their students they were brothers. Kenneth would often let his classes know that he wanted to be able to hear a rat pissing on cotton in the corner of the room when they were working. At that time, we were a faculty that liked to party hearty. 8:00 a.m. hit pretty hard and we all got up, grudgingly, for the morning professional development session. All of us accept Kenneth. "You better get ready," I said.

"I'll go down there when I'm damned good and ready. If they don't like it two tears in a bucket and mother fuck it."

Kenneth has a mind of his own. Besides, professional wrestling was on and he was an avid fan. After a quick continental breakfast with a bagel and cream cheese I attended the session for English teachers. A half hour passed and no Kenneth. Sharon came over during a break and asked his whereabouts. I said he was around somewhere. I pictured him still watching wrestling. I ran up to the room on a bathroom break.

"Sharon was asking about you," I said with some urgency.

"I don't give damn. She's not my boss. The heavenly father is my only boss. He is the one that I am accountable to on this earth. Besides, Lex Lugar is about to take on Yokozuna." I wasn't quite sure whom these wrestlers were as I stopped watching in the days when Bruno Samartino and George

"The Animal" Steele were popular. Finally, in walks Kenneth. One of Sharon's minions was tasked to find out what sessions teachers attended.

"Kenneth," the young lady asked. "What sessions did you attend?"

"Why do you need to know this?" answered Kenneth.

"I am to let Sharon know," she said.

"If you must know I attended the session with Lex Lugar and it was fascinating." Kenneth walked away with the girl searching through the agenda looking for the session with Lex Lugar. At the conference we learned that a community school is a partnership between the school and other community resources, with the major goals being improved student learning, stronger families, and healthier communities.

After the conference the magical last day of school was approaching. I was reading journals of my students as the last assignment was for them to tell me what they wanted most out of life. It was eye opening for me as so many just wanted safety. Safety from guns, gangs, or a sexual predator in their own household. I didn't have time to address all of the issues that were staring at me from the pages of these journals. My eyes were fatigued to the point that I wanted to rub them out of my eye sockets. I really had a passion for this career, but I knew in my heart of hearts that being an English teacher wasn't for me for the long run. Staring at the mound of journals with the insurmountable collection of emotional, physiological, psychological, economical, and spiritual issues facing these students I had an epiphany. I felt in my bones that I wanted to become a counselor.

The last day of school happy hour was upon us and it was the usual rounds of pitchers and chicken wings with the Warrior Family. It was amazing how close knit we were. Sharon liked her rum and coke and she was adamant about staff members attending happy hours. A lot of excellent ideas came out of those moments, with hors d'oeuvre and adult beverages. It was a time to debrief, and there was an atmosphere of family. She, kiddingly, would tell Dave Youngman and I that our attendance was part of us attaining continuing contract. At that time a teacher had to put in three years, and be recommended by their principal, before they could achieve that form of security. A teacher has chosen a profession where they are, arguably, the lowest paid college graduates in the work force. People will say things like you get so much time off. Yes, there is time off, but the majority of teachers work in the summer. I was contemplating summer school or finding a job. Jose mentioned that I could work with him in a Palm tree nursery that summer. I took him up on the offer to work at Gumto's Palm Tree Nursery, which was off of Tenth Avenue North in Lake Worth.

CHAPTER ELEVEN

"THREE DOLLARS AN HOUR"

I was amazed at the rows of massive Sabal palms in this nursery. Many of the customers were from the island called Palm Beach. The first day the owner put a shovel in my hand and taught me how to plant coconuts in the ground. After an hour of digging in the loose soil in what native Floridians call, "sugar sand," it was enough to make me appreciate my teaching job. This was 1988 and I had my first encounter with an illegal immigrant. A man called Elvis B. Pickens, a resident of Belle Glade, arrived to the nursery with a Haitian man with a shovel. The owner of the nursery, Mr. Gumto, came running out to ask his portly customer, "How many palm trees today?"

"Three," he answered with a southern drawl.

"Jose, get the backhoe," Gumto said excitedly.

"No need," said Pickens. "I got my man here, Pierre."

"That's a big job to cut out those palms by hand," Jose said.

"I pay him so I don't get charged the extraction fee," he replied chuckling. Pierre slowly walked out to a huge palm and started to dig. It was 110 with the heat index. He was thin and sinewy with the kind of strength that could hold a lot of leverage and endurance. As I planted coconuts, I watched with amazement at him digging under the huge root ball. After two hours he stopped and drank from a rustic canteen. "That guy is amazing," I said to Jose.

"Yeah, imagine what shape he's in to do that. Slave labor is what it is. I could have dug all three in half an hour with the backhoe. He's probably illegal," Jose said. Pickens climbed into his truck and left. Pierre didn't have a lunch pail. I had a fat tuna salad sandwich, from Marie's Sandwich Shop, in the refrigerator by the barn. I left my shovel and retrieved the chicken of the sea between two pieces of white bread. Pierre continued to dig as he glanced over his shoulder sensing my presence.

"Sak Pace," I said, uttering a greeting in his language.

"N'ap boule," he replied with a smile.

"Would you like half a sandwich?" I asked.

"No," he said quietly.

"I can't eat all of it, are you sure," smiling holding the half toward this sweating man whose muscles were like tight fiber. He took a breath and reached out and took my offering. He let the shovel drop and devoured the thick amount of tuna in two bites. I looked at his calloused hands holding the last bite.

"Thank you," he said his Creole accent evident. He finished one tree and methodically went to another palm. In another hour and change he'd dug it out. He guzzled from the canteen and I was weary just watching him. Pickens wheeled in on the dirt road leading into the nursery with a dust cloud in his wake as he skidded to a halt. Jose was spraying Round Up on a tractor and I imagined that he fantasized spraying the sugar baron from Belle Glade with the poison that is now the subject of class action cancer suits. Pickens sashayed over toward me burping and spitting tobacco juice.

"Pierre's an amazing worker," I said.

"He better be. I'm paying him three bucks an hour," he said with laughter moving his gelatinous belly.

WHAT A LONG STRANGE IT'S BEEN

"Three bucks an hour!" I exclaimed in disbelief.

"He doesn't have any room to complain," he countered.

"At least he's not cutting cane in my fields. Now that's real hot work. Where you from?"

"I grew up outside of Pittsburgh."

"Figures you're a Yankee," he smugly replied.

"Three buck an hour is that all you pay him to do that?"

"Pierre got here illegally. I just saw a bunch of Guatemalans getting on a school bus. I bet 90% don't have green cards. They're going out to pick fruit and vegetables in the best soil in the country. Imagine we had to pay healthcare and minimum wage. That would be tens of thousands more. If they get a paycheck, taxes are taken out. That's why you don't have to pay exorbitant amounts for my sugar. Fruit in the stores is cheaper because of those Guats sweatin'. They all live together and send money back to their families anyway. It works for everyone." That ended our conversation and time passed.

"I'm leaving early; I have class tonight," Jose announced.

"What kind of class?" I asked.

"I'm getting my master's in Educational Leadership."

"Really?"

"I got twenty more years to retirement. Sending kids for B's Quasar hat isn't how I want to spend them."

"Do you want to be a principal?"

"Hell yeah. Why can't a Cuban be a principal?"

"Go for it," I added.

"You should go get your master's."

"I was thinking about counseling," I replied.

"Go for leadership, man. Isn't your dad a principal?"

"Yeah."

"It's in your genes, man. There's more money in administration," he said hopping in his yellow pick-up. Pierre waved from the back of the truck and it still bothers me to this day how he was treated. The US doesn't have a proud history with people of color. What we did to the Indians makes Hitler look humane. Tom Long wasn't allowed to have the kids read *Trail of Tears* by John Elle about the removal of the 18,000 Cherokee from their eastern homelands. That's another story.

CHAPTER TWELVE

"COUNSELOR EDUCATION AND A NEW SCHOOL"

I made an appointment with an academic adviser at Florida Atlantic University for the Counselor Education program. A letter from M. Wayne arrived. I'd put his penmanship up against our founding fathers that wrote the constitution by hand with quill pens. He mentioned the weather and some news from the Neal clan. The P.S. said:

> Dear Jeff,
>
> Enclosed in the small envelope you will find a check for $1,766. This is the amount you have paid, thus far, on your debt for the Monarch. I am releasing you from the $1,234 you still owe. Perhaps, you could put it toward a course on the master's level.
>
> Love,
>
> Dad/M. Wayne

I had some extra money and a sign that a graduate course was in order. In the first class I took a bath in theories from the heavyweights of psychoanalysis like: Sigmund Freud, Carl Jung, B.F. Skinner, Jean Piaget, Abraham Maslow, and Carl Rogers. If I had to point to one of these pioneers in psychology, I'm a fan of Carl Rogers, although, I'm Jung at heart. I was teaching, coaching, and taking graduate courses for two years. My Master's in Counseling was realized just as the news came that the old Lake Worth Junior High was moving to a new site. Lake Worth Community Middle was now being constructed. Sharon hired Jose as an Assistant Principal as his degree in leadership was conferred as they broke ground at the new school. One of her other AP's, Wayne Williams, recently died from cancer. Jose was freaking out about the move.

"This is a nightmare," he said with his husky voice.

"Why is that?" I asked.

"C'mon, I'll show you," he motioned for me to get in his brand-new convertible Ford Mustang. We made the short drive from Lake Worth Junior High to the site of the new building. With his long hair blowing in the wind on the short trek north on I-95 he was a man with a mission. He was chosen by the district to be the school's liaison with the construction company. It was a shame where they chose to build our new school. The land was once a pristine Florida jungle. That summer on my many visits to walk around the construction site I saw the remnants of nature still trying to find their home that was invaded. Sea turtles, Fox Squirrels, Great Blue Herons, gray and red foxes all were scrambling to find sanctuary as land was cleared. The critters eventually found a new home. Lake Worth Community Middle was opened in 1990.

"Jose, it's going to be cool to have a new school," I said.

"Yeah, but you're in the classroom and I am going to be doing discipline. It's going to be a nightmare."

"Why?"

"Sheer numbers. What do we have right now 800 kids? Adding the sixth grade we have three grades and are projected to have a student body count of 1,200 students. I believe it will be much higher."

"Do you think so?" I asked. "Four hundred more students!"

"To add insult to injury we are a cluster for EH."

"What's EH?" I asked.

"Emotionally Handicapped students. The real special ones are SEH."

"What does that stand for?"

"Severely Emotionally Handicapped," he said. "It's going to be a sea of torment for whomever we can get to work with those students."

"Is it that bad?" I asked.

"It's bad. They have a license to do whatever they want because they fall under the umbrella of ESE," Jose said.

"What do you mean?"

"That means that you have kids with behavior disorders that can only be suspended for ten days out of the year."

"Why's that?"

"Education for All Handicapped Children in Act passed in 1975, the Americans with Disabilities Act (ADA), and the Individuals with Disabilities Education Act (IDEA). These good laws had great intentions, like Section 504, that levels the playing field. As with a lot of ideas with great intentions there's mishaps."

"Like what?"

"Ok," Jose said, lighting one of his Benson and Hedges. "Any student who is considered EH or SEH can hit you and spit in your face. The law says their behavior is a manifestation of their handicap. You only can send them home ten times, and if you want additional days, you have what is called a manifestation hearing. This entails getting the parents and the teachers in for a meeting and then you may get a few days added to work with. Hold on to your hat, it's going to be a bumpy ride." I started to read about these behavioral disorders. I noticed that ADHD was the most common. Reading the symptoms of impulsiveness and hyperactivity I was sure I was accurate in my self-diagnosis.

David Youngman always makes a call the night before the first day of school to announce what year this was going to be for us in education. This was year five and he had some bad news, at least for me. He decided to take a position teaching Advanced Biology at Atlantic High School. Later he would go on to become the head of their prestigious International Baccalaureate program. Like gypsies, my fellow teachers and I, packed up and moved our classrooms. There is a feeling of excitement for a teacher to go to a new building with fresh walls. Jose's prediction regarding the student body was spot on as he had to order fifty additional portable classrooms. It looked like Tobacco Row. The district's push for the middle schools to become community schools and to implement the team concept was vigorous. There were two teams, made up of four core subjects, in each building or pod, with roughly 130 students. My team was called "The Producers."

1985-1986 Boys team. Future West Palm Beach City Commissioner, Cory Neering (far right with arms folded).

Getting ready to perform "Alley Oop" at an assembly. Left to right: Jose Garcia, Frank Bermudez, David Youngman, Dave Bingeman (center), Kenneth Long, Tom Long (Alley Oop, glasses), Don Towne, Jeff Neal.

Coach David "B" Bingeman on the PE field.

Jose Garcia in his PE days with David Bingeman. The Butch Cassidy and Sundance Kid of education.

CHAPTER THIRTEEN

"TOURETTE'S AND TYRA"

That year I would have a student that had Tourette syndrome (TS). It was something that had been around, but the awareness of it was in its infancy. His parents brought research papers on the neurological disorder to each teacher. Middle school parents, by nature, are frantic regarding the change from the cocoon of elementary to the ominous middle school. When I met his parents, I could smell the anxiety exuding from them. I did my best to assure them that we were a caring team of teachers and we would do our best to help their son, Mark. What was this complex neurological-developmental disorder characterized by tics and involuntary reactions often laced with profanity? I pored through the articles and learned that the tics occur unpredictably. Alleviating stress for the student was the most effective way to reduce the amount and severity of the spasmodic twitches. Ironically, ignoring the symptoms was highly recommended to demonstrate acceptance and normalize the behavior. It is a fine line to walk.

One day in the middle of silent reading Mark blurts out, "Fuuuccck!" I motioned for him to go in the hallway. He had an empathic way of nodding as if saying he knew this wasn't easy on me. The only incident that caused me some anxiety regarding my experience with him occurred during a competitive assembly. Volleyball, basketball, and a skit were the events that each team was asked to put together. When I asked each class to come up with a skit Mark's group was voted first place. He had the lead and was performing before the entire grade. What concerned me was that he might experience anxiety which could cause the chemicals in his brain to become inflamed. The day of the assembly some added adversity arrived. Mark was playing tackle football and came in on crutches with his joint swollen like a baseball. I asked him if he thought he could perform the skit. He nodded yes, but when he did so his eyes blinked in rapid succession and he barked. He sounded like a collie. "I can do it, Mr. Neal. My friends need me," he said.

"Ok," I replied skeptically. We filed into the gymnasium. Sharon had a way of getting a large group quiet without saying anything. She would grab the mic and gradually the talking and laughing would dissipate. Mark came out on his crutches and greeted each actor as they passed him and went behind a curtain. His head was jolting every few seconds. The student body didn't seem to notice. Each student would emerge from the curtain with some new clothing such as a hat, shirt, pants, and shoes. Mark would ask each student where their new attire came from. They would reply J.C. Penny. A very funny student, called Tiger, emerged wearing only his boxers, seemingly, in a panic. The entire student body erupted in laughter.

"Who are you?" asked Mark without a tic or vocalization.

"J.C. Penny!" Tiger yelled as he streaked out of the gym.

Mark was barking and the student body thought it was part of the skit. They were a hit. A student with Mark's condition is a classic example of being true to the Individuals with Disabilities Education Act (IDEA). He could have been separated for the inappropriate sounds and profanity and suffered from a poor self-image had it not been for his parents. They advocated for their child. Once in a conference a counselor asked if Mark was on medication. His mother replied, "Mark's condition is who he is, and to alter the chemistry of his brain could have adverse effects."

During this time, I noticed a tall, lanky guy who had a beard. He looked familiar. I then remembered the first time we met at a Language Arts workshop my first year of teaching. "Jeff, this is Barry Grunow," Kenneth Long said.

"Nice to meet you," I said, shaking his hand.

"You too," he replied in a quiet laid-back manner.

"I think we met years ago at Loggers Run at a workshop?"

"I taught at Logger's Run," he answered with a smile seemingly pondering something, "Now I know where I saw you. Are you still the coach?'

"No," I replied. "I am going for a master's in counseling."

"Counseling. That's cool. I love to teach English, but if I had to do something else in education, I think being a counselor would be a great way to help kids. Take it easy," he replied as he ambled off with a loping gait. There was a serenity to him, a countenance of tranquility. Back in those days LWCMS needed someone who exuded serenity. The campus was bulging at the seams with almost 1,600 students and the EH unit, with thirty-plus students, was alive and kicking. We were a Title I school. Money is granted by the state based on the free and reduced lunch rate. Ours hovered around 94%. Sharon chose to invest the additional money granted in technology, creating our first two computer labs. I remember seeing the kids glued to those mysterious screens.

On a whim, I walked into a puppy mill. When I picked up a tiny Doberman, she grabbed on to my shoulders trembling. I walked out the door with a crate and a new member of the household. Dobermans are known to be hyper and this dog was no exception. The first night she was in my home I was trying to come up with a name and Tyra Banks flashed on the TV. Tyra it was. I'd just bought a two-story townhouse and there was no yard for this excitable, high-strung canine to run. I began to take her to the school in the evening for runs around the track. Each night Tyra and I would take the ride to the school. No one was on campus with the exception of the custodial staff. One night while I jogged around the track the head custodian, Willie Grimes, called to me. His office was on the east side of the school right next to the cafeteria. When I got there, I noticed another custodian, Ken Phillips, and a Spanish-looking gentleman. They were all smoking. The five female custodians, seemingly, were doing all the work.

"That's the running-est dog I ever seen," said Willie.

"Yeah, she can go for miles and miles," I replied.

"Why don't you get the golf cart and take it around."

The next thing you know I get the cart and Tyra is following me just inside of the track on the grass striding like a gazelle. I remember thinking she could hang with the Greyhounds at the dog track in West Palm Beach, owned by the Rooneys of Steeler fame. I dropped off the cart and decided to engage the mysterious Spanish guy.

"Hi, I'm Jeff," I said to the man.

"Maximo, nice to meet you," he said.

"Nice to meet you to," I answered.

Sharon wanted to see me in her office. She was a smoker and things had changed since the days when Coach Owen could fire up one cigarette after another in his office. I'd grown up like that. Upon entering Dad's office, there was always a thick blue cloud of smoke hovering. Sharon, in the early nineties, had to join the politically correct stance of not smoking on campus. She had some rebel in her as she would stand half-way in her office bathroom and wave the cigarette back and forth feverishly so the stream of smoke would blow up through the fan. "I hear you're bringing your dog on campus and using one of the golf carts," she said waving her Benson and Hedges. She was like a CIA supervisor. How did she know this?

"Yes, I have been bringing her to let her run," I said, thinking this treat for Tyra was ending. "Do you want me stop?"

"No, I don't care. I want you to find out something for me about one of the custodians," she said in a hushed voice.

"Who?"

"Do you know, Max?" she asked.

"I met him the other night, but I don't know him."

"I spoke to him the other day and there's more to him than meets the eye." Sharon had an uncanny sense about people. "I think there is something that we could utilize as a BIA. See what you think."

"What's a BIA?"

"Behavior Intervention Assistant," she answered. "We are going to use some of our Title I funds to hire two or three people because we really need help."

"Help with what?"

"Our EH unit. We need special people to deal with those kids. It is unbelievable what goes on in those portables. I don't know how those teachers deal with it. You have a good sense of people. Just investigate and see if you think Max would be a good fit for that position." The next morning, I asked one of the EH teachers if I could observe a class. I laughed when he said to bring a helmet. He wasn't kidding.

CHAPTER FOURTEEN

"Q AND MAD MAX"

The front portables were nicknamed the bungalows. Passed the flagpole, just inside the gate, I heard this pounding. It sounded like soldiers in ancient times, with a battering ram, trying to break down the door of a castle. The teacher who had advised me to bring a helmet came running down the ramp yelling into his walkie, "Send the police, please! One of my students is in crisis." Six or seven students ran out of the room. They were all laughing, screaming, and cursing about whatever was going on in there. The teacher reluctantly walked back into the room. I followed. It could only be described as a war zone. Ten desks were either on their side or upside down. The blinds were ripped off from the top of the windows, one of which was broken. There was a massive hole in the cheap, vinyl covered gypsum wall where the student was standing in the corner. He was breathing heavily while staring at the teacher.

"Try to calm down, Jerry," the teacher said softly.

"You need to shut the fuck up, motherfucker," he said in a voice that sounded otherworldly. He hissed at me and then let out a maniacal laugh.

I remember thinking he was possessed. "What the fuck are you looking at?" he said to me.

"I'm just visiting," I said in the calm tone the teacher used.

"You can fuck off too," he said. Two officers entered.

"Jerry, are you having a bad day?" one officer asked.

"Fuck you, pig!" he shouted.

Just then a hulk of a man walked in the doorway. I'd seen him around and assumed he was a PE teacher, always in T-shirts and shorts. His name was James Quillian. The kids called him Q. He had a lived-in face that reminded me of an Irish boxer.

"Thank God you're here," the teacher said to him.

"Hi, gentlemen," Q said to the policemen. "I've got this."

"Are you sure," the one officer said.

"Yeah, he'll do better if you two aren't here," he replied.

"Ok, call if you need us."

Q moved in front of Jerry about ten feet away. Jerry said nothing. The other teacher motioned for me to step back. I've seen kids mad and having a tantrum, but Jerry was on a whole other level. He picked up a book and threw it. Q turned like a matador and let it sail right past him. "Jerry," he said with a tone that was firm but calm, "why don't we take a walk around the track?" Jerry didn't think that was a good idea as he ran right at Q and took a swing. It was a right hook and it would have hurt if it had connected. Q leaned back and with his left hand pushed the punch away. The momentum caused Jerry to fall into Q. Ever so slowly he held him in a bearhug until hitting the floor. He then grabbed Jerry's right foot and slowly wrapped it around his leg like a pretzel. "Go ahead, guys," he said on one knee with a smile, "he'll calm down."

"Thank you, Q," the teacher said with relief in his voice.

"Is it always like that?" I asked as we walked away.

"Yes, this is a regular occurrence." I could hear Jerry cursing as I walked back toward the school where students were changing classes. I was rattled and wondered how those teachers did that every day. The daily toll on their psyche had to be colossal. In front of my classroom Sharon was tapping her foot. "I was out in the front portables. I see what you mean about the EH unit," I uttered.

"It's something isn't it? Did you talk with Max yet?"

"No, I was going to try tonight when I take Tyra to run."

"Let me know. I need two BIA's."

That Friday I saw Max in the doorway of the garage. "Hey, Max I was wondering if you want to have a beer?"

"I don't drink that much beer," he replied. "I will have a scotch, though."

"Do you know where Jack's Town Tavern is?"

"Yes."

"Give me half an hour."

"See you then," I answered.

When I arrived, Max was already in a booth smoking and nursing a scotch. I ordered a beer from an attractive waitress who had long brown hair and some jean shorts. As I looked at her walk away Max said with a big smile, "Daisy Duke."

At first, he was hard to understand with his thick accent. I felt like a spy trying to get information for Sharon.

"Max, I don't mean to insult you, but you just don't seem like a custodian."

"Aren't you astute, Mr. Neal."

"I have a story."

"Go for it."

"I was born in Santo Domingo in the Dominican Republic."

"I don't know much about the Dominican Republic," I said.

"DR is great if you can get past the poverty," he answered.

"My mother and sister moved to Flushing, Queens in New York when I was thirteen. My father and I went to San Juan, Puerto Rico. He built boats. We joined my mother in the Big Apple about two years later. I graduated high school in 1967, joined the Navy, and went to Vietnam."

"Did you see combat?" I asked.

"Yeah, I was on a PT boat stationed on the Mekong River."

"How long were you over there?"

"One year and that was enough."

"Then what?"

"I came back home, attended Queensborough Community College and ended up working for the NYPD."

"Wow, how long did you do that?"

"A couple of years. I got divorced and went back to Santo Domingo for a visit and never left.

"What did you do there?"

"I was a policeman during the mid-seventies and then I was hired to be the head of Dominican National Security at the American Embassy. The best part is I met Al Pacino."

"Really," I said astonished, "how did you meet him?"

"He was doing a movie in DR and I was in charge of his security. That was before he got sober. We had a good time."

"So, you worked at the Embassy the whole time?"

"No, I got recruited by the DEA."

"You're shitting me," I said wondering if all this were true.

"I got no reason to lie to you. You want a scotch?"

"I've never had one," I said.

"It's an acquired taste. It will never give you a hangover. I can drink scotch all night and when I wake up, I'm a little thirsty and that's all. If I drink rum all night it takes until about three in the afternoon to feel normal."

"I'll try one," I said.

"Two Chivas and waters, por favor," Max said.

"Go on," I said.

"In the '80s drugs flowed through the island. The DEA was trying to try to battle the corruption as the drug dealers were in control. That's when I had a little problem."

"What was that?" I asked as the scotch arrived.

"In a coordinated effort with the DEA I got into a situation. It was him or me," Max said, lighting another cigarette.

"Did you kill someone?" I asked.

"Yeah, not just anyone," he said with a sigh, "I put down the son of one of the most notorious cartels at that time. I came here to lay low for a while."

"No kidding! Will you be able to go back?"

"Eventually, I want to retire there. It will take some time."

"Max, did you ever talk with Mrs. Walker?"

"Sometimes she comes out and has a cigarette with us." I smiled thinking that was pretty cool of her. My mom always said that two of the most important people on the staff to stay on good terms with are custodians and cafeteria workers.

"Why do you ask?" Max inquired.

"Sharon's looking at you for a position."

"What?" Max said, almost choking on his cocktail.

"She needs someone to be a BIA."

"What the fuck is a BIA?" Max asked.

"It's a Behavioral Intervention Assistant."

"One thing I'm learning about the school system is that you people have more acronyms than police. What's EH?"

"EH is Emotionally Handicapped."

"Is that those kids that are out front?" Max asked.

"Yes, how did you know that?"

"Those portables are fucked up every day. The first time I went into clean them I thought vandals had been there. What does a BIA do?"

"They help to keep a lid on things with those kids."

"Lid on things, huh? Max said as he gulped his drink, "It never fails."

"What?" I asked.

"A long time ago I was in a bad situation on the river in Nam. I had a talk with God who I never really believed in. Atheists, for the most part are atheists until the plane starts falling. Anyway, I prayed."

"What did you say?" I asked.

"Put it this way I made a bargain with God. Pretty soon I heard a boat. I had no idea if it was friendly or the VC. I shot out a flare. There's no way I should have made it, the place was crawling with VC. So, when life brings something like this BIA shit, I believe I'm here to do it. God has blessed me with six wives and I have seven beautiful kids."

"You've been married six times!" I exclaimed.

"Yes, I am still with wife number six."

"Now, I know you are full of shit."

"Here let me show you something," Max said as he pulled a picture out of his wallet with three women on either side of him.

"These are your wives?" I asked.

"Yes, that was on my 50th birthday. They all still love me even the one I shot."

"You shot your wife!"

"It was an accident. I'll tell you that one another time."

"Ok," I said. I paid the bill and we walked out of the bar.

"Those EH kids are wild. Are you sure you want to do this?" I asked. Max crawled into his white OJ-like Bronco and said, "Hey, I was a cop in New York. I answered domestic disputes and saw all kinds of crazy. I'll probably feel right at home."

Max in his days as head of Dominican National Security at the American Embassy.

Maximo Michel heading off to Vietnam at age 19.

CHAPTER FIFTEEN

"LEADING THE LEAGUE IN SUSPENSIONS"

The next day I reported to Sharon that I thought Max would be a good fit for the BIA spot. Like most schools we were struggling with teacher retention, attendance, and punctuality. Sharon implemented a practice that greatly curbed the lack of teacher attendance, although, it probably wouldn't fly today. At this time to procure a sub one had to call an automated sub-locator. Sharon came up with an aplomb scheme to circumvent this practice. She delivered her plan in a stealthy manner at a faculty meeting. "Good morning. We have a district-wide problem with teacher attendance," she began. "Your students don't get the best quality education when you are missing. No matter how good the substitute may be, there is nothing that compares to you being in front of them. Even if you call in the night before, there is a chance there will be a vacancy in your position. We have to ask teachers to cover your class on their planning time. So, our new policy is when you are sick, call me instead of the sub locator."

"Are you saying that we must call you at home?" Kenneth Long asked.

"That's what I'm saying. That way we can find the best possible person to fill in for you. We are starting the Perfect Attendance Award. If you go the entire nine weeks without an absence you will get a certificate for Perfect Attendance and a raffle ticket for a $100 gift certificate at Okeechobee Steak House. This roused some interest as most teachers were aware of this fine restaurant, a landmark since 1947, with perhaps the best-aged steaks in West Palm Beach.

To have to call the principal was wise on Sharon's behalf. It was not an easy affair. She would ask how sick you are and inform you that we are already "scraping the bottom of the barrel." Often the teacher would acquiesce. Sharon would commend them for their dedication and professionalism and there would be one less teacher out that day. She received an award from then Superintendent, Tom Mills, for having the lowest percentage of teachers missing school. It wasn't until I retired and received a payment for my accrued sick hours that I truly appreciated her policy. The one teacher who devised a system around this practice was B. There were nights he knew he didn't want to hear the ear-splitting noise of the locker room the next morning. Jose, Kenneth, Tom Long, B and I were at the El Bandito. B was definitely into his cocktails. He announced he was going to call in sick. I told him that Sharon was not going to like it being that the next day was a Friday. He looked at this watch and said, "It's almost time. You know how organized and methodical she is, right?"

"Yes."

"She takes a shower at the same time every night. It worked last time. It will work right now." He dialed her number. "Hey, Dan it's Dave Bingeman." he said to Sharon's husband. "May I talk to Sharon?" A pause was followed by a wink. "Hey, give her a message for me. I'm really feeling horrible and am not going to make it in tomorrow. Ask her to get me a substitute, please. Thank you, Dan." He hung up.

"She was in the shower?" I asked.

"Oh yeah. I have tomorrow off." Dave was a true character. As crazy as he was, he had a lot of knowledge. Once he assisted me with my counseling degree. I was assigned to bring closure to the members of my Group Counseling course on the last night of class. I was to run the session as if I were the counselor and had no idea how to approach this. Heading to my car I saw him. "B," I yelled out.

"What?"

"I have counseling class tonight and I have to end a group session. Any ideas?"

"The final session of a group, mmm, that's an easy one."

"What do I do?" I asked feeling a glimmer of hope.

"Do the empty chair."

"What's that?"

"You set a chair off to the side and you explain that each person is going to get their turn in the chair. The purpose of the session is to bring closure and send each member off with observations that the group has about them both positive and negative. It's important when they're in the chair that the members confront. That is the essence of counseling, confronting the client. Do the sandwich method. Say something positive and then confront. Tell them to be brutally honest. Then have each client tell the person another positive trait they have. At the end you get in the chair and take your medicine. Some crying and hugging and all of that shit should occur. I'm off to the Rum Keg for dart league."

That evening the technique that Dave recommended worked seamlessly. I explained the process as if I'd run a group session many times before. One by one each member, including me, got in the "chair." This approach did help each member with closure. After the class Dr. Tucker, the professor, asked me, "Where'd you get that idea, Fritz Perls?" It was hard to describe B. About this time Tom Long moved on to another middle school. He earned his degree in Educational Leadership and was hired to become an Assistant Principal at Woodlands Middle. I believe Sharon wanted to hire him, but she was told by the Superintendent, at that time, that under no circumstances would that man be an administrator while he was at the helm. Apparently, Tom had an encounter at Mulligan's in the bathroom with the CEO of Palm Beach County Schools. He asked him to step outside and settle their argument. The Superintendent wisely refused and Tom told him he never would have made it in Vietnam. As soon as the Superintendent retired Tom was scooped up. Tom was pound for pound the best source of discipline on a campus I've ever known. He was fair, firm, and consistent. He took me under his wing, a true warrior, and I won't forget the lessons he imparted.

Sharon masterminded a way to reduce the number of days her teachers called in sick, but there was something beyond her control. The suspension rate at Lake Worth Community Middle was one of the highest in the county out of all middle schools. This is a conundrum for a principal. You don't want to lead the league in suspensions. The hierarchy of leadership at the district office faced immense political pressure to reduce suspension rates, particularly, of minorities. It didn't matter that an influx of gangs was appearing on campuses and they were at war with one another. Each suspension was a red mark against your school. Sharon and Jose came up with a plan. I should have known something was up when they wanted to take B and I out for cocktails. We met at "Flannigan's" which used to be "Mulligans." They were in a booth. Sharon and Jose were having their standard rum and Diet Coke. Dave was imbibing an Absolut Martini that was swimming with olives.

"Sit down, Jeff. Would you like a beer?" asked Sharon.

"No, I think I'll have a Chivas on the rocks," I answered.

"Oooh, Chivas," said Jose. "You are maturing."

Dave downed his martini like it was an ice water and promptly ordered another. Sharon ordered appetizers. Jose was making small talk when Dave cut him off mid-sentence, "All right, what are you two up to?"

"What do you mean, Dave? Can't we just show you guys a good time?" Jose answered with a grin.

"Cut it out, Jose," Sharon interjected. "You're right Dave. We asked you here tonight because I need a huge favor."

"Here we go," Dave said as he looked over at me. Sharon explained the pressure she was under to reduce the suspension rate.

"What is it you want us to do?" I asked.

"We can't just suspend them like before," Jose began. "If we remove them from class without suspension and keep them on campus, we are still supporting the teachers and our rate goes down?"

"We already have Alternative to Suspension," Dave said.

"We only have fifteen seats. ATS can't handle more."

"And we can!" Dave said almost with a snarl.

"Dave, with your counseling background and Jeff's ability to handle kids, you two will be great," Jose countered like the smooth operator he is. "It's only for eight weeks. Just keep them away from the classes. If need be, I'll remove them."

"Are you two willing to do this?" Sharon asked.

"What do you think, Dave?" I asked.

"Fuck it, Dave said. We agreed.

Just like that our teaching assignments changed on a dime for the last eight weeks of school. As I broke the news to my classes that I would not be finishing the year, they were a sea of tires with all of the air slowly let out. I would check on them, but it wouldn't be the same. Dave and I were housed in a small room with ten or twelve desks and two small tables. By Friday we had twenty students in our care. I made the rounds to get work for them. Not one of our detainees were interested in the assignments whatsoever.

Sharon sent reinforcements. His name was Frank Mascara. He was a guidance counselor, a new addition to the Warrior Family. He had a pony tail, earring, and was reminiscent of a young Jack Nicholson. The one thing I did notice about him is that kids loved him. He was always in perpetual motion, like a Pied Piper, with a gaggle of kids in tow. Teachers complained that students always wanted to see him. It was Friday when he came by and you would have thought a celebrity entered our midst. Even the hardened students perked up at the sight of this counselor. Dave, a voracious reader, was reading a thick Robert B. Parker novel and ignored the whole scenario. Frank greeted each student and seemed to know something personal about each of them. He validated everyone in the room. "Sharon, asked me to see what I could do to help. How about I do a little group counseling with a few of them?" Frank asked.

"I just finishing my master's in counseling. It would be good to observe," I said.

"Join in if you want," he replied. Arguments were starting to occur amongst the students being cooped up all day. Students use the term "beef" to describe a disagreement. A conflict resolution is putting out a fire brought on by a "beef." Frank was a masterful fireman. Another type of fire was starting. One of the first modern school shootings occurred at Heath High School in West Paducah, Kentucky. A fourteen-year-old was behind the gun. Coach Owen warned about this type of carnage ten years prior to bullets starting to fly on our school campuses in America.

Mr. Tom Long greeting a disruptive student. Tom passed away in 2021.

CHAPTER SIXTEEN

"Don't Talk about Mamma"

One afternoon Dave and I decided to take the students outside for some fresh air. We had them on the aluminum bleachers beside the track. We had walkie-talkies and could listen to the unfolding drama of a school day. One of the PE teachers yelled 36, the code for a fight. As soon as the words were uttered several male students, all gang-bangers, leapt to their feet and began to sprint. "Fuck!" Dave exclaimed. "See if you can get them back. I'll keep an eye on the rest."

"Okay," I said. After coercing those that fled, they reluctantly followed me back to Dave and the other detainees. I respectfully asked for them to keep moving. One of them said something in Spanish and grabbed his crotch.

"Why do you have to do that?" I asked.

"He's showing you what yo' momma sucked last night," a student named Luis said. The others laughed and high-fived him. A rage began to brew within. I contemplated my next move as the group settled back into the bleachers. Dave came over and asked about the fight. I informed him it was gang related and he nodded saying, "Of course."

"Dave, I need to talk with Luis, privately."

"Ok," he answered. There was an unspoken communication as he sensed something had transpired.

"Come with me, Luis, I need some muscle. We began our short walk to a portable that was not in use. We walked up the wheelchair accessible ramp to a room I thought to be vacant. I was surprised to see a permanent substitute named Gerry Grover asleep in the corner. He was fresh out of college and had a reputation for being out on the town. He wasn't yet on the payroll. This was his hideout. He stirred and raised his head.

"I was just resting my eyes, Mr. Neal," he said.

"That's okay, Mr. Grover. Luis and I are going to talk."

"Okay," he said and exited the other door.

As soon as the door closed, I turned to look at Luis. He knew we weren't there to move desks or tables. His eyes met mine and he swallowed deeply making an audible gulp. He made a quick move and I sprang forward and shoved him into the wall. I decided to go old school with a stiff forearm right under his chin to get him to a place where we could have a discussion. My left hand was against the wall.

"You want to say something about my mother again?"

"No," he whimpered.

"You crossed a line."

He nodded and I released my arm. Immediately he sprinted out the door that banged against the railing of the ramp.

It does them no favors to not confront their aggressions and let things slide. A judge looks at an assault or rape and doesn't care if the student's behavior is a manifestation of their handicap.

As I got back to Dave, he asked, "So how did that go?"

"I made my point," I replied.

That night I wondered if there would be any ramifications for my confrontation with Luis. Sure enough, as I walked through the Main Office, Frieda Proctor, Sharon's Confidential Secretary, told me to report immediately to Assistant Principal, Mrs. Osta's office. Luis's mother and grandmother and several youngsters were there. The mother looked at me as if she wanted to kill me. Abuela (Spanish Grandmother) seemed as if she was pondering a slower act of torture where severe pain could be inflicted. Luis sat with his head down making no eye contact with anyone in the room.

"Mr. Neal, Luis's mother had some disturbing things to say about an incident yesterday. Luis reported that you choked him," Mrs. Osta said.

"Do we need someone to help translate here?" I asked.

"Yes," Mrs. Osta replied. Immediately, I left the office. Our full-time language facilitators were all busy in other conferences. My next thought was Gloria Hernandez, one of the secretaries. I asked her to translate. She said she was busy as her phone was ringing off the hook and people were lined up at the counter like it was Dunkin' Donuts early in the morning.

"Gloria, this is very important. My career is on the line."

She looked at me and nodded and said to give her a minute. Once back in the office Mrs. Osta told me that the mother mentioned getting a lawyer. Finally, Gloria arrived.

"Gloria," I began, "Whatever you do please translate exactly what I say. I know that you are a good Christian woman, but I need you say it word for word, okay?"

"Yes," she replied sensing the gravity of the situation.

"I was physical with Luis," my admittance opening the door to litigation. "I never at any time choked him. I kept him against a wall so that he could get my point." I waited as Gloria translated. The two ladies looked at me disapprovingly as the children climbed on Mrs. Osta's desk. "Gloria, here is where I need you." She nodded. I proceeded to explain how his friend, and fellow gang member, grabbed his crotch and my asking why he had to do that. "Luis replied...." I paused for dramatic effect, "he's showing you what your momma sucked last night." Gloria rendered the words in Spanish, "El te esta enseñando lo que tu mama chupo anoche."

As soon as these words were uttered both the mother and Abuela averted their gaze from me to Luis. To his credit Luis didn't lie when they asked him if he said it. He nodded in the affirmative and with that Abuela stood and pounded him with hammer punches. She screamed in Spanish something that is lost to the ages. The grandmother took him by the arm and wrestled him out of Student Services. The mother apologized and I thanked her clasping her hand with both of mine. I held on as her eyes filled with tears. Gloria said, "She's saying that she doesn't know what is happening with her son. She said he used to be such a good boy, but now he is angry and doesn't listen to her at all. He comes home late every night." I asked if she knew he could be in a gang? When Gloria posed this question, a gasp came forth.

"Ganga? Nooooooo!" she said. I showed her symbols of the six-pointed star that resembles the star of David, and represents the six points of the Crip lifestyle on Luis's tablet. I also asked Gloria to ask if he had a blue handkerchief. Mom told Gloria that he carries it every day neatly folded in his pocket. Tears ran down her face as she gathered the herd of children. The bell rang signaling the beginning of the school day. Dave was having a moment with a student when I entered. He said, "You don't touch me and I won't touch you." Something remarkable occurred through my encounter with Luis. The first time I saw him coming down the hall there was that awkward sense that one experiences after a dispute as to how to respond. To my surprise Luis said, "Hi, Mr. Neal."

"Hey Luis," I said managing a smile. From that moment on, each time I saw him, he always spoke first and it wasn't contrived or put on. It was a warm greeting from a student to teacher. One of my mentors, Lynn Sands-Collins, who was a masterful teacher, and later an outstanding administrator, once told me to demand respect. She said that our students crave discipline because so often they don't get it at home. She was wise in this assertion. I was helping separate two combatants, shortly thereafter, and one of the boys pushed me. He was coming toward me and a student intervened. It was Luis. He put his hand on the boy's chest saying, "You better not try Mr. Neal. He'll go off on you."

It's a shame that educators in order to get a student's attention often have to do something that could be career ending. Throwing a basketball at Gary's head led the entire team to fall in line. Putting Luis up against a wall was a catalyst for him to show some respect. The year finished and Dave and I survived those eight weeks. Sharon thanked us for pitching in and taking some numbers off of her suspension rate. That summer I had my last class in the counseling program. I remember calling M. Wayne to tell him that his son had a Master's Degree in Counselor Education. His reply, "That's good. Now you should go for your doctorate." There was always room for improvement with M Wayne.

CHAPTER SEVENTEEN

"COACH HAS LEFT THE BUILDING"

In July Frieda Proctor called me at my parent's home with sad news. Coach Owen passed away while napping on his couch. The funeral was in two days and I wouldn't be able to pay my respects. Returning to Lake Worth I met Dave Youngman at Harry's Banana Farm to toast the man who hired us. Harry's (Banana Farm is the name so little league baseball teams could be sponsored) is an iconic bar and one that Coach had recommended to me. Playboy once listed it as one of the top ten dive bars in America. I got a tap on my shoulder as Dave and I bellied up for our toast. It was Tim Owen, Coach's son. Coach had introduced us once. I stood to give him a hug and an electrical shock ran through us. "Did you feel that?" I asked Tim.

"It's my dad." He went on to explain that he'd had a dream the night before and Coach was sitting at Harry's with him. Coach told him that he'd be with him just as he was at his baseball games. In the dream Coach went through the back door and Tim couldn't follow. "I just kept my hands on that door because I wanted to keep feeling that warmth that was wherever he went," Tim said finishing his reverie. We all raised a glass to my first mentor.

1998 brought on the birth of the Florida Comprehensive Assessment Test (FCAT). This test was part of Florida's overall plan to increase student achievement. It started out as a really great tool for a teacher to get instant feedback on their student's progress. There was a movement that stipulated students in third, eighth, and tenth grades should be retained who weren't proficient in reading and math. Close to fifty eighth graders would be held back. It was a perplexing situation for Sharon to navigate. I went to school a few days early to get a head start on readying my room. Sharon was on campus and I dropped by her office to say hello. "I am so worried about this year," she said.

"Why?" I asked.

"All of those retainees," she said.

"Sharon, it won't be that bad"

"Oh yes it will be. I'm working on something, though."

"What's that I asked?"

"I'm contemplating getting all of the kids that are retained and create a school within a school. It will be like our Drop-out Prevention only on a larger scale. The question is who am I going to find that wants to work with those students? This is going to be a large group who really don't want to be in school, especially, a second year of eighth grade. I need at least three teachers. If I could get one to teach Math and Science and another to teach English and History, then we would need an elective." I started to think that maybe I could handle this mission. Hell, I always wanted to teach history. So, I took the leap before I'd change my mind. "Sharon, I'll try this assignment," I said. The words had a fatal feel to them.

"Are you serious?" she asked putting down the cigarette she was about to light. "Would you be willing to do that?"

"Yes, I always wanted to teach history. Besides, I imagine I would get plenty of practice counseling students."

"Jeff, that would be great!" she said, smiling. I heard the Main Office door open and shut. There was the sound of footsteps coming down the small hallway.

"Queen Bee?" said a voice that sounded familiar. It was Joe Owsley, the Shop teacher. The only time I saw him was when he would be filling his Styrofoam cup with coffee in the cafeteria each morning. He would say to anyone within earshot, "It's gonna' be all right." He was a stocky guy about 5′10″ with a full head of gray, curly hair. I knew he was from somewhere in the south. "Hey, young man," he said extending his meat hook of a hand that was deeply calloused.

"Hi, Joe," Sharon said. She gave him a warm hug.

"How's Queen Bee?" he asked.

"That's Joe's nickname for me," Sharon said, smiling. "I'm okay, Joe. Jeff and I just talked about a new program we are going to implement."

"What new program are you implementing now, Queen B?"

As she waxed eloquently on how she was creating this new DOP program to help meet the academic needs of "at risk" kids, I could see him smiling. She mentioned that I had volunteered to do the English and History chores and she still needed one other teacher for core subjects, along with one elective. "Queen B you need to stop right there," Joe said with his voice that was a mixture of southern twang and drawl.

"What do you mean?" she asked. Sharon always seemed to have that intimidating force to her being, but Joe seemed to daunt her slightly. "What I mean is that I have been around this game too long. Most of those kids should be in an alternative school. They make it so hard to remove a kid from your campus that it's no wonder you don't have enough room here. Hell, the bureaucrats are too dim-witted to put money into alternative school sites. Imagine giving them real life skills like the old tech schools when we built houses. No, they want everyone to bring up their damn test scores. Poor teachers are busier than a cat in a silo looking for a corner to piss on. I'll teach your damned elective. What do you call it, DOP?" Joe added.

"It would be fantastic if you do that," Sharon said.

"Are you worried about those kids being around your saws?" Sharon asked.

"No, I'll give them OSHA approved safety instruction and the rest is on them. They don't mess with me, Queen Bee, you should know that." Joe stood up and gave me another handshake. Several of the teachers that Sharon had approached blatantly refused to be a part of this project. I wondered if they were much more prudent than myself.

The Owen family. From left to right: Michael Owen, Coach Owen, Betty Owen (wife), and Tim Owen. Sadly, Tim passed away two weeks after he gave me this picture in November of 2021. He was 60 years old.

CHAPTER EIGHTEEN

"DOP with a Kentucky Twist"

The first day most of our students were in attendance. The Wood Shop had twelve long wooden tables spread out over half of the room and the other half was saws. Those that I remember: Basic Handsaw, HackSaw, Coping Saw, Jigsaw, Circular Saw, Table Saw, and the Oscillating Saw. The first bell rang. Joe had a huge chunk of Red Man between his cheek and gum. He had no qualms about expectorating the unwanted juices in the nearest industrial sized wastebasket.

"All right," Joe bellowed like a country auctioneer, "y'all need to listen up." Immediately, the room got quiet as his voice had that loud, clear orotund quality. He continued, "You may be wondering what y'all are doing in this room with Mr. Neal and myself. The reason you are here is that our principal, Mrs. Walker, wanted to have a program called Drop Out Prevention that is designed just for you. The reason why is y'all been designated as "At Risk"! I repeat "At Risk." This conjured up the warden from Cool Hand Luke, who said, "What we have here is a failure to communicate." Joe went on, "Of the seventy-five of you, fifty arrived in the eighth grade once again. This is an intervention not a crucifixion."

"Like a drug intervention?" asked a blond boy with long hair that was parted down the middle, reminiscent of the '70s. In fact, this guy dressed the part with a bright tie-dye shirt and denim bell bottoms. He was at a table with White boys who'd ridden in together on skateboards.

"Someone forgot to tell this boy what decade we're in," Joe said out of the corner of his mouth to me before he continued, "What's your name, boy?"

"Curtis," he said with a voice much like Sean Penn's depiction of a Stoner named Spicoli. Fast times at Lake Worth Middle.

"Curtis what?" asked Joe tersely.

"Curtis Fitzpatrick."

"Ok, Curtis Fitzpatrick. You're absolutely correct in your analogy of a drug intervention with this program called DOP. This is an academic intervention."

"What's it called again?" Curtis said with a broad smile.

"D...O...P," said Joe enunciating each letter.

"Only Dopes do D-O-P," Curtis uttered. The words rolled off his tongue and he went into hysterics. I walked over to his table. It smelled like Jamaica. One boy named Paul, who I later found out was one of Lake Worth's best surfers, told Curtis, "Get it together."

"Stand up," Joe said walking over to the giggling Curtis.

"Only Dopes to DOP. Is that what you said?" He asked moving into what would be called his comfort zone.

"Yeah, like the commercial, man," Curtis replied.

Joe moved within inches of him and asked, "Are we going to have a problem Curtis Fitzpatrick?"

"No man, I'm the mellowest dude in here," he said, still smiling. It reminded me of Gomer Pyle as Sergeant Carter got in his face.

"Good!" said Joe. One more thing don't call me, man. You can call me Mr. "O." You got that?"

"Sure Mr. O," he said, sitting back down beside Paul.

Joe informed them that for now they weren't going to have any electives, except wood shop, and that we were their only teachers. He also said that he would decide if they will use the saws. I gave them the usual protocol regarding the supplies they would need and then took roll. On the way to lunch I saw Max and Q coming across the courtyard. They stopped to see this DOP tribe entering the cafeteria. Joe stayed back in the room to eat his standard lunch he ate every day, thinly sliced ham with no bread and pickles eaten right out of the jar. "What a crew," said Max as he sized up the gang bangers, stoners, Gothics, and multi-ethnic students entering the cafeteria.

"It looks like a great big EH unit," said Q. The first lunch of the year was a crowd favorite, chicken nuggets. There was some action after lunch. A boy ran across the courtyard and punched a girl square in her nose. "Keep on fucking with my little sister, bitch, and it will get worse next time!" he yelled. I grabbed him from behind in a bear hug. The Band teacher, Frank Bermudez, had gotten the girl out of the way. As I walked through the door of Student Services to write a referral the boy began to curse at me. Jose came around the corner, "What's happening, man? Take a breath, dude. You look like a beet. Think of your blood pressure."

"This guy punched a girl right in the face," I said as I began to write his name and student number on the referral. I was mad and the printing on the document reflected this. "He needs ten days at home," I added.

"Hey, man you've got to calm down; it's over."

"Calm down my ass, Jose. He punched a girl in the face. He needs a long vacation," I said with conviction.

"Easy dude, he's under the umbrella."

"ESE? C'mon," I said with disgust, "so he's going to skate."

"No, I'll give him some days. Not what he needs, though."

I went back to the class. To my shock the entire room was dead silent. Joe was up in front of the class whittling and each student's head turned as I walked in. A Black boy named Travis was sharpening his pencil with the biggest shit-eating grin you can imagine.

"What's up, Travis?" I asked. He shook his head and pointed to the cork bulletin board that had a slight indentation.

"That's where Jose's head hit," he whispered. Jose had his head down on the desk.

"What happened?" I asked Joe quietly.

"What happened Mr. Neal," Joe said in a loud voice, "is that Jose had a fit. When a student has a fit you have to grab them to protect them so they don't get hurt. He's okay now. Aren't you Jose?" Jose didn't move. The rest of them sat in silence. Did you take care of that boy who assaulted the girl?"

"Yes, but he's ESE."

"Bunch of bullshit," said Joe. "I'm glad you're here, Mr. Neal. I was waiting for you because I asked the entire class to remain silent after I helped Jose with his fit. It's time that we lay some ground rules, because they just found out they are truly at risk in my presence." Joe moved to the side of the room and asked everyone to look at him. He took off his apron with the ever-present sawdust and tossed it on the nearest table. To my astonishment he lifted his shirt up to his neck, exposing his chest and a rather sizable belly. Joe didn't miss a lot of meals.

"Do ya'll see this hole?" he said, pointing to his lower right abdomen. That was the first time I got stabbed. You see that's what you get when you get in a gang."

"You were in a gang?" asked Curtis. "Cool!"

"Did I ask you to speak, Mr. Fitzpatrick? To answer your question, I was in one of the original gangs called the "Hells Angels" in the beautiful Bluegrass State of Kentucky." He began to tell them he had a choice to fight in the Korean War or go to jail. He explained he fought in the war and got his education from the GI bill. They looked at him like he was from another planet. "One thing the army taught me was that there are rules and laws.

We're going to have rules. Number one we're going to have no fighting. Your right to touch someone ends at the tip of their nose. Are we clear on that?'"

"Yes," an assortment responded.

"I asked everyone if you are clear on that?"

"Yes," came a unison response. Jose's head came up.

"I enjoy teaching my students to cut wood and make beautiful pieces of art. If you play your cards right, I will teach you to make things that you can sell. One boy last year sold wooden jewelry holders at Christmas. He made several hundred dollars." A few of the students, with an entrepreneurial spirit, perked up.

"Cool," Curtis said once again speaking up.

"I told you to stay quiet boy," Joe said.

Curtis made the motion of zippering his mouth shut and beamed. Joe looked at me and shook his head as if to say he didn't know what he was going to do with this one.

Sharon recruited a teacher, Ms. Kimmel-Craine, to join DOP. The kids called her KC. It felt like the calvary was coming to join in the battle. I was teaching History Out-of-Field. This means any teacher who is teaching a subject where they aren't certified. KC would take twenty-five kids to work on math or science while I taught History and English. Joe would take the other twenty-five to the saws.

It was a challenge to present my lessons when Joe would turn the saws on and begin demonstrating how to cut wood. By the end of the school day my voice would be hoarse. The students were surprisingly cooperative in this environment. It was revitalizing to teach history. It amazed me how little information they knew about current events. Many didn't know who the President of the United States was, Bill Clinton. The vast majority of these students were Level 1 readers. Their lack of achievement provided fuel for the argument known as "demographic determinism" that purports that the school really can't do much about those student's low test scores.

Cultural influences do affect student's scores. Students who grow up in an environment that is not language rich directly effects two critical elements of being proficient, language acquisition and vocabulary. The other elephant in the room is the majority of our students lacked background knowledge. Add to that detractors like video games and addiction to social media and you have a prescription for mediocrity. Thomas Jefferson put forth that aristocracy should not automatically inherit everything. The trick for educators is to try to honor that sentiment by bridging the achievement gap.

After a long talk with Joe, we came up with one thing we could do to help our students gain foundational knowledge. Field trips were going to be our panacea. There is a lot of red tape in education that inhibits an excursion with students off campus. We somehow managed to take several field trips that year. We went to the Boca Raton Museum of Art. That was one of the scariest moments of my life as gang bangers, hoodies, surfers, and gothic DOP students roamed around the changing exhibitions and art. Joe threatened a long slow death to anyone who misbehaved.

We journeyed to the South Florida Science Center and Aquarium. That was a big hit with our students, particularly Curtis, who was engrossed in the Journey Through the Human Brain advanced neuroscience exhibit. His tie-dyed clothing wasn't the only thing about him that was in the '60s. Perhaps one of the most interesting field trips we took with our assemblage of academic misfits was to Lion Country Safari. This site is a drive-thru safari with a walk-through amusement park that invites you to spend the day with over nine-hundred animals. You should have seen the faces of the students as they gazed upon some ninety-five species including: lions, zebras, chimpanzees, giraffes, and rhinos. The students were exposed to something that would be akin to visiting Africa. They loved to get away from school and for the vast majority they had never been exposed to these types of experiences.

After the field trip Joe said he had a special treat. When I asked him where we were going, he winked. The school bus stopped before a huge gate that once opened granted us access to a beautiful property with a winding driveway that led up to a gorgeous Queen Anne-style Victorian home. It was the type of residence I would expect to see in Palm Beach. "Joe, whose place is this?" I asked.

"Carolyn's and mine?" Joe answered. Carolyn, Joe's wife, also happened to be the Home Economics teacher at LWCMS.

"Seriously, Joe," I said.

"I'm dead serious," he replied. He waved to a blond guy, who was manning a huge BBQ Smoker that reminded me of the kind used on competitive cook-offs.

"That's a hell of a grill," I said.

"It better be; it cost me almost $4,000." Joe laid out rules that this was his place and if they wanted to come back at the end of the year they'd better stay out of the pool. He warned there were alligators, Florida Panthers, and rattlesnakes waiting for them should they decide to wander. As the students found seats at the tables strewn along the sides of the huge kidney shaped pool I took in the vista of the property.

"Joe, how did a principal or whatever you were in Kentucky come to a place like this?"

"That's a fair question, boy. Why don't we sit down and have a glass of ice tea and I'll tell you my tale," he said out of the side of his mouth. "I left out the part of my youth when I was runnin' moonshine and being chased by the law. It was after those days when I started to teach at Heath High School that I met a sweet blond country girl who was the Home Economics teacher. She wanted nothing to do with me because I drank too much."

"Did you drink too much?" I asked.

"Hell yeah, boy. The bartenders used to tell me it's time to go home. You done drank all the liquor. So, I quit drinking and a year later we got married. Carolyn coerced me to get my Master's. Lo and behold, yours truly became the new principal."

"Did you like being principal?" I asked.

"Yes, I did. Something was missing, or so I thought."

"What do you mean?" I asked.

"I came from the wrong side of the tracks. Mom would buy new soles and glue them on my old shoes to help keep your feet dry on the way to school in the winter." Delicious beef brisket, pork shoulder, and ribs appeared. It was mouthwatering as he used wood from orange trees to smoke the meat. There were ample sides of potato and macaroni salads. The students ate as if they hadn't eaten in weeks. It was the quietest I'd ever seen them.

"Anyway," Joe continued, "I guess you could say the lure of the world got to me. The years were passing by and like most educators, I suspect, I got disgusted with my financial picture. I had a nagging feeling that I should have been a businessman. So that's what I did. I quit my job as principal and started selling farm machinery. I joined up with John Deer & Company. I sold tractors, combines, sprayers, every type of farm equipment known to mankind. Made a million dollars in a couple of years. Mrs. O and I traveled the world. We bought a deluxe Winnebago for about $200,000 and started to go across this country and you know what we found?"

"What?" I asked.

"We were miserable. We both missed the kids and going to school every day. So, we sold our house and all the stuff we accumulated and moved to Palm Beach County. That's how we ended up here."

"Wow!" was all I could say.

"We are building a lot of equity here today," Joe said.

"What do you mean?"

"I'm not talking about market value. These kids are going to remember these field trips. They're damn sure going to remember this food. Nobody's done this for them. The way to get to these kids is through their stomachs. While I took in Joe's words, I looked at the smiling, happy faces of the kids. They behaved differently toward us after our excursions. It also paid off instructionally. Sharon and Jose were amazed as the DOP crew did fairly well on a Winter Diagnostic test that was administered before Christmas.

CHAPTER NINETEEN

"COUNSELING A HIPPY IN THE '90S"

Christmas break arrived and as I watched large snowflakes falling from the warm comfort of my parent's dining room the phone rang. It was B. "Dave, are you calling to wish me a Merry Christmas?"

"I wish it was that," he said torrid with emotion.

"What happened?" I asked thinking the worst.

"It's Mary Anne Hedrick," he remarked about his friend and colleague in PE. "She was going to the Palm Beach Airport and her van flipped over several times. She's in intensive care and Natalie told me that she's going to be a paraplegic. I just can't believe it." I was stunned. Mary Anne, with her Irish features, was the epitome of health. She ran marathons and swam competitively. She regularly snow skied the greatest slopes of our nation. Skydiving was another hobby and her softball teams in West Palm Beach were always competing for a championship. I remember her running the track on her planning period, always in perpetual motion. She was a great example for our students.

My assumption was that we lost a great teacher. I was going to miss her laugh and that vibrant smile below those bright, healthy eyes. Imagining her in a wheelchair was beyond my comprehension. There was no way she could come back and teach PE, not from a wheelchair. Guess what? I learned something from Mary Anne. You can't keep a good woman down. As she recovered, I noticed a change in Dave. He wasn't calling in sick while sleeping off a big night out. I went with him to see her in the hospital. She said she would be back soon. I nodded and tried to speak encouraging words. Deep down I doubted her comeback. I didn't know about the spirit and heart of the resilient, Mary Anne Hedrick.

"It's coming, soon," Joe said.

"What's that?" I asked perplexed by what he meant.

"Have you ever noticed how they group themselves at the tables. You got the three or four gang-banger tables, you got them devil worshipping Gothic kids with the black fingernail polish, and you got the skateboarder stoner table."

"Yes," I said.

"That's the way it is inside. Everything's broken down by race. The Whites eat together and the Blacks eat together, as do the Hispanics. Whites use the White barber and Blacks use the Black barber. Prison is like going back to the 1950s. Only thing they do share on the inside is a water fountain and shower. I spent a little time there when I was young. You develop a radar for things that are going down."

"Really?"

"Stay on your toes, boy."

Joe went back to whittling. One thing police will tell you is that during a full moon all hell is going to break loose. The lunar gravity exerts a stronger pull on the parts of the Earth closest to the moon. One night, shortly after Joe's prophetic warning, I drove my Thunderbird along the ocean. There was a massive moon staring at me that shimmered on the water. I became transfixed by it. I knew that something was going to happen the next day at school. That blood beast in the sky would see to it. The next day seemed uneventful until after lunch.

Just before we were going to break off for the afternoon KC was talking with a group at the Gothic table. I was talking with the skateboard crew. One of our students, named Ricardo, walked into the room with an entourage of girls beside him. He was a pretty-boy who never joined up with one of the three gangs that were represented in our DOP population. All of the sudden I heard a door open behind me from one of the three supply rooms. A group of male students filed out forming a long chain. None of them were in our class. I asked what they were doing as Joe took off his goggles that were resting on his head. Apparently, one of the top guns in a gang's girlfriend had been with Ricardo. It didn't surprise me as a multitude of young girls were vying for his attention each day.

"C'mon you Mexican, motherfuckers!" Ricardo yelled and started to bounce on his feet like a boxer. He looked like he had been training for this moment all his life. Seven or eight made a run for him. I admired his courage in the face of this onslaught. He threw about every punch I'd ever seen connecting with a left and right hook to the first attackers. Joe and I ran toward the fray. The sheer numbers got to Ricardo. They were pounding on him with hammer fists. Joe grabbed one boy under his arms and threw him hurtling backward to the ground. I did the same. We were systematically grabbing and throwing them like one would throw buckets of water off of a sinking ship.

I pushed the button for assistance. The rest of the class looked on not getting involved, with the exception of Paul. Paul was the dirty-blond surfer who rode his skateboard with the stoners each day. He was a fighter and started to wail on Ricardo's attackers. I was glad to have his help as these students kept coming, seemingly, out of nowhere. Larry Ludwig, Assistant Principal and two policemen burst through the door. As the boys were being lined up against the wall face first with legs spread, the police searched for weapons. Joe had a boy who was kneeling in front of him with his hands cupping his face.

"You aren't even in my class, boy!" he yelled with anger.

"Joe!" Larry yelled. Joe didn't move as he held the boy's face with one hand under his chin, and the other behind his head. I was wincing looking on at this because I pictured Joe doing a neck twist snapping the boy's vertebrae. He thankfully let go. "Better not grab me like that, old man," another combatant remarked to Joe. Joe backed him up against the wall. "Make your move, boy!" he yelled as he put his left foot forward and leaned back holding his large fist by his right hip. The boy was not expecting this and neither was I. Fortunately, for the boy he made a quick move and ran out of the room."

"Boy is lucky he ran. I haven't beat anyone's ass real good in a coon's age." Another country saying and another full moon at Lake Worth Middle. Our suspension rate went up that day as sixteen students were suspended. Ricardo was the only one suspended from our class. Joe and I had amnesia regarding Paul. Later on, Bruce Wasserman, Guidance Counselor, waved me into his office. He had taken over the coaching duties when I decided to go full blown on my master's degree. Bruce was a dedicated counselor and a good coach. He won the county basketball championship with, arguably, the best all-around athlete to ever go through our school, Charles "ET" Frederick. "Heard you guys had quite a fight in there today," Bruce said.

"Breaking up a one-on-one fight is one thing, but that was a whole other ball game," I replied.

"I have some news for you. This is going to be my last year here," he said.

"Where are you going?"

"Jupiter High School."

"Good for you," I added.

"Anyway, I wanted to give you a heads up. I know you have your counseling master's. Maybe you could take back the coaching duties"?

"Thanks, Bruce. I just might, I've missed it."

"One more thing," he added as I headed for the door. "What do you think about Curtis Fitzpatrick and his crew?"

"Actually, I like them. Paul helped Joe and I breaking up the fight today."

"That's not what I'm talking about," he said. "They're all using drugs. I smell it on them every morning."

"Yes, I know," I answered. "The police periodically search them, but they're too smart to bring it on campus."

"Did you tell them to stop using drugs?"

"I talked about the effects on their sexual reproductive systems and brains."

"I am going to confront him. Would you like to be present?"

"Sure, sounds like a good idea," I replied.

When I mentioned it could affect him having kids his reply was typical Curtis. "Bob Marley had twelve kids that we know about, Mr. Neal. The actual estimate is much higher." When I told Joe that Bruce wanted to confront Curtis, he smiled and said, "Good luck with that." The next day I made my way to Bruce's office and Curtis was already there in all his glory with his Grateful Dead tie-dyed shirt, complete with the teddy bear.

"Whoa, Mr. Neal, what's up, dude? I guess I must be in trouble, right?"

"Curtis, I'll get right to it," said Bruce leaning forward.

"We know you're using drugs."

"Well, yeah everyone knows that," he replied.

"Have you ever thought about the serious harm you are doing to yourself?"

"Is this about the balls thing we talked about, Mr. Neal?"

"Have you thought about the ramifications to your health?" Bruce repeated undaunted by Curtis' sarcasm.

"Yes, Mr. Wasserman, but I think I'm going to be A-Okay."

"What makes you think that?" Bruce asked.

"For one, I'm starting to get away from chemicals."

"Chemicals?" Bruce said with alarm.

"Yeah, you know man-made chemicals," he said.

"Like what chemicals?" I asked.

"Yeah, like LSD, you know acid."

"Are you telling me you are also using LSD?" asked Bruce.

"Noooo, what I'm saying is that I'm getting away from chemicals and am only doing natural stuff. I already am trying to cut down on smoking weed to twice a day. I will eat a magic mushroom if it comes my way, though."

"How many times do you think you dropped acid?" I asked.

"Oh, Mr. Neal I would say," he closed one eye and tilted his head as if calculating a number. "I probably have at least fifty hits under my belt."

"Fifty!" I exclaimed.

"That's probably a low-ball number it could be more. It was always pretty clean."

"This is worse than I thought," said Bruce looking at me. Lawyers should never ask questions that they don't know the answer to and the same holds true for guidance counselors. Bruce asked, "Curtis, do you realize you could have a flashback at any time?"

"Is that like when the high jumps back on you later?"

"Yes," Bruce with a dyer tone. "It could happen at any time."

"Well, Mr. Wasserman I'll tell you, I've never had a bad trip. If one comes back on me, it's a bonus!" Bruce was as confounded as I was. Curtis stood and move to the door.

"Hey, I like your shirt," I said.

"Yeah, do you like the Dead, Mr. Neal?"

"I like a couple of their songs?"

"Which one is your favorite?"

"Truckin' is a pretty good one," I replied.

"Yeah," he says and proceeds to break out singing really loud like Bruce and I requested an intimate concert.

"Truckin', like the do-dah man.

Once told me You got to play your hand.

Sometimes the cards ain't worth a dime.

If you don't lay 'em down.

Sometimes the light's all shinin' on me

Other times I can barely see

Lately it occurs to me

What a long strange trip it's been.

I love that last line, long strange trip," Curtis said. "Guess what, Mr. Neal?"

"Yes, Curtis?"

"I'm going to make you a present with the help of Mr. O."

"I'll look forward to it," I said, still digesting his solo and the fact that in all likelihood he dropped over fifty hits of acid. The endurance for anyone to sustain that was bewildering.

"Do you believe what he just told us?" Bruce asked.

"I'm pretty sure of it," I stated. "I don't think there is an untruthful bone in his body. Not sure about what's going on in his brain, but he's not a liar." When I got back to class Curtis was examining some wood that Joe cut daily for the student's projects. I pondered what he was going to create.

CHAPTER TWENTY

"PIZZA AND A MOVIE"

It became too much to attempt instruction in the shop; we needed a classroom. A ramshackle portable in the back of the school that was permanently soiled from years of neglect was our only option. The first day a student remarked, "Mr. Neal, this portable is ghetto." While we were settling in our new home a student, Aliya, let out a blood curdling scream. I calmly asked, "Aliya, why do you do that?"

"We're all crack babies, Mr. Neal," Shanice uttered. For a moment I had no idea what to say. The entire class was quiet. At first, I assumed she was joking. The faces told a different story so I asked, "How many of you think you're a crack baby?" Aliya and Shanice were the first with their hands in the air. Then other students slowly raised theirs until eight of twelve were testifying that they had been born to a mother that smoked crack cocaine during pregnancy. I needed to understand what I was dealing with in that room. My first inclination was to speak with Sharon Purce. She was an immensely popular teacher. A Black woman who came of age in the 1970s, in Washington DC. She'd seen a lot on the streets of our capital. She always moved at one pace in a Zen state. After school I made my way to her classroom. She was reading aloud to a boy on the basketball team. Sharon, seeing me, motioned for me to enter. I sat down and she continued reading. As she finished the text the boy packed up and hurried off.

"I didn't mean to interrupt," I said.

"No, I read with him every day. We were just finishing."

"That's cool," I said.

"What's up? You haven't been to see me for a while."

"DOP's been challenging to say the least."

"I know. I've been praying for you," she said with a smile.

I proceeded to tell her my tale about the "crack babies."

"All hands on deck, really?" she said. "I believe it. The devastation of that period is just beginning!"

"Is there something that you recommend to help?" I asked.

"They're a totally different breed of challenging students. They're coming to us with brain damage. This is a whole new ball game."

"Is there a remedy?" I asked.

"The problem is more complex than just their exposure to cocaine in the womb. Chances are they've had inadequate health care and poor nutrition. It's hard to know where prenatal damage leaves off and the environment takes over in the carnage. The problem is they've already fallen through the cracks. Early intervention in elementary school would have been ideal, but the system wasn't ready for this plague. In the last few years, I've noticed they are more irritable, almost hypersensitive. You want a little game plan, Jeffrey?"

"Please!"

"Change your playbook instructionally. Try not to have a lot of stimuli in your room. KISS (Keep it Simple Stupid). Have your lessons short and sweet because of their short attention spans. Play classical music and let them draw, doodle, write whatever. They will revolt at first, but this music will calm the savage beast. Work one on one with them as much as possible, especially, with the ones that are most agitated. Get Frank to come to talk one on one."

"That's a good idea," I said.

"He's a beautiful man. Have you gotten to know him?"

"A little bit," I answered.

"Besides shorter lessons, anything else?"

"There is something you can do, but it's a bit risqué."

"What's that?" I asked drawn by something deviant.

"Movies," she said. "That's the key."

"Movies?"

"Think about it. These kids have never been out of Lake Worth. No one has read to them in their youth. They haven't seen the world. You have to show them movies. Take them on magic movie journeys. Whatever you are studying find a film and watch it."

"We have to have the permission to show movies?"

"If you don't break a rule once in a while nothing changes. You'll be amazed at the movies you can find that correlate with whatever topic you're teaching. The right movie can open up the world for them."

As I left her room, I already knew my first movie to show. We had just finished reading, "The Outsiders." A movie directed by Francis Ford Coppola came out in 1983 with a young cast of future stars. It became my mission to start aligning movies with what we were studying. I drastically shortened my lessons. This worked well with their short attention spans. I began playing classical music. To my surprise they liked Mozart. I taught them to pronounce it correctly by drawing a castle on the board with a "moat." I decided to implement a reward system. I announced that if they did all their work, I would be treating them to pizza and a movie on Fridays. I could see the lights go on as they argued about which Pizza we would be getting. Dominos versus Papa Johns was the basis of this dispute. I settled it by telling them we would be getting Lake Worth Pizza.

It's amazing what a little incentive does in a classroom. A few of the students would start to veer off task and Aliya and Shanice would intervene reminding whoever was acting out that pizza was on the line. Getting the Pizza was a challenge because Sharon had a policy that all classroom "parties" had to be approved. Lake Worth Pizza is a family business and three of my former students owned it. They delighted in meeting me at the back gate of the school to hand the contraband pies over the fence. It had the sleazy connotations of a drug deal as I passed the money through the fence. The smell of garlic floated through the portable.

We watched "The Outsiders." Jesse said that Ponyboy, the main character, didn't look like he pictured him. I stopped the movie and we discussed that a big part of reading is visualizing the characters. They particularly liked the gang fight. A couple had tears in their eyes when one of the characters named Johnny dies. I had them think of their favorite part of the movie and write it down. Then they were to find the poem by Robert Frost, "Nothing Gold Can Stay" and write it out word for word. They all completed this task. On Monday we had a discussion of the symbolism in that poem. I was amazed at their responses as Travis, probably the most streetwise among them, captured the essence of the text. "We only are young for a time and have a chance to be happy in this world for a bit. Then we all die." Since we were studying poetry, I decided to go with *Dead Poets Society*, starring Robin Williams as our next movie feature. Aliya asked a poignant question, "Mr. Neal, both them movies you picked out had all White actors. When are you going to show us a movie with Black people in it?" I was so preoccupied with finding movies that related to our topics, that this hadn't occurred to me. They were clamoring for *New Jack City*, *Menace to Society*, and *Boyz n the Hood*. It was time to get a movie for History.

We were studying the Civil War. I rented *Glory*, the story of the first all African-American regiment, the 54th Massachusetts Volunteer Infantry. When I told them Denzel Washington was in the movie the girls were excited. The movie started and all were glued to the screen. In the scene where Trip, played by Denzel, is flogged with a whip in front of the whole unit, he ripped off his shirt revealing the large scars that were old wounds from whippings he received as a slave. The class gasped. As Denzel's character, Trip, stood there taking his beating he didn't make a sound. Gradually, his one eye filled with a tear that slowly came down his cheek. Shanice wept openly. I thought it would be a good time to stop the movie and discuss. "I would have killed that man," Travis said. We discussed how slaves were treated. For the first time, I think they actually thought about what it must have been like for their ancestors to be slaves.

Another scene in that movie that caught their attention was with Morgan Freeman. His character was a gravedigger and he was a father figure in the unit. He confronts Trip with a slap to the face after Denzel's character was calling another Black soldier a chimp and mimicking him with the grunting sounds of a monkey. Freeman's character tells angry Trip that the White man he so hated were dying by the thousands for him. He explained he knew this because he buried them. He also gave Trip a stern warning to watch who he was calling nigger. This was timely, as my students all called each other "nigga." We had an in-depth discussion on why Freeman's character resented the word. I believe they began to think about the connotations of that word that had become acceptable in their culture.

CHAPTER TWENTY-ONE

"CATCHING TRADEWINDS WITH "B"

Through sheer determination in rehabilitation MaryAnne returned to work. I went to say hello to her in the gym and out of the blue Dave asked me if I wanted to accompany him to downtown St. Augustine. He and his best friend Black David were going to be guest bartenders at a tavern called, "The Tradewinds." Dave told me he talked to Sharon and got permission for us to leave in the middle of the school day. I was elated and Joe agreed to watch my class while we beat the traffic. The next day after the students ate lunch, I was shotgun with "B" at 80 mph in his 1973 white Cadillac Fleetwood 75.

"I told you a little white lie," he said quietly.

"What little white lie?" I asked.

"I...I never got permission from Sharon for us to leave. We had to beat the traffic so we can make the celebration."

"What!" I exclaimed delivering a sharp blow to his upper left triceps. My fist hit square in a sweet spot.

"Take it easy," he said rubbing his arm.

"Take it easy," I said. "You're risking my livelihood."

"Don't get your panties in a knot. Have a good time."

Our first stop was at cabin that was owned by a gentleman named Walt Slater. He was something of a legend at Saint Augustine High School as the football coach who won multiple championships and a state title. He was a standout football star at the University of Tennessee and enlisted in the Army Air Corps during World War II as a navigator on a B-24 bomber. Then Dave dropped a bomb. Walt had been a Pittsburgh Steeler. "What! The Steelers! No way!" I was enthralled. Growing up in Western Pennsylvania parents train children like the Hitler Youth to be Steelers fans. Even though he was in his seventies Walt looked in shape. "Dave told me you played for the Steelers."

"Yeah, I played there for one year. I led the league in punt returns in 1947. We were the first Steeler team to go to the playoffs. We had a contract dispute over $500," he said, smiling. "That was a lot of money back then." We talked about coaching.

"Let's get to the Tradewinds," Dave commanded. The tavern was packed and everyone gravitated to B calling him White David. "These are my friends," Dave said. "We all got smacked in the face with sex, drugs, and rock and roll in the late '60s." A man at the bar stool stood up and lifted Dave in the air.

"You must be Jeff," Black David said before we were introduced. "I've heard a lot about you." He then stunned me as he gave me a hug that had strong leverage. He told the bartender to give me whatever I wanted. They were toasting to everything you can imagine and both hit the bar with their glasses before drinking.

"We are bartending in one hour," Black David said.

"Should be fun," B said. "I've got to see a man about a horse." As he moved to the bathroom Black David motioned for me to sit down. He had a beard and wore dark glasses.

"How do you like the bar?"

"It's nice," I said as I looked around the rustic place. The bar was old and made out of wood with a bamboo edge. The people looked good-natured in a sea of denim with many wearing cowboy hats.

"Nice crowd," I said, thinking of something to say.

"You teach with Dave, huh?"

"Yes, unfortunately," I replied.

"I know he's a piece of work. I knew him when we were young."

"I thought you were a Black guy from your name."

"You aren't the first one to make that assumption," he said with laughter. "We became White David and Black David as we divorced simultaneously and moved in with each other. This was before caller id and every time we answered the phone it was a pain in the ass to figure out which Dave. We were saying Dave's not here before Cheech and Chong." The owner, named Terry, gave the two Daves instructions on how to run the bar. I smiled as Dave cupped each woman's hand while lighting their cigarette. A couple he kissed on the lips still thinking he was a young lion. After an hour the crowd gave them a drunken ovation as they came back on the side of the bar where they were most familiar.

"Are you hungry?" Black David asked.

"Starving," I answered. In moments we were crossing the famous Bridge of Lion's. We went to a restaurant, the Worth House, built in 1790. We got menus. A beautiful waitress appeared and White David says, "Well hello darlin', why aren't you gorgeous."

"Would you gentlemen like a cocktail before dinner?"

"I would like a Perfect Manhattan," said Black David.

"A Perfect Manhattan sounds good," replied White David.

"And you?" she asked.

"What the heck, I'll try a Perfect Manhattan," not having any idea about this cocktail's ingredients. The Captain's Platter was just what the doctor ordered. I drenched the fried fish with Mango Tartar Sauce and devoured everything. The conversation that usually lulls when food arrives kept going between these two old friends. I couldn't keep up with these guys as the Perfect Manhattan's kept coming throughout the dinner. White David retreated to the restroom leading Black David and I alone at the table.

"So how was White David when he was young?" I asked.

"He could have done anything. You name it acting, sales, modeling, he had it all. Then he realized that he was good looking and it all went to hell."

"What do you mean?" I asked.

"He literally could walk into a room full of people and every woman wanted him. The man couldn't say no to anything, especially whiskey and women." Black David worked on an assembly line of a GM plant in Detroit. He was going to retire in a few years and build on the property he had in Vilano Beach, a quiet coastal community just north of Saint Augustine. We went back to "The Tradewinds" and the debauchery continued. Black David had to catch an early plane to Detroit in a few hours and gave B one of those quick hugs men give, and he came over to me.

"Take care of that crazy old bastard," he said.

Back at Walt's I made my way to the couch after I grabbed a bottle of water from the refrigerator. I was curling up in the fetal position under an Indian blanket. Closing my eyes, I saw Dave sitting on a tall stool by the counter lighting a cigarette. He seemed to have no interest in sleeping. He motioned for me to join him in the kitchen and I waved him off. Sleep came over me. I could feel my entire nervous system shutting down. Then it happened.

"Hey," he said, startling me. "Look what I found?"

"What Dave? I'm sleeping!"

"I found the faculty directory in my gym bag. We can call anyone we want."

"Knock yourself out." I pulled the blanket over my head. Many of the members from the Warrior Family received drunk dials from B. I figured he'd bother Jose or Tom Long. I heard the rhythmic sound of a digital phone being dialed. I couldn't believe he was still awake let alone calling anyone at that hour. I looked at him, a true rascal, spinning on the bar chair at the kitchen counter.

"Hello, Dan," he said. "It's Dave. Um, it's 2:45," he said as he looked at his watch and winked at me. There was a silence. "I really need to talk to Sharon. It's about Jeff Neal. There's been a horrible accident." I sat up my heart beginning to pound and I remember thinking he was evil as he grinned. Then in a serious tone said, "Sharon, it's David. I'm really sorry to call you so late, but it's Jeff. No, he's not dead. Jeff has fallen off the couch and we're not sure, but we think he broke his pecker." A bolt of electricity shook me. He walked over with a malicious smirk on his face and handed me the phone saying, "She wants to talk to you." I reached for the phone praying for a dial tone and there was only silence.

"Hello," I said as sheepishly as anything I ever uttered.

"So, you broke your pecker!" she said with her tough voice. Wide-eyed I looked at Dave who had gone back for yet another drink. She then said, "Get some sleep, Jeff."

"Are you trying to get me to kill you," I said.

"Relax," he said. "Sharon loves that stuff. Get some sleep we are invited to Brunch tomorrow." My head hit the pillow. Walt had coffee going when my eyes opened. He was such an old school gentleman. The coffee was strong and I drank it black. In minutes Dave emerged from the bathroom looking fresh as a daisy. I hopped in the shower and the warm water was heavenly. Never underestimate the power of a shower. Surprisingly, I didn't feel that bad even with less than three hours of sleep.

We pulled up to Terry's brick house that had a cornfield and a small pond in the back by the woods. The awesome smell of bacon permeated my nostrils. Terry told me, in a hoarse voice, to get a plate and help myself. She also pointed to a small table with pitchers of Bloody Marys and Mimosa's. Moving along the table I helped myself to ample amounts of eggs, sausage, bacon, biscuits, gravy, and grits. I did have a Bloody Mary for the V8 effect. David and I were seated on the back patio that overlooked her back yard. Terry sat down across from us.

"How long have you owned "The Tradewinds?" I asked.

"Twenty-five years," she answered with pride in her voice.

"Wow, that's quite a run," I added.

"Tell him what happened in 1976," Dave said.

"Fuck you, David!" she said.

"Terry has the distinction of firing Jimmie Buffet."

"Jimmy Buffet," I said. "You fired him?"

"He didn't draw a crowd. Every time he played no one was sitting there. That was before Jerry Jeff Walker took him under his wing and took him to Key West and taught him about life. I still can't believe he made it." The greasy food hit the spot. I thanked Terry for her hospitality. Our next destination was St. Augustine Beach.

"I used to take my two little girls and Coleen here when they were babies," Dave said with a trace of regret. It was like pavement as we pulled on the beach and rolled down the sand. Huge trucks were parked with grills, coolers, and loud music. It was a tropical tail-gate party. Dave bummed a couple of beers from the people who were enjoying the sun and surf.

"I have a lot of ghosts here," B said as he unbuttoned his shirt and took off his shoes and walked down to the water. He threw his wallet and glasses on the sand and walked right into the ocean. He took something out of his mouth and bent over swishing his hand back and forth. He turned and smiled. One of his incisors was missing giving him a look of a deranged pirate.

"Did I tell you I played hockey in Canada," he said fitting the tooth back in the space that was empty.

"No, I just remembered baseball."

"Probably had a better chance of going pro on the ice than I did in baseball." Jet-Skis were noisily bouncing off in the distance. I got in and floated in the waves. I looked up to see a plane flying over with a banner advertising a local happy hour.

"We've got to be at The White Lion for happy hour.

"Dave, I need a nap."

"Nonsense," he replied. "Let's go."

We started back the road leading to Walt's. As I drove my eyes started to close and I was struggling to keep them open. Being out in the sun made the fatigue even worse. "Dave, I need sleep. In fact, I am going to skip the happy hour," I said.

"You better take me, Neal. You aren't shit unless you are at the happy hour by 4:00. Everyone is going to be there."

"I don't care if the Pope is there, I'm not going."

"Ok," David said as reached into his glove compartment. He rooted around under some papers and in his right hand a Smith & Wesson appeared. "Are you going to take me to the happy hour?"

"Are you fucking kidding me? Put the gun away!"

"Are you going to take me to the happy hour?" he asked.

"No, I am going to nap." We weren't that far from Walt's cabin. Dave moved closer to his window that was down. We locked eyes. Neither of us smiling as he now had his arm propped up with the gun almost out in the wind.

"Ok," and with that he stuck the gun out of the window and fired. Thank God we were out in the country with no homes to be seen. Being that this is arguably the most powerful handgun in the world the sound was deafening. A huge cloud of smoke blew into the window filling the car. I coughed and thought he was out of his mind.

"Are you taking me to the happy hour?"

"Fuck you, Dave!" I answered. Once again, "Bam!" Another shot out of the window and once again we were engulfed in smoke. I pulled into Walt's driveway, white knuckling the steering wheel. Skidding to a halt on the gravel I got out of the car.

"You're fucking up," he said.

I said nothing and entered the house. Grabbing a bottle of water, I drank it with deep gulps. I went to the couch. Dave said one more time, "We can still make the happy hour." I turned over and it was as if I'd ingested a powerful sleeping pill. I was going down fast. B was muttering as he headed back to his room. The next thing I know I see Walt in the kitchen. I had no idea I'd slept through the night. B did as well.

"Good morning," Walt said. "Get some coffee."

We talked for a while and B announced that it was time to head to Lake Worth. I thanked Walt and got into the car this time on the passenger side. We made our way south on A-1-A. I looked at my insane tour guide, in his Ray Bans, the same crazy bastard who fired a gun in this car. We drove a long while before Dave spoke, "I told you we should have gone to the happy hour," he muttered. You don't know the conversations you missed out on."

"Dave, I really needed some sleep."

"Sleep," he scoffed, "Sleep is just little snatches of death. Once you push through you will be amazed at how much you can take and you live more."

"Snatches of death, huh?"

"You're the English teacher here, have you ever heard of Jack London?"

"Of course, my students read, The Call of the Wild."

Dave began to quote part of London's credo:

"I would rather be ashes than dust!

I would rather that my spark should burn out

In a brilliant blaze than it should be stifled by dry-rot." That's why I never give into the snatches of death. I shall use my time," he said, smiling and gave me a playful push. Dave was a voracious reader. I asked him who his favorite writer was. He said that's like asking who's the most beautiful woman in the world. He fired off a litany of authors. You name it he read it. "Reading's just an escape for me now," he answered. We stopped and got lunch on the water at a place in Cocoa Beach. I recalled my trip home from the Keys and my conversation with Tom Long. Dave lived quite a life and I knew he had a brain to pick. We were on the road again. "Dave, I may have a chance to be a guidance counselor next year," I mentioned.

"No, you don't," he answered.

"Why do you say that?" I asked.

"Did you ever look at Frank and those other counselors? They're highly paid clerical people."

"What do you mean?" I asked.

"Very little of what they do involves counseling. Take scheduling for instance. That's a full-time job. Most of the tasks they give counselors are administrative. Lunch duty, bus duty, hall duty, scheduling, and countless others that don't involve counseling. Trust me, you will be a highly paid clerical person, period. To talk to a student, you will have to somehow fit that in amongst your administrative duties. The teachers don't want them out of their class because they're worried about their test scores. They don't even factor that the kid could be in crisis."

"I never thought about it like that," I added.

"I don't mean to bring you down. If you want to be a counselor, go for it. Just remember you are in a system that is solely guided by testing."

"I may actually be learning something from you," I said.

"You can't afford to pay me what I'm worth," he said, smiling and taking out his last cigarette. Dave wheeled the Cadillac like a Higgins boat invading Normandy at the next Seven Eleven. He got Marlboro Lights and a six-pack of Bud. He poured the beer in a cup with ice that he had from the small cooler and then added some tomato juice.

"Red eye is one of the best things to drink," he said. "What else do you want to know?"

"Give me your thoughts on education in general?"

"It's one of the noblest of professions, especially, given what they pay us. The task of an educator is to give the student a plan by giving the essential features of the career they are pursuing. A school should offer a view. They should teach them to understand other cultures and provide the tools necessary for expanding their horizons." He drove on sipping his red-eye.

"Any good stories from your counseling days?" I asked.

"Did I ever tell you about the time I went with thirty counselors on a plane to California to counsel kids coming back from Vietnam? This is when the term post-traumatic stress disorder (PTSD) was coined. It was shell-shock before. Someone in the government decided that since the warriors were so young, they should get help from young people who had backgrounds in counseling. I was picked because Ball State had a great counseling program."

"Did you help them deal with flashbacks?"

"It wasn't just flashbacks. There was a boatload of PTSD. Hell, we lost 69,000 of our youth in that war. That's a lot of death to process. The recurring nightmares didn't let those guys sleep. Most of them suffered from acute anxiety. Do you know what was really interesting about that whole experience?"

"What?" I asked.

"So, there we were, all of us flying to California. This was back in the day when you could smoke and drink on planes. They weren't paying us but Uncle Sam said we could have all of the liquor we wanted. We were ripped to the tits. We started to talk about our signs?"

"You mean astrological signs?"

"Yeah, you know you would walk up to a girl and ask what her sign is? It was hip to do that back then."

"What happened?" I asked.

"Everyone of us on that plane had the sign of Cancer."

"What, no way! All thirty of you?"

"Every last one of us, Cancers. We thought we might be able to achieve Cosmic Consciousness together."

"I'm a Cancer," I said.

"No shit, what's your birthday?."

"July 22."

"I'll be damned," Dave said. "You're on the cusp of Leo and could be a good counselor with that sign?"

"Why is that?"

"Cancer is receptive and highly sensitive, and capable of huge amounts of empathy. Those are important traits for counselors." Dave went back to his tale, "This one kid, he couldn't have been more than nineteen. He kept his head down like a dog that's been beaten. One day he just started to cry and fell on the floor in a disheveled heap. I thought his head would split from the pain. He got drafted along with his childhood friend, in something they called the "buddy system." They got ambushed. He was separated from his unit and was running through the jungle. Eventually, he found a path that was worn and described it as a gauntlet. He had no idea where he was going, so he decided to just keep running. Then he saw it."

"Saw what?" I asked.

"A stick in the ground with an American army helmet hanging there. It had some dog tags hanging loosely from it. He stopped and saw the tags belonged to his childhood friend. He removed the helmet and there was his friend's head carved like a pumpkin. Sometimes there is only so much a counselor can say." Dave changed the topic to Mary Anne saying how glad he was she was back teaching. It was quite a weekend. Dave getting me to leave school early and meeting an old Steeler. On to Black David and the bar owner who fired Jimmy Buffet. Let's not forget calling Sharon at 2:45 in the morning. All of this courtesy of this Canadian who seemed to thwart any type of prudence and temperance in his life. Proverbs of Hell, William Blake says, "The road of excess leads to the palace of wisdom." Dave traveled that road and if there is any truth in the proverb, he was one wise soul. It occurred to me that I'd never seen him ill. I inquired, "B, I don't think I've ever seen you sick, not even a cold. What's your secret?"

"What germ wants to live in me," he replied.

CHAPTER TWENTY-TWO

"What a Long Strange It's Been"

Sharon's reaction after the call in the wee hours of the morning sat at the forefront of my mind. I took my regular seat at Monday's faculty meeting in the back with the PE department and athletic coaches. Dave was taking one of his patented three-day weekends. To my dismay Sharon started the meeting by saying, "I received a call this weekend from Mr. Bingeman and Mr. Neal. Apparently, Mr. Neal had a fall. Are you doing okay, Jeff?"

"Yes, thank you for asking," I said clearing my throat.

"That's good to hear," she said as she began to run down the items on the agenda. After the meeting it was like the paparazzi were after me as I fielded questions about the alleged fall. "Sorry, I couldn't resist," Sharon said.

"Sorry about that call," I uttered.

"It was funny. You're here, so make a difference in a child's life today." Joe Owsley introduced a technique this day that would prove invaluable to me. After testing we decided to let the students use the staff bathrooms by the faculty dining room since they tended to roam the campus if they got out of sight. What could happen? They're just using the bathroom. About twenty minutes later a mournful wail came from the dining room. I entered to find Maria, a cafeteria worker, with her hands over eyes.

"Someone stole her purse," Fran uttered. "She just went to the bathroom for a second. It had to be one of your kids."

"Ok," I said. "I'll find it."

"Please, Mr. Neal. Maria doesn't deserve this. She had her paycheck in the purse." I'd often pick Maria up as she walked to school. She would tutor me in Spanish on the short ride. Every day as she got out of the car she always said, "Thank you, teacher." She was a good Christian lady and the thought of one of our students stealing her purse enraged me. I told Joe what happened.

"Unrighteous bastards," he muttered.

"I'll search everyone," I said.

"These career criminals wouldn't have brought it back here. This is going to take a special tool to get this done. I have to go to the office." I wondered what card this old country boy had up his sleeve. They settled at their tables. Moments later Joe yelled, "The cutpurse bandit is in here!" Silence befell the class. Just then a piercing beep came over the PA system. It was Frieda.

"Mr. Owsley," her voice came over loud and clear.

"Yes, Mrs. Proctor."

"The Sheriff's Department are on their way."

"Thank you. We'll be here."

"Joe, what's up?" I asked.

"This is the old lie detector technique," Joe whispered. He began loudly, "The Sheriff's Department is on the way because someone in here decided to steal a cafeteria worker's purse today." They looked on with interest. "So, the sheriffs are coming with a lie detector to determine who took the purse or if they know who took it."

"Can they do that?" asked Curtis. "Don't we have rights?"

"Yeah, boy you got the right to take this test," Joe replied. "If you refuse you will not leave the room. You see, being that the item stolen had money and valuables, this is not a petty theft. The sheriffs are handling it. Take the test. If you didn't do it, you're free to go. If you did do it, well then lie detectors don't lie." Joe whispered to me, "Search the room and look for the nervous one. This can work with this age group." I did as Joe asked. After a moment they were back to chattering. A boy named Eric walked over.

"Mr. Neal," he stammered.

"Yes, Eric."

"What if I might know where that purse is?" he whispered.

"How could you know where it is?"

"This boy came up to me in the courtyard when we were coming back to Mr. O's room. He told me he took the purse. He said he put it underneath one of the portables in the front."

"Really, what's the boy's name?"

"I don't know. We just talk sometimes."

"So do you think you can find it?" I asked.

"I can try," he said as if he were an altruistic volunteer. We walked to the front of the school. "I think he said he put it under this one," he said getting on his knees, crawling like an infant, disappearing under the portable. After a few seconds he reappeared without the purse.

"Wasn't under there, huh?" I asked.

"Nope," he said rubbing his chin as if pondering where it could be. "Maybe it's under this one," he said. A moment passed as he rolled out from underneath the structure with the purse held high.

"Wow, you found it!" I said with fake astonishment.

"Yeah, I did," he said as if he were surprised.

"Let's give it back to the kind lady." We went to the dining room. Maria was sitting with her eyes red from crying. When she saw the purse in my hand she cried out, "Oh, Dios mio!" Nothing was missing.

"Guess what Mr. O," I said. "Eric found the purse."

"Well, that's just dandy. I suppose you want a reward?"

"Ah, yes please," said Eric with a sheepish grin.

"C'mon, step into my office. I got your reward."

I watched as Joe and Eric entered the threshold of the office. The door closed and there was a thud. Joe's voice was barely audible. The class looked on as if they understood. There was no protest just a sense that Eric was getting what was coming to him. Part of me thought I should intervene and then I remembered my experience with Luis. Sometimes you have to cross over that fine line to drive a point home. I knew Joe wouldn't hurt him. He had too much of the old school living within him to not send a message from the real world. In a few moments Eric came out and said, "I'm sorry that I stole the purse."

"That nice lady didn't deserve that," I added.

"I know. Mr. O wants me to write her an apology letter. I'll bring it tomorrow." Joe came out adjusting his apron and said, "Nothing like the 'ole lie detector threat to get a confession. Feel free to use that one in the future." The bell rang. It was the last day of testing. The next morning as I was signing in by the teacher mailboxes Carolyn, Joe's wife, said, "I hope you two don't do this DOP program next year."

"Why?" I asked.

"I've noticed a change in Joe. He's different and I believe it's the stress of working with those kids." Moments later Jose was walking toward me and motioned for me to stop.

"I'm heading off for high school, my man," he said in his raspy rock and roll voice that sounded like Joe Cocker.

"Are you serious?" I asked taken aback.

"Yeah, I've been here seventeen years and it's time. I've accepted a position as an AP at Santaluces High."

"You already have the position?"

"Yeah, they can't pass me up," he said with a grin. "I speak Spanish."

"Wow, good luck."

"Do you remember Lake Worth Junior High?" he asked.

"Yeah," I said with a sigh.

"Those were the good old days." We had developed a friendship. Once we got dropped off in Daytona and rode bicycles back to West Palm Beach. The coastline is beautiful from the vantage point of a bike. It was on that ride that I learned some things about Jose. His dad, whom I meant once, was a very intense-looking gentleman who was head of intelligence in Cuba and worked for the CIA when Kennedy was President. When the Bay of Pigs fiasco occurred, they had to abscond to Florida in the middle of the night to avoid being killed by Castro. Jose had bodyguards in kindergarten. He possessed a sharp mind and had an interesting approach to being an administrator. He went on to become a principal at both the middle and high school levels. I had to agree with his sentiment about the smaller Lake Worth Junior High. There was a purity to the energy in that school. The year was coming to a close and on the last day of school the DOP students were surprisingly emotional as they said goodbye. The last student to bid me farewell was Curtis. He walked up with his standard tie-dye shirt holding something behind his back.

"Hello, Curtis," I said to the "wonder boy."

"Hey, Mr. Neal I have the present."

"Where is it?" I asked pretending not to notice his right hand tucked behind his back.

"Right here!" he said as he swung his arm around dramatically revealing a perfectly carved rendition of the lightening bolt skull, a Grateful Dead Logo. He had painstakingly painted the red, white, and blue lightening bolt complete with the rose. It was intricately carved. He beamed as I marveled at this most precious gift.

"Wow, the Grateful Dead, huh?"

"Yeah, and I put something on the back."

"Did you?" I asked. I turned the painted side over to read:

To Mr. Neal,

What a Long Strange It's Been!

Your friend.... Curtis

"Curtis, I think you might have left a word out," I stated.

His forehead knitted in concern and I could see his lips moving as he read the inscription. He looked up at me and said in a serious tone, "Oh, wow I forgot to write "trip." It's the most important part!" he exclaimed. "I'm going to fix it right now."

"No, I like it just the way it is. It's more authentic."

"You mean like valuable," he said.

"Yeah, valuable. I will cherish this, Curtis."

"Yeah, Mr. Neal I get it now. It will be more valuable like one of those baseball cards with a flaw. Maybe it will be worth more if I become famous."

"Exactly," I said, surprised he knew anything about baseball cards. What he was going to do to become famous outside of enduring the most acid trips at a young age was the question.

"I have to fly now, Mr. Neal," he said, picking up his skateboard. "Thanks for everything and don't forget to "Rock On!" In an old-school hand shake, he grasped my hand as if we were arm wrestling. I went to the window and moved the blind. I watched the only hippy I ever taught skating away and wondered what would become of our "wonder boy."

Reflection after a school year is something I've always done. Sharon needed some people to run the DOP program and it didn't hurt that Joe and I were both deviants to some degree in our youth. Joe's stint with the Hell's Angels and running moonshine was a little more colorful than mine. A disproportionate number of the students we had that year were males, minorities, and came from low socioeconomic backgrounds. If their stories are to be believed, many had been exposed to "crack" in the '80s. The lessons I was getting are won through shedding the fear of working with challenging students. They weren't like the students years ago. Finding that one thing that is their passion is mandatory. For Curtis it was rock music that created our bond. That year of DOP helped pave the way for the next leg of my journey, becoming a guidance counselor.

CHAPTER TWENTY-THREE

"WELCOME TO COUNSELING"

Bruce moved on and it came time for me to interview for the counseling position. Sharon was at the head of the table in the power position. AP's Ian Saltzman and Larry Ludwig were present as was Frank. Sharon had a belief that Coordinators should be involved in the hiring process and have a stake in the new hire's success. Larry asked why I wanted to make the move from teacher to counselor. My answer centered around the fact I didn't see myself teaching for the next twenty years, and I enjoyed helping kids with their problems. Sharon asked if there were any incentive programs that I was thinking of implementing. Frank had prepped me for this question as my response was his idea.

"We have a problem with attendance," I began, "I want to introduce a program called the "Breakfast Club." How it will work is once a week you get donuts or pastries and juice and reward those who are attending school. Food is a good motivator."

"You can't take kids out of class to eat. Every moment of instruction is critical," said Saltzman.

"I was thinking about doing it in the morning before school starts."

"I like that," added Frank.

"Where would you get the food? You can't finance that on your own all year," said Sharon.

"I was thinking of donations," I said, thinking on my feet. "Publix throws a lot of stuff out once the sell by date passes. The donuts are still good. Who knows, maybe this incentive could make a difference." Sharon nodded with approval and then asked Frank if he had any questions. He asked, "What are the three most important duties of a counselor?" This was the last question and I wanted to knock it out of the park. I only had to look across the table at Frank. I described what I saw him do on a daily basis.

"Conflict Resolution is a very important duty for a counselor, especially at our school, where kids are ready to fight at the drop of a hat."

"Good," Sharon replied. "Two more."

"Individual and group counseling," was my next response. "Kids that have similar issues can find solace in a group setting as they realize they're not alone. Other kids need that one-on-one work. I would have to say that being an advocate for students, teachers, and parents would be my third answer."

"Ok, thank you Jeff for your responses. We will let you know about our decision," Sharon said. It was the night before the first day of pre-school. My usual tossing and turning while trying to sleep was not present that evening. I was dreaming with rapid eye movements when the phone rang. I looked at my digital clock on the nightstand. It was 2:45 in the morning. It had to be a drunk dial from David. I picked up. "What do you want you want, asshole?"

"I wanted to inform you that you are our new counselor."

"I'm sorry, Sharon. I thought you were Dave."

"I knew you would," she said with a gleeful laugh. "Don't be late for the first faculty meeting. I'll be introducing the new guidance counselor tomorrow."

"Thanks," I said.

At the faculty meeting I sat in the back by Dave and MaryAnne Hedrick. Sharon did some kind of ice-breaker activity that is common to help ease the shock of being back to work after a two-and-a-half-month hiatus. As she was wrapping up Sharon said, "We have a new addition to the guidance department. Stand up, Jeff." As I did a round of applause came. Frank stood and clapped hard saying, "I'm going to put you to work, buddy!"

"The shit has hit the fan now," said Dave. "Be careful what you ask for." I moved my accumulation of teaching supplies out of my room. The pre-school week was not the usual setting up the room. My world had drastically changed. I was now in charge of doing over five-hundred schedules for my grade level. Frank's office was controlled chaos. There were course numbers for all grades in math, science, language arts, social studies, and electives.

"I will show you how to build a schedule, okay? This is where the work comes in. I've been working for weeks on these babies."

"You were working before pre-school?" I asked.

"We'd never get done if we didn't. The real challenge is to tailor each schedule specifically for each child's needs. Also, there is legality involved with ESE students. If you don't provide the services demanded by the law it could mean a lawsuit. You have to help assure all of the kids who have 504 plans are being given the services that are needed. We will talk about BIPs and FBAs later. Kriss Huff will school you on ESE matters." She was over that department and married a math teacher by the name of Bill Huff, a true character from Pittsburgh.

"What's a BIP and an FBA?"

"Behavior Intervention Plan and Functional Behavior Assessment." Frank replied as he began to weave through various screens examining data on a student. He looked at test scores, grades, and if he had ever been retained. Also, if he was ESE or not. "Poor kid," said Frank. "He doesn't get an elective. Test scores are too low. Intensive Math and Reading for him. He punched numbers and asked, "Are we done?"

"Looks good to me. Four core subjects and two electives for the first semester and second semester. Yes, it's done."

"Not so fast," said Frank. "Two more steps. There's a little thing called classroom size. We put him in a science class that has thirty-four kids. That's a lot if the teacher is going to do labs. The teacher across the hallway only has thirty. So, we switch him to the other team. Delete and enter the new numbers."

"That took a lot of time for just one's kid schedule," I added.

"That's why I'll be here to 6:00 or 7:00 tonight. We'll probably need to come over the weekend to make sure all schedules are complete for the first day. Jeff, you'll get the hang of it. I'll be helping you. We Pittsburgh guys have to stay together." I'd forgotten that Frank was from the "Steel City." I was so focused on the computer and the schedule that I failed to notice the portrait of the skyline view of the city with the three rivers merging with the confluence of the Monongahela, Allegheny, and the Ohio River.

Dave's words haunted me that counselors were highly paid clerical workers. I began to punch numbers. Number after number for each course for hours upon hours. My eyes hurt at the end of the day. As I tried to sleep a series of the course numbers flashed inside of my closed eyes. Thursday came and it was time for all Counselors of Palm Beach County Schools to meet for a professional development day. This meeting was being held at Royal Palm Beach High School. The auditorium contained a sea of counselors, a truly eclectic bunch. There was a morning session where pertinent issues were addressed. One topic was a counselor's responsibility reporting abuse. One statistic in this workshop that caught my attention is that 2.9 million cases of child abuse are reported every year in the United States. The presenter then broke it down even further. He asked us to write the total number of students in our school. Then he asked us to do a little math. It turned out at Lake Worth Middle that year nearly two hundred kids have been molested or abused by a family member or a close adult at some point in their lives. I saw a lot of abuse stories in the kid's journals while I was in the classroom but this number seemed astronomical. Most teachers, once they suspect abuse, turn it over to the counselor to do the reporting. I went in on Saturday to finish the task of scheduling. The first day was about to arrive.

CHAPTER TWENTY-FOUR
"A SIMPLE CONFLICT RESOLUTION"

As I walked around the corner approaching Student Services there were four language facilitators working the long lines of parents explaining the registration process. Our school has one of the highest rates of English Language Learners (ELL) in Palm Beach County. These are students who speak another language at home that is not English. Some of the countries represented by the parents in line were: Guatemala, Haiti, Jamaica, Dominican Republic, Nicaragua, Honduras, Bahamas, Barbados, Grenada, Guyana, Panama, Mexico, and more. The wonderful secretaries who run Student Services were doing a heroic job of handling the bureaucratic nightmare of registering a child for school. Birth Certificates, proof of guardianship or custody, proof of residency, record of immunizations, are all in play.

"Welcome to the machine," said Frank already at his desk.

"Did you see all those parents outside?" I asked. "Why did they wait for the first day of school to register?"

"It's like that every year," Frank said not looking up. Sharon entered the office. Her face was all business. "Why aren't you scheduling?" she asked.

"I'll get right on it," I said going to my office.

"You better, all those kids need a schedule today. The eleven-day count is ten days away." I turned on my computer and signed in. On the 11th day of school, the district does a "head count" to measure the population of each school. Depending on the number we may qualify for more teachers. More teachers equal less crowded classrooms. If I were still in the classroom, I would be sipping coffee while readying my room in relative peace. Now, I was in the hustle and bustle of Student Services with a swath of parents trying to navigate the registration process. The larger more looming challenge was where to put the students. We were busting at the seams in all classes with a student body over 1,600. PE was the only elective that had room. It was a dumping ground.

My morning post was in the bus loop. Being out and about with a walkie was a brave new world to me. Each bus was three to a seat. It's quite a sight to see that wave of students moving on the first day of school. They are excited, nervous, and most are wearing shoes that cost more than my car payment. Cell phones are out in full force as they enter through the cafeteria for breakfast. Eventually they gather in the large courtyard. When the first period bell rings the sixth graders are like lost sheep. Most can't understand a schedule, let alone find the building where they have to report for their first class. There is a look of absolute terror in their eyes. A sigh of relief on their pained faces is automatic when you offer to show them to their class. After the transition I returned to the pandemonium of Student Services. Frank was talking to a bus driver. "Jeff, do you want to take a break from your scheduling and do a counseling chore?" he asked.

"Sure."

"Do you see those three over there?"

"Yes," I said, as I looked at a White girl, a Hispanic girl, and a small White boy. Frank continued, "There was a little skirmish on the bus with no punches thrown. It should be a simple conflict resolution and you can send them back to class in a few minutes, okay?"

"Got it," I said. I walked by the kids and motioned for them to follow me into my office. I spread the two girls apart and sat between them. The boy was to my right. I took a breath and began my first conflict resolution at Lake Worth Middle. "We are going to have some ground rules. My role is to try to understand what happened and see if we can come to an agreement and settle this in a peaceful way. Are you guys willing to do this?" They nodded their heads in agreement. "Everyone is going to get their turn to talk and the one rule is to listen to the other person's side of the story without interrupting. Are we in agreement?" Again, the heads nodded.

"Ok, who wants to go first?"

"Do you really want to know what happened?" said the White girl.

"Yes," I answered, leaning forward.

"Well, her brother molested me last year, and last night her mom," she said, pointing to the Hispanic girl, "got into a fight with my mom in the front yard and the police came. This morning the conflict continued and we almost fought. We didn't throw punches, so you can't suspend us." I looked over the top of my glasses at this girl who just said the magic word that I wasn't expecting to hear on the first day of school, molestation.

"Is that true?" I asked looking at the Hispanic girl.

"Yes," she said nodding in the affirmative.

"What's your part in this?" I asked the boy.

"He likes her," said the White girl, "and he thought I was going to kick her ass."

"You were not," said the Hispanic girl.

"Yes, I was," she countered, her voice rising.

"All right we're not following the rules I laid out. I'm going to turn this over to an AP and you'll get a bus suspension."

"Sorry," said the White girl. I decided that the boy was just a bit player in this drama and sent him back to class. Time to consult Frank. "What's up?" he asked.

"That situation on the bus was a little more than a simple conflict resolution," I said with my voice in a hushed tone. "The girl said she was molested by the other girl's older brother and the mothers got into a fight last night and the police were called."

"Oh, shit," said Frank. "Do you want me to handle it?"

"No, you gave me the task to do. I just wanted to get your advice. I need to report this to Children and Families, right?"

"Try to get a hold of the mother of the girl who said she was molested. See if, in fact, she was molested, and if it was reported. Maybe it was and that would be the best of all scenarios right now."

"Ok," I answered and went back into the office. The girls were waiting patiently. Before I could begin to speak Sharon appeared in the doorway.

"How are the sixth grade schedules, Mr. Neal?"

"I'm doing a conflict resolution right now, Mrs. Walker."

"You can't spend all day on conflict resolutions," she said motioning me to my doorway with her index finger. "Do you see all of these students waiting for schedules?" She pointed to thirty-plus kids seated in the wooden chairs around the edges of Student Services. "Get those kids to class."

"But..." I said before she cut me off.

"No, butts. Your first priority is scheduling right now."

"Ok," I said. I went back into my office.

"About the comment you made about the older brother. Did he really molest you?"

"Yes," she answered.

"Does your mom, know?" I asked.

"Yes," she answered emphatically.

"Was it reported to anyone?"

"My mom said I am not supposed to talk about this with anyone and that includes you."

"Okay, I am going to send you to class, but we aren't done with this. You two aren't going to have any problems as far as fighting, are you?"

"No," they both answered. They went off to class. On the contact screen there was the mother, grandmother, and a neighbor. After a ring there was an automated recording that says, "We're sorry you have reached a number that has been disconnected, or is no longer in service, if you feel you have reached this recording in error, please check the number and try your call again." My first experience with trying to reach a parent for a counseling issue. I had yet to build a schedule. Miraculously, I finished one just as the bell rang. In the hallway Frank, with his entourage of students, was at his post. I made my way through his groupies and asked in a loud voice over the clamor, "The mother's number was disconnected."

"Of course, it was," Frank added. "That's typical. Try all of the numbers on the contact screen and see if you can get someone. If not, you'll have to make the call to Children and Families. Sorry about that on your first day." Period 2 was strictly devoted to scheduling. I punched course codes as fast as a courtroom stenographer. Then I tried the grandmother's number and it was like déjà vu all over again with the number out of service. Last number on the contact list was a neighbor. The phone rang, and I was hopeful if not elated to be getting someone on the other line.

"Hello," he said with a voice filled with agitation.

"This is Jeff Neal, Guidance Counselor from Lake Worth Community Middle and—"

"On the first day of school are you kidding me! First, I told that damned elementary school that I don't even know this girl. I want you to take my number out of that computer. No wonder the education system sucks. Get your shit together."

I went out to Ms. Castro, who handled data for contact screens, to have her delete the number only to find her inundated with parents who were confused as to why they couldn't just drop off their kids at school.

"When is that Q'anjob'al facilitator going to get here," Ms. Castro said to Ms. Niskanen.

"Multi-cultural says they will be here soon," answered Ms. Niskanen in her calm manner.

"They better because I speak Spanish," she replied. Q'anjob'al is a Mayan dialect spoken by most of our Guatemalan parents. Three numbers and three strikes. Time to make my first call to the Department of Children and Families (DCF). Thankfully, the phone was working and someone answered. I answered a litany of questions from the caseworker. She said she and a sheriff would be at our school before the end of the day.

I felt a sense of accomplishment just to have fulfilled my legal requirement to report abuse. I was off to my first lunch duty. Feeding middle school kids in the cafeteria is an adventure. When I first started my career, I used to wonder why the kids were running to get their breakfast. The lines would bottleneck as they couldn't wait to get that food. Coach Owen enlightened me that for many, school breakfast and lunch were the only meals they get all day. Assistant principals run the lunch. It's a challenging process feeding three hundred kids in thirty minutes. To get them their lunch, keep them seated, and dispose of their garbage is a work of art. The cafeteria workers are angels. They put up with the screaming, cursing, food throwing, and other behaviors of ulcer breeding monsters. They wear a smile on their faces and have a real desire to get kids a healthy meal.

Saltzman was running my lunch and he had news. He'd earned his doctorate the year before and just found out that he was named Principal of one of our feeder schools, South Grade Elementary. He would be leaving the next week. I ate a school hamburger on the run. Later I was on a roll building schedules when Ms. Niskanen popped her head in my office and told me the DCF case worker and sheriff were waiting to see me. They sat down in the Parent Resource room and waited. The girl looked at me as if I betrayed her as the door closed and she sat down to be interviewed. Frank and I made our way to the bus loop. We both were armed with a list of bus stops. Sixth graders have a hard time remembering what bus they ride. We ask them where they live and then search for a bus stop near that address. A vast majority don't know their address. Many don't speak English and with my broken Spanish and nonexistent Creole these factors make locating a bus very challenging. It was August in the high 90s and sweat was pouring down my back in steady little streams, like legs on the side of a glass of wine. Frank and I led a caravan of unsuccessful riders back to Student Services to call their parents.

"Are you the one who called DCF on my baby?"

"Excuse me," I said to a woman in her early thirties.

"Why in the hell would you call DCF? This thing was investigated a year ago."

"Your daughter didn't tell me that. She only mentioned that she was molested from another boy and that she wasn't allowed to talk about it at your request."

"Damn right I told her not to say anything! Nobody's fucking business what happened. She was molested and it's done. It didn't help that she gave that boy a blow job. You should have asked me!" she said her voice rising.

"I did try to call you and all numbers were disconnected."

"I will pay the bill when I get paid this Friday."

I waved at the girl as she followed her angry mother out of Student Services. She smiled slightly.

"How was your first day counseling?" B asked.

"Interesting," was all I could muster.

"I bet it was. I'm going down to the Rum Keg and have an ice-cold draft beer and throw some darts with the life-guards."

The sun was going down as I got in my Thunderbird to go home. Most of the teachers had gone home hours before, save a few that never leave their classrooms until the custodians leave at night. The next day I was summoned to the 100 Building. A sixth grade female student refused to go to class. "Let's see if you can work some of that counselor magic," Saltzman said.

"I'll give it a whirl," I said.

"Hey," Saltzman yelled before I got through the door. "I'm leaving on Monday to take over my new school. A new AP should start on Monday. Good luck on being a counselor."

"Good luck on your principalship." I walked to the small, thin girl in a tattered yellow skirt, seated against the wall. Dirt was edged in her fingernails and her face was pale almost the color of milk.

"Hi," I said softly, looking for kindness to flow from me to her. She said nothing while just staring straight ahead. "I'm Mr. Neal. I'm the counselor for the sixth graders. Are you in sixth grade?" Still nothing. Then I noticed she wasn't blinking. In fact, it was as if she were in a hypnotic state. I waved my hand in front of her face and there was no response. She finally looked up at me.

"Go away. We don't like you."

"We don't like you?" I repeated.

"No," and she went back to staring. The bell was going to ring. Mrs. Craft, a sixth grade math teacher, looked out her window.

"The kids tell me her name is Charlotte," she said. "I tried to get her to come in and all she did was stare. You should call her parents and get them to pick her up. She can't just sit in the hall all day."

"Go away," said Charlotte to Mrs. Craft.

"I'm sorry sweetie, this is my job and I can't just go away. If I could, I would." The bell was going to ring any second.

"Hey, I don't want to call your mom. Why don't we get some McDonald's?" She broke her gaze and looked at me.

"My treat. What do you say? C'mon, follow me," I said and to my surprise she came right behind me, staring calmly amidst the chaos. She sat in my office. I pulled her file. She had been a little bit of everywhere:

West Virginia, Georgia, Louisiana, Texas, and now Florida. Interestingly, psychological evaluations were underway with each school district but were never completed. Frank walked by my office.

"Frank, I need to consult with you about this one in. After explaining everything he smiled saying, "You better get to McDonald's."

"I know, right?" I said, smiling. "Charlotte, what would you like from McDonald's?" I started to rattle off the menu and when I got to the Quarter Pounder with Cheese she nodded. I ordered two Quarter Pounder with Cheese meals and thought of John Travolta in Pulp Fiction calling this burger a Royale with Cheese. I hurried back to school a little unsure about how to help this student that referred to herself as "we." The smell of the fries got her to turn her head as I entered the office. Immediately, she grabbed the burger and took two huge bites. I tried to ask a few questions that were designed to be innocuous and they went unanswered. Finally, as she squeezed ketchup on her fries she said, "Please don't call my mother."

"Ok, I won't right now, but you have to go to class."

"I will," she said and steadily munched on the burger.

"Have you made any friends yet?" I asked.

"Sarah doesn't want me to have friends."

"Who's Sarah?" I asked. She stood and said nothing.

"Do you know where your next class is?"

"Yes," she answered. The bell rang and as I watched her exit Frank appeared. He saw her go by and asked, "How did that go?"

"She ate her burger, fries, and downed her coke. Don't know much more. Doesn't say much."

"Yeah," Frank said. "She's got that look."

"What do you mean?"

"She's got the mind parasites."

Sharon interrupted, "We need to get these kids in classes."

"We should have all schedules done today," Frank replied.

Charlotte stayed on my mind. Maybe she'd been abused? Sexually? Physically? Obviously, there's some neglect going on from her lack of hygiene. I decided to call the last middle school she attended in Amarillo, Texas. I was patched through to her guidance counselor from last year. "Oh, that poor little waif," said Ms. Robinson with a strong Texan twang. The woman spoke to me at great length reiterating all they did to try to help Charlotte. Their School Based Team brought her up for the school psychologist to do an evaluation and then she moved. "There's a strange dynamic going with the mother," Ms. Robinson stated. "That girl is suffering."

CHAPTER TWENTY-FIVE
"INTRODUCTION TO A BAKER ACT"

The next day Frieda Proctor called my office and said, "Mrs. Craft requested you to come to her room. Something about a Charlotte." I entered the same hallway. "Charlotte, hey it's me, Mr. Neal, your McDonald's buddy." She turned to me with a venomous sneer, and took a pair of scissors and stabbed it into her right thigh. Blood flowed freely from the red circle on her leg. "Charlotte!" I yelled. I grabbed her under her right forearm before she could administer another thrust. I peeled the scissors out of her hand and she tried to bite me. Once I had the scissors, I asked for the nurse to come. Charlotte began staring again.

"We need to Baker Act her," Officer Baxter said as he called dispatch and in moments the Mobile Crisis Unit was en route. A simple case of what I thought was school refusal morphed into institutionalization and examination. Paramedics arrived in moments as their station is a stone's throw away off of Detroit Avenue. It was sad to see her strapped down on a gurney with her blood-stained dress.

"What's going to happen to her?" I asked the nurse.

"They'll treat her at the facility at JFK Hospital. They have thirty-one beds over in Atlantis.

"Baxter, what exactly is the Baker Act?" I asked.

"The Florida Mental Health Act is called the Baker Act. This allows for involuntary institutionalization for anyone who shows a substantial likelihood to do bodily harm to themselves or others without treatment."

"How long will she be in there?"

"The usual time is seventy-two hours."

"Then what?" I asked.

"Then they go back home. They'll probably assign a therapist for her. She's got some deep-seated issues."

My mind kept replaying the scissors going into her pale white leg and the blood running down her thigh to the floor. Her face showed no sign of pain. It was as if she were enjoying the affliction in some sadistic way. This was day three and already I was with DCF and a Baker Act. Thursday and Friday passed with relatively few mishaps. Monday morning an attractive Hispanic woman with long, dark hair was introduced to me as Charlotte's therapist. Her name was Liliana. Frank winked at me as we passed by his office.

"Do you mind if I close the door?" Liliana asked. "We did a thorough psychological evaluation."

"What are the findings?"

"It's too early to tell, but our best psychiatrist thinks she has DID," she answered.

"DID. What is that?"

"Dissociative Identity Disorder."

"Ok, that explains why she was saying "we" instead of I."

"She likes you, Mr. Neal. If fact, you are the only one she mentioned at the school that she likes." I nodded thinking of the power of a Royale with Cheese. Liliana continued, "(DID) is a mental disorder characterized by the maintenance of at least two distinct, relatively enduring personality states. This is usually a reaction to trauma from the past and the personalities help a person avoid bad memories."

"So, she was abused?"

"It's likely that she experienced trauma," she answered.

"What are the symptoms of this condition?"

"Depression, substance abuse, eating disorders, anxiety, and self-harm, are a few of them. I believe you witnessed the latter. One of the things that occurs is memory loss. Charlotte may not remember the scissors incident. A person with this disorder will detach from themselves."

"So, what is the plan?" I asked.

"She is going to see me once a week. If you could do some "talk therapy" that would be great," Liliana said.

"Talk therapy, that's a Cognitive Behavioral Therapy, right?"

"It focuses on getting her to talk about what she is avoiding. Exploring her past could benefit her more than the pills they are prescribing."

"What medications will she be taking?" I asked. I have mixed emotions about this phenomenon. If they had ADHD drugs when I was growing up, my elementary teachers would have had me mainline them.

"She is taking antidepressants and anxiolytics," she said as she stood up to leave. "I hope you have time to counsel her." Liliana left. As I scheduled times to counsel Charlotte Sharon walked in with a big man with red hair. He was tall and had to weigh 250 or more. "Jeff, this is Bob Hatcher. He's going to be our new Assistant Principal." We shook hands. His hand shake was firm. I sensed he was an athlete. He stepped outside the office to greet someone. Sharon stepped closer.

"Bob is just what we needed," she said.

"Why?"

"He was a PE teacher at Omni Middle School for a period of about eight weeks. They pulled him out to do discipline and he did a great job. He has the same mark that you and I have."

"What's that?"

"His daddy was a principal at South Tech High School."

Bob settled into his office with pictures of he and his wife on a boat. He was an avid fisherman. He even had a side business selling, "Red Eye Lures." I knew nothing about fishing, but this big red head was an angler. Later I was to find out that my suspicion of him being an athlete was spot on as he had a baseball scholarship to the University of Alabama and was drafted to play for the Philadelphia Phillies. If not for a shoulder injury, he and I wouldn't have crossed paths.

On Friday of that week, I went into Frank's office. He was scheduling a new student who was sixteen. The boy was as hard core of a gang banger as I had laid eyes upon. His folder read that he was from the Southside of Los Angeles. Frank was trying to engage the kid in conversation. I saw a tattoo just off the side of his right eye that was tear drops.

"That's an interesting tattoo," I said. He scoffed and shrugged his shoulder and shook his head as if I was dismissed. Max was walking in just in time to hear this exchange. He sat down directly beside the teen. It was like a scene out of a movie.

"What do we have here," said Max. "A real gang banger. Where you from, boy?"

"Don't call me boy, old man," the kid snapped.

"Old man is right. You'll be lucky to be an old man. Who do you run with MS-13?"

"Fuck no," the kid said sharply as this struck a chord. Frank looked over his glasses at the new student.

"So, who do you run with?" Max said crossing his legs and clasping his hands around his knee. "Are you ashamed to say?"

"Eighteenth Street," he sighed as if he was bored.

"Oh, the big boys," Max said with a slight laugh.

"What's so funny old man?"

"Nothing. Just you kids in your gangs. You commented on the teardrops on this boy's face, Mr. Neal? Those indicate certain things. Being humiliated, serving time, or for someone one who has killed," Max said and then he looked at the boy. "Which one are you?"

"Fuck you! Can I get my schedule?"

"He'll get your schedule when he's ready," said Max. "This isn't the street. You don't run this shit. We do." The boy's cold stare was icy and alive with hatred. Frank finished the schedule quickly and changed the subject going over to the classes with the student. Max and I walked out together. "How did you know that shit about the tattoos?" I asked.

"This ain't my first rodeo. I came up in New York. That boy probably hasn't done time yet, and he don't look like the type to be humiliated. My guess is that fucker killed someone. The tears are for who he killed. Frank and I made plans to go to the beach and watch the sun rise. It was still dark as we crossed over the Robert A. Harris Bridge that leads to Lake Worth Beach. Frank fed the meter a bunch of quarters. Light was etching its way over the horizon, but the sun wasn't up. "This is perfect. We are about to see something sacred," Frank said as he spread out his towel. I placed a large beach blanket that had an elephant on it and sat down. Frank closed his eyes and took a deep breath. He was in a ritual.

"Are you practicing a yoga pose?" I asked.

"Yes," he said opening his eyes, "right now I am in the Seated Dandasana. We westerners always sit in chairs and our muscles are tight and our hips are too stiff." He took deep, slow breaths. I decided to cross my legs American Indian style, and took some deep breaths myself. I opened my eyes and just as I did the top of the sun, that looked like a giant, bruised tangerine was coming above the water.

"That's what I'm talking about," he said. "Thank you."

"I feel totally relaxed," I replied.

"You are going to need to do that with your new role."

"As a counselor you mean?" I asked.

"I didn't understand middle school. I worked in elementary my entire career. I was like a rock star with all of those kids running up wanting attention. I wasn't ready for middle school."

"Ulcer breeding monsters is what my dad calls them," I said. "He always says I would think I died and went to heaven if I made the switch to elementary." Frank laughed. "Did you always want to be a counselor?" I asked.

"My path was counseling."

For some strange reason Tom Long flashed in my mind. Somehow, I knew that Frank, with his ponytail and earring, was going to be another mentor. We made our way to the ocean. I went into interview mode the same way I did with B on the way home from St. Augustine. "Frank, I know you are a PA guy like me," I said.

"Steel Country," he said as he dunked his head under.

"Where were you born?"

"Bell Vernon. I went to high school at Belmar."

"Did you play sports?"

"In high school I was a half-back. Then I played safety at West Liberty State College.

"Did I hear your dad's a congressman in Pennsylvania?"

"Yes, he represents Washington and Charleroi. He takes care of the working people along the Monongahela River."

"Is he a Republican?"

"No, he's a Democrat. He's not a typical politician either. He eats at McDonald's. His view is that the people don't need to spend their money on fancy dinners for him."

"How did you end up being a counselor?" I asked.

"I was in college in the late sixties. Maybe you don't remember all of the stuff that was going on at that time with Vietnam and the counter culture."

"You'd be surprised. Your generation interests me. I think you guys will look a lot better than my generation, the yuppies of Wall Street. Your time will be looked at the same way as the French Revolution."

"Okay," he said. "Now you're talking to me. Jeanne, my wife, and I went on a journey together. At that time the Beatles were going to India and everyone was wanting change. The war caused us not to trust in the institutions. Opening my mind made me want to be a seeker. Yoga and meditation, whatever could lead us to be enlightened. I heard a guy speak at the University of Pittsburgh. His name was Richard Rose. He was enlightened. We joined a group that he formed in Wheeling, West Virginia. I was reading esoteric books like "Cosmic Consciousness and "Be Her Now." It was powerful to be around Rose as he had that awakening. He was like a witness for us from the source. I wanted to tread on that path. I got into Transcendental meditation and even went to New York for EST in 1971."

"What is EST? I've heard of it."

"Erhard Seminars Training. We'll have that conversation another day. This is my second year in L-Dub (local slang for Lake Worth) and this gig is no picnic. It is one of the most challenging environments I've seen. The fighting and street laws these kids live by, well you know how it is, you've been there longer than me."

"It's true," I said. "Something can jump off at any moment."

"Sometimes there are nights that flame like fire in my mind thinking about one kid," Frank continued. "The one who could try to commit suicide. You can take all of the steps: report to DCF, parent conferences, have them sign a contract, all of it, and still you know that little one wants out." Frank looked up at the sun and said, "It's almost 9:00. I have to take Jeanne to breakfast."

CHAPTER TWENTY-SIX
"LAST CHANCE FOR JIMMY B"

For every challenging student there are ten outstanding kids who work hard and are respectful. One of these superlative students was a girl named Kelsey Burke. Ms. Beebe, a master ELL teacher, brought her to my office. There was throng of female students who wanted to fight her. Kelsey was cute and the boys noticed. I call this phenomenon the, "Mirror, Mirror on the Wall" syndrome. Many melees are born of envy.

"Talk to Mr. Neal," Ms. Beebe said, exiting like a tornado.

Kelsey sighed and sat down. She was wide-eyed as she read the motivational posters that were strewn around the walls of my office. I wondered where she came from.

"Where are you from, Kelsey?"

"Honduras."

"How long have you been in the United States."

"A few months."

Her eyes darted around the room. I could sense she was intelligent. We called a few of the jealous peers in and I performed a textbook conflict resolution. Kelsey and I formed a friendship that day. At the end of the year, she gave me her picture with a kind note on the back. It would be years later when Senator Dick Durbin, of Illinois, would tell her story on the floor of the United States Senate. Her graduation picture from Florida Atlantic University with the United States flag was in the background as Durbin spoke. He recounted her harrowing journey, alone with her brother, from Honduras through Guatemala and Mexico, that eventually landed her in Lake Worth. He mentioned her attending the Criminal Justice Program at Lake Worth High School and how she put herself through Florida Atlantic University and Palm Beach State College. Not being a citizen, she wasn't eligible for any school loans. Her strong will and determination were her only support. In 2008 she was given protective status under the Dream Act. Durbin used her as an example of how our immigration system, if someone proves themselves worthy, should be allowed a shot at the American Dream. Durbin's bill is called the, "Kelsey Burke Dream Act." As I said in my ten to one ration with productive kids there is always that one that tries everyone's patience. That one was Jimmy B.

"Good morning, Mr. Neal," said Larry Ludwig.

"Good morning, Mr. Ludwig."

"Mr. Neal this is Jimmy," he said, pointing to a skinny, Haitian boy standing in my doorway. "Mr. Neal, we're having a big problem with Jimmy. He just can't behave. In fact, he has worn out his welcome in just about every elective we have. PE doesn't want him near the locker room as he is a safety issue. He flooded the toilets the other day."

"Mmm, that's not good," I said. My opus at Penn Elementary surfaced in my mind.

"Mr. Neal if you would please give Jimmy a ride home I'd appreciate it. He is suspended for the next three days."

"I'll take him home," I answered. Jimmy lived right on the outskirts of the hood on a street beside the graveyard. We got into my Thunderbird.

"I'm hungry. I didn't eat lunch," he announced.

"I don't think that's in the cards today, Jimmy."

I tried to make small talk and he just looked out the window saying nothing. We pulled up to his house. He opened the door and got out. "Jimmy, is anyone at home?"

"No one's home," he said as he got out his key. "Come in and see for yourself." Inside the house there was barely any furniture. A dilapidated couch and a small table were all I could see. Old, tattered blankets served as draperies. Jimmy went into the bathroom. Opening the refrigerator, there was not a bit of food in sight with the exception of one bottle of Sunny Delight juice. This pricked my conscience.

"Since your mom isn't here, let's go get some lunch."

"Can we get Kentucky Fried Chicken!"

"Yeah, there's one over on Lantana Road," I said. Jimmy ran to get in my car. His mood became upbeat after he found out we were going to visit the Colonel. I looked over at his left leg bouncing up and down.

"Are you hyper, Jimmy?"

"What's that?"

"Do you have a hard time sitting still?"

"Yeah, that's why I get in trouble all of the time."

"I get it," I said. "I was hyper too."

He looked over, sizing me up. I could see his wheels turning. Who's this tall, White dude buying me KFC? We pulled up to the drive-through. I ordered a two-piece meal for me and turned to my copilot and asked, "What do you want, Jimmy?"

"A three-piece meal," he yelled into the speaker.

Just as he uttered the words the employee who was taking our order said, "Is that you, Jimmy?" Her accent was Haitian-Creole.

"Yes," he answered.

"You is a bad boy, Jimmy."

"You're popular," I said, smiling.

"That's my neighbor," he said as he rubbed his head with both hands going back and forth. I could tell this one was a live wire, trying to calm his mind.

"I want to change that order," I said as we pulled up to the window. "Give us a bucket and a large order of mashed potatoes and some corn."

"Family size?"

"Yes, ma'am," I said. Jimmy's eyes bulged as he looked over at me. The aroma of fried chicken spread throughout the car. There was a small plastic table beside Jimmy's driveway. We got out and opened the bucket of chicken. He ate ravenously. I told him to slow down, although, I usually eat too fast myself. I finished a couple of pieces and told him to save some for later. Just then his mom got dropped off. She was in a maid's outfit from Motel 6. I greeted her. She had an annoyed look.

"She doesn't speak English," Jimmy said.

"Well, tell her that you're suspended for the next two days and you're welcome back on Thursday." As Jimmy spoke to her in Creole, she wound up with a right hook, open-handed, and clocked him over the top of his head. She cursed him out in a language I didn't understand.

"Thanks for the chicken," Jimmy said as I got in my car.

"You're welcome, Jimmy. See you on Thursday."

In the rearview mirror I saw him holding the bucket of chicken. Never underestimate the power of food when dealing with a student. When I got back to the school Larry asked if I could find an elective for Jimmy. I made my rounds to the teachers and none wanted him back. The only one that hadn't had him was Joe Owsley. I headed to his shop.

"Joe, what's up my man?"

"Well, Mr. Neal or is it Coach Neal?"

"I haven't been asked to coach yet," I said.

"Oh, Pattison is going to ask you," Joe said. "He just asked me to coach the girl's team."

"Are you going to do it?"

"Of course, I am. I'm from Kentucky, boy. Hell, I knew Adolf Rupp—876 wins and 190 losses makes him fifth of all-time in college hoops. We're going to start a dynasty in Warrior Country," he said with a smile.

"Joe, I have a favor. It's a scheduling issue."

"It's hard to get those little chickens in the proper pen."

"I need you to take a kid in your shop class. I'm not going to lie to you, this one is special."

"What's his deal?"

"I went to seven teachers and none want him back."

"He's that special, huh?"

"He's this skinny, Haitian boy who's hyper as hell. I took him home the other day, and God as my witness, he doesn't have a lick of food in his house."

"You mean to say he doesn't have a pot to piss in or a window to throw it out of."

"That's about it," I said admiring Joe's way with words.

"Bring him by, I'll straighten him out"

The bell rang. Kids were entering Joe's domain eager to get to the saws. On Thursday Jimmy was sprinting through the cafeteria going for the powdered eggs and silver dollar whole wheat pancakes. They weren't that bad with a lot of syrup. I told him to come to my office fifth period. He nodded and kept eating those cakes.

"Jimmy, you know that they're putting together an Alternative Education Packet for you," I said as he entered my office later that day.

"What's that?"

"You are going to be sent to another school. C'mon Jimmy, you just can't do whatever you want. I had seven teachers tell me that you disrupt everything they do."

Jimmy sighed, "How long do I have here?"

"I think it's up to you. If you keep acting up, I'm sure that Mr. Ludwig is going to put your packet on the fast track and you'll be attending South Intensive before you know it.

"Is that the school by Barton Elementary?"

"Yes."

"I don't want to go there."

"I don't blame you. It's all portables. No electives. They take your cell phones every day. You have to walk through a metal detector. It's not a fun place to be."

"What do I have to do?"

"For starters you need an elective. We are going to see, Mr. Owsley. If he agrees to take you in his class your chances are a lot better at staying."

"Who's Owsley?"

"It's Mr. Owsley. He doesn't have to take you in his class. Be respectful, Jimmy! He's old school and if you say something slick you can forget it."

"Ok," he said. We made our way to the shop. Joe was whittling and his blue apron was covered with sawdust. A wad of chewing tobacco was sitting like a tennis ball inside of his right cheek. "Is this the little shit you were telling me about?" Joe said, standing while spewing a perfect spiral of spit out of his mouth into the waste basket. The juice ran down on a piece of white paper like a slow, brown stream. Jimmy's face contorted.

"What's your problem, boy," Joe said moving closer to him. Joe wasn't exactly brandishing the knife, but it was in his hand. Jimmy's eyes were glued to it. "I'm talking to you, boy. What's your problem?"

"I don't have a problem," Jimmy said with his head down.

"Look at me, boy."

"I'm not supposed to."

"Why's that?"

"In my culture it's disrespectful."

"To look someone in the eyes! What culture is that?"

"I'm... Haitian," Jimmy said almost stuttering.

"Well, I'm not Haitian and you're going to look me in the eyes."

"Yes sir," Jimmy said with his chin rising upward.

"That's better," Joe said gesticulating with the knife to make his next point. "You can come into my class, but don't mess with me."

"No, sir," Jimmy said.

"You obey all my rules, especially, regarding safety with the saws. You understand?"

"Yes, sir."

"Good. Now you get along. This is my planning period and I like to whittle." Joe winked at me and said, "He'll be all right Mr. Neal. Jimmy and I have an understanding. Don't we Jimmy?"

"Yes, sir."

As soon as the door closed and we were in the courtyard, Jimmy gave me a backhand in my forearm and said, "What was that? Was he going to stab me? That man looks crazy."

"Truth is, Jimmy, Mr. O is a little crazy. You better follow his rules. He's your last chance."

"What's wrong with his mouth? Was that blood?"

"Yes, Mr. Owsley never took care of his teeth. That's what happens when you don't brush and floss."

"I'm going to start brushing my teeth more." A week or so later I checked on Jimmy. I pulled up his schedule and as fate would have it, he was with Joe. Upon entering the shop, I saw Jimmy covered with sawdust and Joe was giving him one on one instruction. He had on goggles and looked like a little astronaut or a mad Haitian scientist.

"How's Jimmy doing?" I asked.

"He's doing great!" Joe said, shutting down the saw. He's one of my most talented students. In fact, he's helping the other students with their cuts. He made a nice jewelry holder he's going to sell at Christmas. If he plays his cards right, he might be a carpenter or a cabinet maker."

"Wow, Jimmy, I didn't know you had all of this skill." His smile spread wide on his face as he turned the saw back on and replaced his goggles.

"The little shit is talented with wood," Joe said. "I told him that I would be checking with his academic teachers and if I got any bad reports, I would take away his 'saw' privileges."

"Ludwig said there's been no bad reports on him," I added.

"I told you he was going to be all right," Joe said getting back to instruction. Jimmy was talented and demonstrated this by making me an Irish Clover that he painted green at the end of that year. The leaves were cut perfectly.

Dennis Pattison, PE instructor, was just about to enter the gym when he spotted me saying, "Mr. Neal, hold up."

"What's up, Dennis?"

"You interested in coaching?"

"I am."

"Good, meeting tomorrow at 8:00, later," he said.

The next day after a coach's meeting I was walking with a fellow named Brett Packard who coached track and field. We began our career the same year at the old Lake Worth Junior High. "Who are you going to ask to be your assistant coach?" Brett inquired as we walked down the hall after the meeting.

"I haven't thought about it, yet?"

"Why not ask, Barry?" he said. "He can hoop." Moments later as God and the universe would have it, I heard Barry's voice in Frank's office. "Hey, Barry," I said. "I was going to ask you if you wanted to be my right hand this year in basketball. I'm coaching again. There's a stipend this year."

"Anything would help. We just bought a house in Lake Worth and every penny counts."

"Sounds good," I said.

"Thanks for thinking of me," he said and the bell rang. Tryouts were around the corner. I'm the most easy-going person in the world, but basketball causes me to go Dr. Jekyll and Mr. Hyde. The game played such a huge part of my growing up that something comes over me at the first practice. It becomes my mission to teach them the sport that truly is a preparation for real life. The coach becomes your future boss. The players on your team are your coworkers. Teamwork is essential or your team/business will fail without it. Hard work is essential and you're not always guaranteed the thrill of the victory as there's also the agony of defeat. The next morning Barry came by, "What time is practice?"

"4:00 sharp. Don't be late!" I said with a grin. Frank just acquired a CDL chauffeur's license to transport kids on the activity bus. He wanted one for field trips. He agreed to drive to the away games. I love it when a plan comes together.

Mr. Joe Owsley educating another student to work with wood and craft it into a useful item.

Jimmy "B" made this for me in honor of my Irish heritage.

CHAPTER TWENTY-SEVEN
"MISSION IMPROBABLE: GANGS AND EH"

On Monday Sharon said, "I have some missions for you and I'm not doing you any favors by asking you to get involved with these two assignments."

"What assignments?" I asked as for some strange reason Peter Graves of the original Mission Impossible came into my mind. Sharon wasn't asking me if I chose to accept the missions.

"We need a guidance component in the EH program. They have mental health counselors, but we need to do something from the school site."

"What is it that you want me to do?"

"Anywhere you can see to help."

"What's the other assignment?"

"You know we have a gang problem."

"Yes," I answered with a hint of trepidation in my voice.

"Lake Worth Police are working in coordination with Officer Baxter to be proactive. I want to see what you can do from a counseling perspective." The phone rang and Sharon waved me off. The two new assignments of working with Emotionally Handicapped Kids and Gang bangers was a place I hadn't been before. It's like having two options where one is bad and the other is worse. I chose to go out to the front portables to see what Q and Max were up to with those special kids. I knocked at the fourth portable and asked James Smith, a Black EH teacher, where Max and Q were hiding. He smiled and said, "Follow your nose." He pointed to the last two portables that were closest to the track. As I got closer there was the pungent smell of meat on a grill. Max was standing in a cloud of smoke that was coming off of burgers and hot dogs.

"What's up, Mr. Michel?"

"Ah, Mr. Neal you coming out for some lunch?"

"It does smell good," I replied.

"What's up, Bubba?" he said.

"Sharon wants me to help out with this program," I said.

"Things are going good now."

"Why is that?"

"The Bicycle Academy and our barbecues."

"What is the Bicycle Academy?"

"You should go see it. Q is in Portable 4 with seven kids."

"You barbecue every week?" I asked.

"Yes. If they don't fight all week or have to be restrained, they get the barbecue. Between the Bike academy and the burgers, we have found a formula for survival," Max said. He piled the dripping burgers and blackened hot dogs on a tray. I could hear the sounds of movement inside the portable as I walked up the ramp. The door was locked and a Black boy named Charlie opened the door. He blocked my entry.

"Q, someone's here," said Charlie.

"Well, who is it?" Q asked.

"Who are you?"

"Mr. Neal."

"He says he's Mr. Neal."

"Well, let him in. He's cool."

The other boys eyed me suspiciously. I could tell they didn't like a stranger in their midst. Q had two boys holding a bike upside down as he worked on a chain. Each student was totally immersed in their work. It amazed me when I did an inventory of the tools strewn across the floor: Allen wrenches, tire levers, chain brushes, and Open-end wrenches. Most could be used as a weapon. Just then Max opened the door and said, "Dinner is served."

"It's lunch, dumb ass," one of the kids yelled.

"Watch your tongue," said Q pointing a wrench at the boy. The kids put down their tools and followed Max to Mr. Smith's portable who had already poured juice in red Solo cups. They lined up in an orderly fashion.

"I'm impressed," I said to Q.

"They know better than to fuck around with food," Q answered. "The first time we cooked for them they got into a fight and we made them watch us eat. They got nothing." Every student grabbed a plate and a burger. It was the first time that I really had a talk with Smith. He played basketball at Palm Beach Atlantic University and we had a mutual friend named Kyle Woolum, a devout Christian who is a missionary man. James was a serious Christian himself. I saw him saying grace before the hamburger went to his lips.

"Tell me about this bicycle academy?"

"I started going around to my neighbors and asked if they had old bicycles to donate," Q answered.

"Where do you live?" I asked.

"Delray. Sort of in the ghetto, but it's changing and we are taking it on our own to revamp the neighborhood. You'll have to come to my "Art in the Alley" day. Local artists display paintings in the alley. We also have a mango festival. Anyway, I started to show these knuckleheads how to repair bikes. I gave them the first one as long as they completed the work. It turns out that most of these kids, who everyone thinks can't do anything, can actually fix bikes with the best of them."

"We aren't dumb, Q. We just have brains that ain't wired right," said Charlie. "Least that's what my Auntie says."

"Amen," said Mr. Smith.

"I didn't say you weren't smart," Q chimed in, "if you paid attention other people may think that about you, not us. Officer Debbie got wind of what we're doing and the Lake Worth Police Department is donating a helmet for every bike that's made. We are starting to donate them to needy families in Lake Worth." It did my heart good to see these kids with labels eating burgers and dogs. Their demeanor exuded pride. "You guys can be proud of yourselves. You're going to make a lot of kids happy with this project," I said.

"Thank you," they said in unison. When I walked out Bob Hatcher and Officer Baxter walked by with a man-child.

"Who's that?" I asked Max.

"That's Dizzy, a whole other story."

The bell rang and I felt good about my first venture to EH land. Those three men had rapport with those kids. The whole enterprise was rather ingenious. They got them to do something with their hands and not only got a bike and a helmet for themselves, somewhere deep down in their hearts, they were getting some intrinsic rewards. Also, the same dynamic that worked for me in DOP with the Friday Pizza parties was flourishing. Officer Debbie, who was our school D.A.R.E. Officer (Drug Abuse Resistance Education) was someone who cared about them and gave them helmets for their bicycles. The kids didn't see her as the PoPo. At the end of the day, I gave Sharon a positive report of what I saw in EH land.

"I know they're doing a great job," Sharon said.

"Remember there are still ten other boys out there. The other ten are with Dr. Meyer and his assistant, Mr. Maley. Touch base with them as well. There are a couple that just don't belong at our facility."

"I hear you, Sharon."

"Jeff, I have something for you," Sharon said opening her middle drawer. She handed me a business card. "Here is the name of an officer of the Lake Worth Police Department. He is on the gang task force. Set up an appointment."

"Appointment?"

"There is a teacher's planning day coming up. See if you can set a meeting."

"Ok," I said. Part of me was excited to learn about gang-bangers. I'd observed them for years and studied their graffiti. Something was forbidden and yet alluring about their world. What would make a kid want to get involved in a gang in the first place? There are shootings upon shootings. Often on the local news the newscaster usually ends the segment with, "the police suspect gang activity was involved in this incident." I called the officer and we decided to meet over lunch.

We met at "The Farmer Girl," owned by a Greek gentleman named, Pete. It has old-fashioned, homestyle cooking with some wonderful Greek dishes. Pete's claim to fame is that each year at Thanksgiving, pro bono, he opens up his restaurant to the homeless of Lake Worth. The police come by and deliver meals to the elderly or shut-ins. Once Pete got to know me, he offered meals for needy students at our school. Counselors would take them dinners on Thanksgiving Day. The spirit was moving the first time I saw kids tearing open Styrofoam to get to the turkey, mashed potatoes, stuffing and gravy. The Lieutenant arrived promptly at noon, in a crisp, decorated blue uniform. We shook hands and moved to a booth in the back of the restaurant. We ordered cheeseburgers with double-dipped fries. He began, "Your principal wants you to work on the gang situation at your school. I'll give you an overview of the current gang activity, okay?"

"Yes," I replied. "I don't know much about them."

"There are many gangs in Palm Beach County. It has come on strong since the end of the 1980s and it's getting worse. People think that Lake Worth is bad, but there are gangs operating in Boca Raton, Wellington, and

Jupiter as well. This phenomenon has permeated all socio-economic classes. You my friend, don't have an easy task at Lake Worth Middle by virtue of your demographics. You are a recruiting hotbed."

"Why is that? Is it the poverty?"

"No, it's that your student body comes from many of the countries where the gangs have originated. Your campus is a melting pot for various gang cultures that have a lot of tension right now. You know about the Bloods and Crips?

"Some."

"They originated in California in the 1960s. Most membership is African-American. They are easy to identify by their colors. Crips are blue and Bloods are red. Bloods are Crip Killers and vice versa. You'll see them flashing signs."

"What is all of that?" I asked.

"It's like sign language. They both deal drugs: mainly pot, coke, and crystal meth. Also, extortion, robbery, prostitution, and human trafficking are part of their playbook. Their weapon of choice is an AK47."

"Wow!" I vociferated.

"Most of the gangs are set up like the military. The Bloods and Crips are incredibly organized. A lot of them learned it in our military. It is estimated that 2% of the United States Armed forces belong to criminal gangs in the United States. A recent report states that more than fifty-three gangs are represented in our army. They are encouraged to join the military to learn warfare techniques. They found gang graffiti on tanks after The Gulf War. Gangs are set up with three Generals and three captains underneath. The rest of the bodies on the streets are known as soldiers. Next we have MLK."

"I always see their graffiti."

"MLK stands for Making Life Crazy. This is another American gang that originated in Selma, Alabama. They are associated with the Crips.

Often, gangs will have affiliates in their criminal enterprises. Mexican Mafia is another that operates in Lake Worth."

"I've seen that one on the bathroom walls a lot. I wasn't sure if it was real. I always think of mafia as Italian."

"Oh, no they're a real gang," the officer continued, "One of the biggest, with over 47,000 members. They were born out of the violent prisons in California. They are ruthless. Cutting off fingers, beheadings, all sorts of niceties are perpetrated by this crew. One of their affiliates that pay taxes to them is a gang called Sur 13. The Sur comes from Sureños that is Spanish for Southerners."

"That is spray painted everywhere on the walls," I added.

"Some of those criminals are pretty damned artistic," the officer added. "Okay, another that is getting larger in Lake Worth, is the 18th Street Gang from El Salvador. They are the reason that country has the second highest murder rate in the world. A nice feature of their culture is that you have to kill a rival gang member to get into the gang. Their motto is Vida Loco, the crazy life. They are little killing machines. Our government helped train MS13."

"Really? What does the MS stand for?" I asked.

"Mara Salvatrucha. In the 1980s Reagan sent troops over and trained ten-, eleven-, and twelve-year-olds to fight in their civil war against communism. What happened is that Salvador got so chaotic that they fled the country and landed here. They started to get bullied by American gangs. Unbeknownst to them, these kids from Salvador were hard core killers. Have you noticed them flashing this sign? He made a fork with his index and little finger?"

"Yeah, I've seen that," I answered.

"Guess where they got that?"

"I don't know the devil's pitchfork."

"Close, while MS13 was getting Americanized they went to heavy metal concerts. While these little warriors were watching the crowds of

Black Sabbath and ACDC, with their tattoos and hands making a pitchfork, the gang decided to adopt that as their sign. So, every time you see a MS13 flashing that sign, just know it's brought to you by ACDC," he said with a smile.

"Wow," I said as the irony set in.

"There's the Spanish Cobras from Puerto Rico and Folk Nation from Chicago. They are violent and their main rival is the Latin Kings. Finally, we have Top 6."

"Top 6, what kind of a name is that?"

"They are a Haitian gang. They are not well organized, but they have numbers,"

"What do you mean?" I asked,

"The large Haitian population in Lake Worth has formed a large gang. It's a perfect storm at your school. It's going to get worse before it gets better."

"So, what do you think I can do to help?" I asked.

"Keep your head down," the Lieutenant said. "What would you like to do as a guidance counselor?"

"I'd like to get them to leave the gangs. I didn't grow up with this culture, but to me they either get killed or go to jail."

"I wouldn't waste my time trying to convince them to leave the gang," he said, sipping his coffee.

"Why?" I asked surprised by this comment.

"I've been doing this a long time. You'll be wasting your time and precious energy trying to convince these kids to leave."

"So, we just look the other way as these kids join up in criminal enterprises? Hey, that's cool be a gang banger."

"I understand what you are saying, Jeff, but you don't understand. Once they're in that world there is no turning back. They won't listen to you."

"Really?"

"They have to disappear to get out. Blood in and blood out is the code for the real gangs. There is a price to be paid. They don't want to leave, either."

"Why?"

"All I know from my fifteen years watching this plague on our society is that they are in there for life. It becomes their family. Your best bet is to try to stop the recruiting."

"What do you mean?"

"Mrs. Walker told me you coach basketball. When you are conducting tryouts, you look for talent. That's what the top dog of each gang is doing."

"What do you mean?"

"As you look at talent with your players, the gang leader is looking too. Scanning the campus like a shark smelling blood."

"What are they looking for?"

"They are looking for someone of the same race. They're looking for heart. You know how it is when you can sense a kid's tough. He's not afraid. He doesn't back down. That's who they want on their side. Spot the recruiting and intervene is about the best you can do. Hey, I have to get back. I'm not sure if I helped you or not," the officer said.

"No, you did thank you so much. I learned a lot today."

"I appreciate what you do," the lieutenant said softly. "My mom was a teacher. I know how hard she worked. No one ever gave her the credit she was due. Take care, Jeff."

CHAPTER TWENTY-EIGHT

"ANT MAN AND SAMMY LEE"

The intense pressure and scrutiny put on teachers to raise their student's test scores was fervent. High-stakes testing and Governor Jeb Bush's A+ Plan were married and brought forth the grading of schools. Our grade never fell below a C. I can only imagine how the F schools felt. Imagine being a kid from an F family living in an F neighborhood and attending an F school. That's how we build confidence. Ishmael Gouldbourne, a member of the first team I ever coached, and Barry were helping me find fifteen players from four-hundred. The sheer numbers guided tryouts to be no easy task. I was in the cafeteria when a student says, "Coach Neal, you need to get Ant Man."

"Ant Man?"

"He's over there," he said, pointing to a tall, Black boy who was carrying his tray walking my way.

"Are you Ant Man?" I asked.

"Yep," he said as he dumped his tray in the basket.

"Why aren't you trying out for basketball? Today is the last day of tryouts, come on out." He smiled and walked away. Through sheer serendipity I met another athlete that day. That afternoon as I was about to pass the #400 building a student kicks the door open. I had to swing my head to the left, although, the door caught me on the shoulder. A tall, lanky one screams at the top of his lungs, "Fuuuuckk!"

"Watch your mouth," I said rubbing my arm. "Get over here," I commanded. He ignored me and started to jog to the back exit. I ran in front of him and backed him up against the locker. "First you kick the door into my shoulder, and then you run away, what's your problem?" He had fear in his eyes. I eased my arm and slowly put it down. He took a deep breath and I saw his heart pumping through his shirt.

"C'mon, let's take a walk."

"Sorry I hit you with the door and cursed."

Then I saw his calves with large veins running all the way down to his heels. I stopped dead in my tracks and watched him walk. He moved with grace and his shoulders were broad and his arms were extremely long. My coaching instinct kicked in, "Do you play basketball?"

"Nope, I wanted to but I didn't go," he said quietly.

"Well, you're coming today," I said. "Be there at 4:00."

"Yes sir," he answered.

"What's your name?" I asked.

"Sammy Lee."

"Ok, Sammy Lee. I'll see you at 4:00"

"Ok."

"What got you so angry?" I asked.

"She always makes me read in front of the class and she knows I have trouble," he said. My heart went out to him.

"Guess what, Sammy Lee. You're going to play basketball and you are going to learn to read. I promise," I said, thinking Sharon Purce would have a new pupil.

"That would be great," he said a big smile.

"Let's shake on it," I said extending my hand. A friendship was formed that is still intact to this day. Little did I know that he would end up with a scholarship and play pro ball throughout Europe and in China. I entered the gym for the last day of tryouts. Balls were soaring and careening off rims at all six baskets.

"I found a couple of prospects today," I said.

"Who?" Ishmael asked.

"Some kid named Ant Man."

"Oh, yeah," Ishmael said. "That's Anthony Marshall, my neighbor. He can play."

"The other kid is right there," I said just as Sammy Lee walked through the doorway."

"He looks like a player," Barry said.

"Sammy Lee, get over here. I thought I told you to be here at 4:00. You're late."

"Sorry, I had to call my mom to let her know I was staying after school." I grabbed his shirt and lead him through the maze of kids firing up jump shots.

"Sammy, do you see that rim up there?"

"Yes," he answered.

"Can you touch it jumping off of two feet?"

"I think so," he said.

"Do it."

He crouched down and threw his arms over his head. My face turned upward as I watched him grab the rim with both hands and hang on it. I looked at Barry and Ishmael who both had the same look on their faces that was part astonishment and part excitement. "Let go of that rim!" I yelled. He dropped gracefully back to the hardwood. I blew the whistle and the hundred or so boys that were left on this final day of tryouts gathered on the baseline underneath the basket.

"We have a diamond in the rough with that one," Barry whispered, pointing at Sammy. The playing began and we watched intently trying to identify the best talent. We had some tough decisions to make that night. I always tell the story of Michael Jordan, who didn't make the varsity team as a sophomore as an attempt to provide inspiration to not give up. After some serious deliberation the 1998-1999 basketball team was picked.

At that time, I was living in Lake Worth on a street called North Palmway. "O" street was the next street over and is where Barry bought a house with his wife Pam. Theirs was a quaint house and his yard was like a tropical jungle. Barry hosted a faculty party one evening and I remember it being a beautiful night with a full moon. Everyone had a good time.

"I have the best house on the best street in the best city," Barry said. "This town is great. There's hippies, a gay community, the beach, and just good old Florida stuff. It's like Key West without the drive."

"Barry, do you want your kids to go to Lake Worth Middle?" asked B.

"Of course, I would. We have great teachers. Also, I think it would be great for my kids to learn about other cultures. Attending our school would give them an advantage when they get out in the "real world." Barry seemed content that night. He had his hands on his hips observing the get together he had orchestrated. Everyone was bathed in the moonlight. He put on a CD and I recognized the unmistakable sound of Locomotive Breath from Jethro Tull.

"You like Jethro Tull?" I asked.

"My favorite band," he answered. "Jeff, do you want to play in a basketball league? It's pretty good competition."

"Where do you play?"

"Over at the Norman J. Wimbley Gym in Lake Worth.

It's a nice gym. Our team is the Beatniks," he said.

"I just bought some Dennis Rodman Nikes. I need to break them in."

"Great, I'll let you know when the next game is."

I liked the sound of Beatniks. The first time I walked into the gym it was packed with students. Barry was joking with them as he buried jumpers with his flawless shooting form. His brother, Kurt, was on the team and he was an ace shooter as well. One of my favorite characters on that team was a tall Jamaican guy, Patrick. We were talking when a student walked by with a RIP T-shirt with a picture of one of our students who had recently been killed.

"What happened to that kid?" asked Patrick, his Jamaican accent prominent.

"The kid stole a car and was being chased and ending up killing himself. Not a real nice kid," I added. "He and his buddies roll Guatemalans all the time."

"Really? How?"

"Many of the workers get their paychecks cashed downtown near the courthouse on payday. Sometimes they have a few beers before going home. This boy and his crew wait to jump them and take their money."

"Everyone loves Barabbas," Patrick said.

The students were surprised to see these old White guys battling on the boards for rebounds. Barry and his brother Kurt had a chemistry that was probably due to playing ball for decades together. They were basketball junkies and had the kinship that brothers have. I flew home to see my folks at Christmas. It was good to see my childhood friends. You know you have a true friend when you pick right up where you left off.

The night before I was to fly back to Florida, I rented a movie from Blockbusters called, *Colors*. Robert Duvall and Sean Penn were in this gritty movie about an experienced cop and his rookie partner patrolling the streets of East Los Angeles that were teaming with gangs. How little I knew of the lives of our gang kids. That was soon to change.

CHAPTER TWENTY-NINE

"LESSONS FROM ANGEL"

A fight breaks out in Student Services. Bob Hatcher and Office Baxter got between two combatants who were in rival gangs. Hatcher guided one boy into his office and Baxter asked me to take the other. His name was Martin. I asked him if he needed to see the nurse. "I don't need no fuckin' nurse, what I need is to kick that putas ass." Hatcher entered the office and said, "You guys have a beef, you need to settle it out there, not on this campus. Hand over the bandana."

"That's mine. You can't have it."

"Yes, I can. It's gang attire and it's causing a disruption to our campus. In a moment Bob had it in his hand and the boy stood up quickly and moved toward him.

"Give it back," the boy said.

"Nope it's going in my collection. Mr. Neal would you mind taking this guy home? I just spoke with his uncle."

"Okay," I said.

"I'm not going home with him."

"Let me explain something," Bob said, "Right now you're going home to cool off. If you want, I'll give you ten days for disruption of a school campus and code it gang related. You can take a ten-day vacation or you can let Mr. Neal take you home. Which one do you want?"

"Ride home with him," he said, pointing at me. Passing Hatcher's office, I noticed him tying the new bandana to his collection.

"How many of those do you have?" I asked.

"Over fifty. It really pisses them off when I tie them together. All the colors mixed up is an insult to them. That's the way I like it," Bob said with a smile. He draped the knotted bandanas over his bookshelf.

"C'mon, I'll take you home," I said to Martin.

He sighed and followed me to my car. As we drove out of the parking lot I asked, "You like being in your gang?"

"Of course. They're my homies. My street's right up there," he said, pointing at a house with a neat front yard.

"Martin, is your dad at home?"

"He's in prison," he answered.

"Your uncle's home, right?"

He nodded as I turned the car off. Making sure an adult was home was protocol. As he opened the door a beautiful little girl came running at Martin. He scooped her up and it was then that I noticed his tattoo on his bicep that said "Madre." I remember thinking here is this hardened kid giving love and affection to this little girl. Beauty and the beast.

"What's up? You ditching school?" Martin's uncle said in a deep voice from a room that had beads hanging in the doorway. He put his hands together and spread the beads evenly down the middle and entered the room. The beads slowly came back together. He was wearing a wife beater and khaki pants with sharp creases that were ironed to perfection.

"Hi, my name's Coach Neal. I'm a counselor at the school," I said, extending my hand. His arm was covered with tattoos.

"Pleasure, my name's Angel," he said as he looked at Martin. "What did this little fucker do now?"

"Martin got into it with another boy today. It wasn't a full-blown fight, but the Assistant Principal asked me to bring him home so that he can cool off. He's welcome back to school tomorrow."

"Why'd you do that?"

"The boy was talkin' shit," Martin said.

"So, you going to fight every motherfucker that talks shit to you? I told you, don't take care of business at school."

"Thanks for bringing him home, Coach Neal. I will let his mother know. She's out back."

"Would you mind having a word with me outside?" I asked.

"Sure," he said. "What's up?"

"I'd like to talk about his gang affiliation," I said.

"This is not the time to have this conversation," Angel said, looking around. "Why don't we have a proper tête-à-tête over dinner. My sister is an excellent cook."

"You don't have to make dinner," I said impressed he threw out a French phrase with perfect enunciation.

"I insist. You want to talk in my house, you're going to have dinner. You like Mexican?"

"Yes."

"You want to come tonight?"

"I wouldn't be able to get here until after 6:00."

"See you at 7:00. "Latinos usually don't eat 'til late." Bring beer if you like. It will go good with the Burritos."

"Will do," I said.

After practice I showered and dressed. I stopped at a corner store and bought a six pack of Corona. It was a new fad where everyone drank it with a wedge of lime. There were a lot of cars: Monte Carlo, Ford Fairlane, and a big red Cadillac were amongst the fleet. A long powder blue Impala, with California plates, pulled up. It was a lowrider that startled me when the 3,000-pound vehicle jumped up due to the magic of hydraulic systems. I knocked and the little girl, Valentina, opened the door. Her brown eyes were luminous. Angel, in a bright blue and red plaid shirt, was on the couch watching a Heat game. His mustache was the imperial sort, bushy like Juan Valdez on the coffee can. The smell emanating from the kitchen gave a spicy hint to the air.

"Have a seat, Coach," Angel said his accent thicker than I remembered. "Martin, take those beers to the cooler out back."

"You like the Heat?" Angel asked.

"Yeah, I've been a fan since they started the franchise."

"So, you remember Tony Seikaly and Grant Long?"

"Yes."

"Margarita!" Angel yelled. Martin's mother came from the kitchen wiping her hands with a towel. She was an attractive woman with jet black hair. She had a deep scar across her forehead that had healed. She smiled and nodded.

"Margarita, este es Coach Neal, el que yo te había hablado. El trabaja en la escuela.

Margarita says, "Bienvenido, ven a mi Cocina para que veas lo que estoy preparado para nuestra cena."

"She says welcome and for you to come see what she made for dinner," said Angel. "Martin, go translate for your Mami."

In the kitchen the smell of garlic and cilantro was powerful. She had prepared a feast. There was a stack Burritos that looked like little missiles.

"Que es eso?" I asked, utilizing what little Spanish I knew.

"Carne Asada," she answered, which Martin informed me meant "roasted meat." There was a Quesadilla. I love to eat dishes from other cultures. There were Chilaquiles, which is corn tortillas cut in corners and lightly fried and served with salsa. There was also a large sauce pan with something called, Birria. It was a spicy stew where the main ingredient was goat meat. The mother was proud as she showed me the various dishes. I could tell it meant a lot to her preparing this meal. Her forehead was beaded with sweat.

We sat down to eat and Martin's sister, Emilia, asked grace. She was a fourth grade student at one of our feeder elementary schools. Angel and I talked basketball. He was a student of the game. We were both in our midthirties so we remembered the rivalry of the Boston Celtics and the Los Angeles Lakers. Angel was a Lakers fan as he was from LA. He snapped his fingers at Martin and pointed to my empty Corona. Martin jumped up immediately.

"Bring him lime, Martin. There's some cut in the fridge," Angel commanded. The food was excellent. The Burrito was so fat that I had to struggle to finish it. I didn't want to insult Margarita who had worked so hard to prepare the feast. They did have a little fun at my expense. Angel offered me some Cholula Hot Sauce. As I reached for its Angel said, "I have something hotter, but you may not be able to take it."

"What is it?" I asked.

"It's homemade and the Ghost Pepper lives in it," he said.

"I never heard of it."

"It's too hot for Gringos," Martin said with a laugh.

"Don't say that to him, it's disrespectful," Angel said, pounding on the table.

"Sorry, Coach Neal."

"That's okay. Not the first time I've been called a Gringo."

To ease the tension that had become the main energy in the room I asked, "How about some of that hot sauce?" Martin looked up at me and then at Angel.

"Get the man some hot sauce," Angel said. Martin left for the kitchen and returned with this green sauce that was in a purple bowl. There was a small white plastic spoon on the plate underneath. I still had a fourth of my Burrito so I grabbed the spoon and poured a small dollop.

"A little goes a long way," Angel said a smile forming on his lips. Everyone had their eyes on me. Men have the affliction of the male ego. It's like the command center in our brains linked with our self-esteem. Mine was engaged and I wanted to show this Mexican family that a Gringo could handle their hot sauce. I dumped a hefty spoonful on the outside of the Burrito which fell like a tiny waterfall. The first bite went down. As I chewed my throat closed for a second. I closed my eyes that were filled with tears. Upon opening them, through blurred, salty vision I could see Martin giggling with his sister. Angel had a big grin. Margarita uttered something and went to the kitchen and returned with white bread. I reached for the glass of water beside my beer.

"Don't drink that water," warned Angel. "It will make shit worse." I ate the bread and it did help. About that time in my life was when my hair started to run a race back to my ass. I just turned thirty-three and there was a circular clearing on the crown of my head. The sweat formed in that spot. I decided to slap the top of my head where a tiny puddle had gathered. I had no idea how much sweat was up there. It shot out like a sprinkler. Valentina laughed and Martin was in hysterics.

"That is good hot sauce," I said with a hoarse voice. Margarita started to clear the table. "I thought maybe we could both talk to Martin," I mentioned.

"No, we men are going to talk first."

Margarita brought a beautiful marbled Tres leches cake and it was just what the doctor ordered to eradicate the damage from the hot sauce.

"Let's step out back, Coach. You want a cigar?"

"That would be good." Until that time I could count all the cigars that I'd smoked in my life on one hand. Angel was about to introduce me to what would become an obsession for me, the pursuit of a good cigar. Angel went to his humidor. I could hear a party in the back yard next door. There was the dancing light of a fire, laughter, and loud voices. Spanish music played and the smell of weed was carried over by the gentle breeze. Angel returned with two long and very dark cigars. I looked at the yellow label to see the name Cohiba. I turned it over in my hand and with the light from the torch that was beside my chair I was able to see the intricate rolling of the leaf.

"This is a real deal Cuban from Habana," said Angel. "Not one of those knock-offs from DR or Nicaragua.

"Thank you, I've never smoked a Cuban cigar."

"Here let me cut it for you," he said as he produced a silver cutter and made a perfect slice in the back of my cigar. "Let me show you something," he said as he cut his cigar. "To light a cigar properly you should use a wooden match. A cigar differs from any other form of tobacco, it's truly organic. The binder, filler, and outer leaf are all plant. None of that shit that is in cigarettes. So, you light the match and you turn the cigar slowly in the flame." I watched intently as he demonstrated. "Then once you make sure the flame has burned the entire surface at the end, you can stop turning it and just puff like you would naturally. That way it will burn evenly." He struck a match and I followed his instructions and the rich taste of tobacco filled my mouth. It was a flavor bomb.

"So, this is a Cuban?" I asked.

"Yeah, but Castro fucked up the water system and they're not as good as they used to be. Dominicans are growing some beautiful leaf right now. I love a good Fuente. Enough about cigars. What's on your mind, teacher?"

"I'm not sure where to start. My principal asked me to help with the gang problem we're having at our school. There is a lot of tension between the different gangs. Like what happened with Martin, arguing with a kid from another gang.

"This surprises you. That is the law of the jungle, mano a mano. How much do you really know about gang life?"

"I'm learning as I go."

"Where are you from?"

"Near Pittsburgh."

"In the city?"

"No, north, near a city called Butler."

"Did you have gangs where you grew up?"

"Motorcycle gangs, but nothing like this," I answered.

"So, you are working on something you don't know about."

"That's true."

"Coach Neal, I was drawn to talk to you," he said as he dug deep into the Coleman cooler and retrieved two white cans of beer. "Fuck that Corona, Modelo is the best Mexican beer. I'm going to share my knowledge because I lived that life, and still do to some degree. The problem is that you don't understand why kids join gangs. Is that true?"

"That's for sure," I added.

"You came to the right place. I have a PhD in gang life. You see these kids in gangs are the result of urban decay, poverty, familia breakdown, cultural differences, and interracial conflict. You hear that party over there?"

"Yes," I said as the music seemed to get louder.

"They all grew up near each other and one gang ruled the street they live on right now. You understand turf?"

"That's where a gang owns the area to deal drugs?" I asked.

"Something like that," he said, smiling. "It's more like they fight for neighborhoods and street corners." The light from a torch illuminated some scars on his cheek, right above his mustache, that I hadn't noticed before. He continued, "What happens is that a kid like my nephew Martin grows up in a neighborhood and he has a choice to join or be on his own. Do you know what it is like to be on your own on these streets?"

"I guess not," I answered, sensing how little I did know.

"Imagine you are a typical kid, from this neighborhood."

"Okay."

"You may have a piece of shit dad like the asshole Nicaraguan my sister married. Did you see the scar on her forehead?"

"Yes," I said.

"That fucker came into the house drunk and brought a machete across her head and opened her skull. Little Martin was seven or eight and got up to help his mother and the fucker threw him into the wall. Knocked him out! So, you're little Martin and you got that in your head. You don't like school and you are longing for something. Do you know what that is?"

"Revenge," I said, thinking of the violent father.

"No, coach you know what Martin and all of those fuckers in the back yard over there are longing for? C'mon, it's the most powerful force in the universe." I shrugged not knowing what to say. After a pregnant pause he said, "What they're looking for is love. Love and family. That's what a gang offers them. The gang is the only real family most of them know. Add to it protection, social status, and you get laid. Love, protection, and family are a powerful trifecta."

"What about getting shot or going to jail?"

"That's the life. You know when you enter you could go out early. It's a status symbol to be in jail. Those boys look up to me because I did my nickel. We have laws that we live by, our code."

"Like what?" I asked.

"You can't be a rat or a coward. You can't raise a hand to another member without approval. No disrespect like having sex with another member's wife or girlfriend. You can't steal, and you definitely can't be a homosexual. You can't cause dissension in the ranks. This is a big one, membership is for life. It is mandatory. La Eme comes first, even before your family. Those are the hard rules that must be obeyed." I remembered the lieutenant's admonition to not bother with trying to get them out of the gang.

Angel got up and took a piss in the back by a wooden fence. I kept hearing the thud of Mango's dropping on the earth. The Cohiba had me reeling with the nicotine surging through my bloodstream. I felt like I was flying around on a magic carpet made out of tobacco. "I don't know if our conversation helped you or not, Coach Neal. I know you want to help. You aren't going to stop it. The best thing to do is lay down the law and don't let them operate on your campus. Do you have any questions?"

It seemed surreal that the gang task force officer basically said the same thing a few days before. For a moment I thought about Angel's words. The whole love and family thing wasn't even on my radar. The one thing that I wasn't comprehending was the protection thing. It seemed a little over dramatic. So, I asked, "The idea of the gang protecting Martin. Is that really necessary? If he didn't join the gang, would he really need protection?"

"You don't understand the fear?"

"No, I guess I don't," I replied.

"C'mon, bring your cigar. I want you to meet some people." We walked through the backyard to a double door that opened up into the yard where the party was taking place. There was a huge fire pit with flames that lit up the yard. There were probably forty people. All were dressed in the same red plaid shirts. The girls were pretty but had that hard edge to them. They all turned to see the gringo in their midst.

"Come enjoy the fire," Angel said with the cigar in his mouth. Do you want another beer?"

"No, I'm good," I replied. A dark energy enveloped me. The hair bristled on my neck. Angel raised his hand and the music stopped. Then in Spanish he yelled like a general in an army. Just as the words were out of his mouth I watched as all of the females started walking to the house. They glared at me upon passing. As this migration was going on some males who were present made an exodus to Angel's backyard. The door to the house where the females exited closed as did the double doors that allowed passageway to the other yard. The guys who remained slowly formed a semi-circle around me. My back was to the fire and it was hot. I looked at the badass crew staring at me coldly. The flames danced on their faces as an eerie beat grew louder from the speakers. These street outlaws had that vacant look that I saw on the boy with the teardrops tattoo. I counted thirteen guys, including Angel.

"You feel the changes in your body, Coach?" Angel said above the music. I dropped my cigar. He continued, "I'm sure you feel the changes. That's the adrenaline being pumped by your brain. All that pounding of your heart is redirecting your blood to your muscles that causes a surge of energy. Pretty soon your limbs start to shake." It was all true. I started to sweat profusely feeling a droplet running all the way down my back.

"You feel that, Coach?"

"Yeah," I uttered with shallow breath. Angel then spoke and the stares stopped and each one approached me. They drew me in and gave two hard quick slaps on my back, flashing grins as they backed away.

"Coach, you all right?"

"I'll have that beer now," I said.

"That's my man," he said and he yelled into the house and over to his yard. The people started to file back. The music with the ominous beat disappeared and a lively Salsa tune took over. The laughter and dancing resumed. Angel and I retreated to the chairs by the cooler. I gulped cold Modelo and the effervescent quality made me burp.

"Now you know what Martin or any of those homies over in that yard feels when a rival gang comes up on them. If a gang knows you don't have protection, you're just a sheep among wolves."

"I get it," I said, finishing the rest of the beer.

"No hard feelings, Coach."

"None. I am going to head home, though."

"Ok," said Angel. I'll walk you out."

I thanked Martin's mother for the meal. She gave me a kiss on the cheek. I like this gesture that is practiced in the Latin culture. Angel followed me to my car. He extended his hand and said, "Be careful out there. I told my boys if they ever see you in trouble to get your back. Not everyone out here on these streets is going to do that. Good luck to you, Coach Neal."

"Thank you, Angel. Dinner was great and thanks for the Cuban. Even more thanks for the lesson."

"Sometimes a teacher needs a teacher, right."

"All the time," I said as I got in my car. I waved and looked at him with the cuban cigar still bellowing out clouds of smoke. I wondered what possessed him to have me over for dinner. It was as if he were trying to protect me. Maybe Angel was truly being an angel.

CHAPTER THIRTY

"THE THEFT OF OJ'S BUST REVEALED"

En route to retrieve a child from class I did a double-take. There Barry stood outside his door, dressed in a full-length bright, white toga as he greeted each student. There was much laughter and taking of pictures. I put my hands out to the side, speechless, as I looked at him. "I do this when we read Greek Mythology. It's amazing what this garment does to stir things up," he said with a smile. The bell rang and he rubbed his hands together, signifying high excitement saying, "Time for the show." I could hear him telling his students what page to turn to in a story about Odysseus. He was in his element engaging students with his toga. Each of his classes acted out plays. I smiled as I closed his door to let him do his magic.

My day was starting out a little different. There was a young boy who was allegedly being abused by his mother. He was a slight, Haitian boy who was painfully shy. Finally, with the help of another student, I got him to pull both pant legs up above his knees. I stared intently at the two perfect circles that looked to be infected. It was revealed later that his mother made him kneel on tuna cans on the front porch and scream to all passers-by that he was a liar. Often cultures from other countries don't understand the disciplinary boundaries in the United States. The nurse confirmed my suspicions that both knees were infected. I called DCF. After that unpleasant task, I left my office to head out to EH land when Sharon stopped me and said, "I asked Q if he would take his truck to get some desks that the West Palm Beach National Armory is donating. We need desks! Give him a hand," Sharon said.

"Ok," I answered. Q pulled around in an old Ford F150. It was creaky and the white paint had its share of rust. There were tools, papers, unopened envelopes, cans of paint, and just about anything else one could fit in the cab. "Just throw that shit behind you. As you can see, I'm not a neat freak," he said, smiling. We passed the Palm Beach International Airport and a siren sounded.

"That's for me," Q said whipping his head around, one eye closed, looking like a pirate. It was a cool day and I had on an old leather jacket that I had since high school. It felt like an old friend. Q was digging for his wallet. I instinctively put my hand inside my jacket to get my billfold.

"Don't move!" the cop says as he wheels around parallel to Q's open window with both hands on his gun that was pointed at me. Take your hand out of your jacket!"

"I was just reaching for my..."

"Just follow my directions and both of you put your hands on the dash." The policeman called something into his walkie by his chest and then asked Q, "Do you know why I pulled you over?"

"I don't know, it could be for any number of reasons, I've been arrested like a dozen times in life," he replied. The officer I don't think was quite ready for that response.

"Your back right tail light is out," he said, studying Q.

"I know, I keep meaning to replace that."

"You!" he said, pointing at me, "don't ever put your hands in your jacket when a police officer is approaching you."

"Yes, sir," I said.

"Yeah, they don't like that," Q said, handing over his license and registration. I looked over at him humming as if he were getting his oil changed.

"Have you really been arrested a dozen times?" I asked.

"Oh yeah, probably more," he said, laughing.

"For what if you don't mind me asking?"

"Mostly for aggravated assault. A couple of times in college for public intoxication, you know, stupid shit like that."

"So, you were a street fighting man?"

"I had to be. I grew up in Opa-Locka."

"I've heard of it, but I don't know much about it."

"It's an urban community in North-Western Miami. It was named originally by the Native Americans who called it 'Opa-tisha-wocka-locka' meaning 'a big island covered with many trees and swamps.' We're one of the most violent parts of Miami."

"Really?"

"There weren't a whole lot of white folks on my street so I had to fight my way to school every day. That's how I got my job in college."

"What was that?"

"I was a bouncer at Uncle Luke's club."

"Uncle Luke?" I asked.

"Have you ever heard of 2 Live Crew."

"Yeah, I remember, *Nasty as They Wanna Be*, right?"

"That's the one," Q said nodding. "I got a job as a bouncer at his club because of me growing up where I did. I was home for the summer from the UCF and my mom said I had to get a job. I saw this advertisement that Uncle Luke needed bouncers in his night club. So, I walk in and there's this big Black woman interviewing all of the candidates for bouncers. I was the only White guy. The lady looks up at me and it went something like this.

"Do you know what kind of night club this is?"

"Yes, ma'am," I answered.

"So, you know this is a Black night club?"

"Yes, ma'am."

"No offense, but I don't think you'd be a good fit."

"I can do this. I've been fighting Black guys all my life."

"Excuse me."

"I grew up in Opa-Locka."

"Okay."

"I'm serious. Here's my license. She grabbed my license and looked at it and then back at me. She had family there.

She said, "I don't want nobody sayin' we prejudice, you got the job."

"How did it go?" I asked.

"I loved the action and they loved me. They called me Opie," Q said, laughing as the police officer came back with the ticket.

"Get that light fixed, Mr. Quillian," the officer commanded.

"Will do," Q said grabbing the ticket and tossing it in his glove compartment. He started the truck and said, "My crowning achievement was when I made national news."

"This has to be good."

"I graduated from college in 1995 when the O.J. Simpson murder trial was going on. So, three of my college football buddies and I decided to give ourselves a graduation present and go to the Hall of Fame in Canton, Ohio."

"Okay, I've been there."

"Remember where the bronze busts are lined up?"

"Yes," I said recalling that part of the museum.

"Anyway, we were really drunk and I was leaning on one of the busts and all of the sudden it lifts up. I realized that all of them can be picked up. This was at the height of the most controversial court case of the twentieth century. One of my friends says we should take O.J.'s bust. I thought that sounded like a good idea and I picked it up."

"Was it heavy?"

"No, it was like 70 pounds."

"So, you were just able to walk out with the damned thing?"

"This was before cameras were everywhere. There was construction going on. They were getting ready for enshrinement week or something. I walked right out the door."

"Did you get away with it? Do you still have it?"

"I could've gotten away with it, but my buddies panicked and drove out of the parking lot away from me. I walked a long time. I saw this big pile of brush that waste management people pick up so I placed O.J. behind it. My plan was to wait until morning and get it before absconding back to Florida."

"What happened?"

"Unfortunately, an ODOT crew came by and returned it. The hall of fame got real strict after that and bolted everything down. That night Tom Brokaw starts out his broadcast with, 'Someone has stolen the bust of O.J. Simpson from the Football Hall of Fame today.' My mom knew it was me," he said, laughing. In moments we were pulling under I-95 on Belvedere Rd. into the armory. I don't know how he did it, but he tied twenty-two desks with bungee cords to the bed of the truck. We looked like, "The Beverly Hillbillies" on our way out.

One of the things that being a counselor afforded me was the opportunity to spend time with people like Q. When you're in the classroom, in your own world, there is an isolation and often one doesn't get to see what your neighbor is doing. There was excellent instruction going on as the staff was packed with master teachers. Future chefs were being trained in Home Economics and being funneled to the culinary program at Lake Worth High. Eighteen electives were offered to students and we were a well-oiled machine. Today we have only a handful of electives. The incessant need for higher test scores on the FCAT was the culprit of this murder of our curriculum.

James "Q" Quillian the Renaissance Man. Q is holding a sunflower he grew on campus with Gardening Club.

CHAPTER THIRTY-ONE
"FIRST CHANCE FOR THE BIG DANCE"

The season was moving toward the playoffs and we were undefeated. The team had jelled. Barry spent extensive hours working with Ant Man and Sammy Lee on their jump shots. A fellow named Justin O'Neal came on strong as a power forward. Alex Hernandez had a good shot from the corner and Terrence "Pac" Diaz was a fire plug of a point guard. Little Jarvis Jackson, the sixth grader, wasn't afraid to mix it up with the eighth graders. Jules Noel, who was the fastest sprinter in Palm Beach County, was learning the game. His defense was aggressive and brought good results. We'd amassed a 10 and 0 record in the regular season and won two playoff games. It came down to us playing against Roosevelt at home, for a chance to go to the county championship.

I'd never been to the big dance, as they call it, and I thought with this team we had a shot. JFK from Riviera Beach and Roosevelt in West Palm were usually in the hunt to be champs. Often when a team goes undefeated there is a pressure that manifests itself. Everyone asks if you think you are going to remain unbeaten. We were working hard and preparing at the practice the night before the big game. Barry was upbeat and encouraging the kids. I stayed after practice with Ant-Man and fed him jumpers.

"Are you nervous about the game tomorrow?" I asked.

"Nope coach, we got this. We're going to win."

"That would be nice."

At 3:30, the following day, the Roosevelt bus came around to the back of the school. We always asked them to park there for safety reasons. A team bus in the front, after the game, is a gauntlet of rowdy fans. I watched as the team filed off the bus with their maroon uniforms and was amazed at their size. During warm-ups I could sense that my boys were a little intimidated as they watched the tall team go through their pre-game drills. Many of them were laying the ball over the rim, and it was obvious they could dunk. At half time we were tied. It came down to the last few minutes. We were trailing by four with a minute to go. Ant-Man hit a three-point shot and we were down by one. I started to get that feeling we were coming back. At fifteen seconds we were still down by one. I instructed Sammy Lee to pressure the ball on the inbounds pass and they had to use another time out to avoid a five second call. The second time they got the ball in and Terrance Diaz fouled a player with five seconds left on the clock. I called a short time out and reminded them of a play we had to push the ball up after foul shots.

The player made the first shot. He missed the second one and Sammy Lee grabbed the ball and threw a perfect baseball pass full court to Ant Man. He let the ball go as the buzzer sounded. The gym went silent as it rotated in the air in a great arch. The ball hit the rim and ricocheted back and forth before falling out. The crowd sighed. They had worked hard and now it was over. In the locker room many were filled with tears. I was searching for something to say to take the sting out. Barry entered the locker room enthusiastically as he shook each kid's hand.

"Who wants to go to Jupiter with me tomorrow morning and play in some pickup games with varsity players? The only way to get better is to play against good competition," he announced. Their heads came up and many players raised their hands. The kids wrote down their addresses and had something to look forward to the next day. This gesture was healing in that moment. So, it started that Saturday with Barry driving into the hood with his friend, Tim, picking up athletes and taking them to his former high school in Jupiter. He then would treat them to lunch at Wendy's after the games. He did this all summer long.

I was going to miss Ant-Man. There was something special about him. Believe it or not recruiting goes on at this level, and Ant-Man was no exception. I would see coaches from local private high schools with hungry eyes and pens dancing on their clipboards. A private high school named American Heritage came knocking on his door. It is an excellent school that, at that time, had the highest number of National Merit Scholars in Palm Beach County. I kept my mouth shut when he was making his decision as to whether to go there. He played there for a year and returned back to Lake Worth High to play for Coach Dana Drummond. I always like to see a kid go to the school he is assigned and play in front of his community. Recruiting should be for college. By the way, Ant Man earned a scholarship to Georgia Southern and was a stand out there. Today he works for the City of Lake Worth Recreation department and passes on his expertise to youth aspiring to be basketball players.

I was spending time in the local gym with Sammy Lee and others. The gang Top 6 was a presence. One night a shooting occurred right outside of the gym just as Sammy Lee and I were walking into the evening sweating and slurping Gatorade. Young kids came running in the gym screaming. The sound of bullets spraying, a block away, on Washington Avenue. Jarvis and his brother Colby lived at the end of that street by the railroad tracks. It seemed surreal that AK-47s were blasting into the night so close to the Wimbley Gym. That night I heard a voice of a young Black boy who ran up to my car. I'd seen him in the gym hoisting jump shots.

"Are you Coach Neal?"

"Why, yes I am, and who might you be?"

"My name is Jeffrey and my mom named me after you."

"What?"

"She was your student."

"What's your mom's name?"

"Bernadette."

"Bernadette Remmington?" I asked as I only remembered one Bernadette from my first year of teaching.

"Yes, I'm Jeffrey Remmington."

"Wow, pleased to meet you, Jeffrey. How is Bernadette?"

"She's doing good; she's a school bus driver."

"Tell her I said hi."

"You can tell her yourself. I live right down the street," he said, pointing to where the shooting occurred less than thirty minutes ago.

"I don't think I will tonight."

"No, it's okay. The police are already there and the bird will be coming soon."

"The bird?"

"The helicopter the police use." Sure enough, just as that came out of his mouth, I heard the unmistakable sound of the whirring and chuff of helicopter blades. A huge spotlight searched a few blocks away. Jeffrey was so calm about it all and he seemed eager for me to say hi to his mom.

"How far is your house?"

"It's the fourth house on the left," he said, his eyes wide.

"Do you want a ride?"

"I have my bicycle. You can follow me," he sprinted to a bike that was hidden in the hedge beside the gym. He jumped on his bike and waved me to follow. I smiled as he was pedaling like he was in the Tour de France. We pulled up to an apartment building and I got out of my car and looked around. The police in two SUVs and one patrol car were interviewing a group of boys that looked to be in their late teens.

"Mr. Jeffrey Neal," I heard Bernadette's voice. How are you?"

"I'm good, Bernadette. I hear you're a bus driver."

"Yes, I am," she said proudly. "I couldn't believe when Jeffrey told me you were out here."

"Hey, did you name him after me?" I asked with curiosity.

"I sure did. You were my favorite teacher," she said.

"You want to play ball?" I asked Jeffrey.

"I do."

"How are your grades?"

"I could do better," he said, putting his head down.

"Your books have to come first. That's why they call it student/athlete."

"You hear him, Jeffrey!" Bernadette said.

"You have a nice shot, but there were two things I noticed."

"What's that?"

"You need to keep your shooting elbow straight like a dart shooter." I imitated how dart shooters put their elbow straight up and down before going for a bull's eye. "The elbow has to be straight and you need to move the ball up to your forehead and not your chest. You have to develop a jump shot. Jump, pause, and release."

"I'll work on that. Thanks!" Jeffrey did work on it as he went on to play pro ball in Japan, Puerto Rico, Mexico, and Canada. As I drove past the police, I recognized a few of the boys they were interviewing. At the end of the block where it winds around and runs parallel to the railroad tracks, I saw Jarvis and Colby walking into their house. I beeped and they waved. It dawned on me that these kids have to navigate in a war zone. Little did I know that another place would become a war zone across the country the next day.

Larry Ludwig informed me that there was a mass shooting at a school in Colorado. That night I watched the news. Columbine High School was in Littleton, Colorado. The news footage showed that chaos reigned that day. There were SWAT team members escorting students and staff outside of the building everyone walking with their hands clasped behind their heads being ushered to safety. Two students named Eric Harris and Dylan Klebold went on a forty-nine-minute rampage with two dozen pipe bombs. Also, a TEC-DC9 mm semi-automatic handgun, Hi-Point model 995 carbine rifle, Sawed-off Savage Springfield 67H shotgun, and others all added to the carnage. They trapped victims in the cafeteria and library and executed twelve students and one faculty member before committing suicide. The initial coverage stated that they were part of an outcast group called, "Trench coat Mafia" that hated jocks and were bullied. That was flawed information.

Distinctly, I remember thinking how horrible it would be for a school to experience that savagery. In the background of the news footage students seemed to never stop hugging each other. I shut off the news and wondered what the hell was going on here. Jose Garcia's new school, Conniston Middle, experienced a shooting in 1997. A student was murdered. Joe Owsley's former high school in Paducah had a shooting where a student shot and killed three students while wounding others that same year. Now there was Columbine. There was something different about this one. It stayed with the nation and it stayed with me. It was April 20, 1999. Later I was to learn that the two killers planned the bloodletting on Hitler's birthday.

CHAPTER THIRTY-TWO

"Farewell to the Matriarch Rosie"

May passed and another last day of school. On the way to Pennsylvania, I stopped in Memphis for Dan Melore's 40th birthday. Dan, one of my best friends, was like an older brother when I was growing up. The chance to go experience Memphis that summer was enticing. We celebrated at B.B. King's Blues club in style. Catching up with an old friend was a good way to kick off the summer. Friends are family that we choose. The humidity was in full force when I got back to L-Dub. The only place for a respite from the solar oppression was the ocean with the hopes of a breeze. A few days before school began, I saw Barry walking with his son, Sam, around the block. I jogged out to say hi. "I have a daughter now!" he exclaimed.

"Congratulations! What's her name?"

"LeeAnne," he said, smiling.

A new counselor named Kevin Hinds was hired who was young and energetic. He gave Kayak lessons as a side job. As the year began the job seemed to entail more intricate problems than I remembered. There was a boy named Harvey, in sixth grade, who refused to go to class. He had an acute case of school anxiety. His mom reported he often complains of physical symptoms before it's time to leave for school and if she lets him stay home the manifestations disappear. About two to five percent of the student population have this malady called "school refusal." I assigned him a therapist as I couldn't devote all of my time trying to coerce this kid to go to class. She exposed him to school in small degrees. Eventually this helped to ease his fear. He bonded with a science teacher named, John Carroll, and actually started to enjoy school.

Next a girl, from a foster care home, was having suicidal thoughts. Her Language Arts teacher flagged a few pieces of writing that concerned her. The art teacher gathered pictures she drew of her hanging herself or big bottle of pills with the skull-and-crossbones poison sign. Foster children are often a challenge to educators. All of the multiple changes and placements in their lives leave them with emotional scars. A lot of systemic problems in child-protective systems leave a child languishing there for years without a permanent home situation. God knows what led this girl to be removed from her original home. It could be abuse, neglect, death, incarceration, drug abuse, you name it. The good thing is that she tipped us off with her writings and drawings which is known as suicidal ideation. The foster care people I contacted knew about her risk factors. They said she was seeing a therapist at the shelter. Then I was confronted with a student who had Prader-Willi syndrome. One of the characteristics is that students with this disorder have ravenous appetites. We had to watch him at the waste baskets in the cafeteria as he would rummage for snacks that were thrown away.

While that was going on, I had a sixth grade girl inform me that her new stepdad came into the bathroom each morning and watched her shower after the mom has gone to work. "He says it's to make sure I'm clean, but it makes me uncomfortable. Please don't tell my mom! She's happy for the first time." As if this one wasn't bad enough, another girl shows up at my office and tells me her friend in seventh grade is pregnant and is afraid to tell someone. I called the young girl down and sure enough she was pregnant. She begged me not to tell her dad who was raising her on his own. The boy who impregnated her was a charismatic eighth grader. He was quite the "player" with the ladies. She was just another one he deflowered. "Please don't tell him, please, please, please...." That was just four scenarios out of the entire grade.

Frank was plugging along with a sea of children following him everywhere. Kevin Hinds was young and clean cut, like an altar boy, who became a middle school counselor. The weight of the job didn't seem to affect him whatsoever.

We as a faculty, like a great sports team, started to jell. Many of the old guard from Lake Worth Junior High had retired. Sharon was in her fourteenth year leading the Warriors. I was no longer the young one on the staff. I liked that feeling of the changing of the guard, one generation giving way to the next.

I entered Barry's classroom on his planning period to see if he still wanted to be my wingman and he was with Social Studies teacher, Brett Packard. Brett has a sense of humor, always quick on the draw, with a witty comment. I hadn't realized what good friends he and Barry had become. They both were music junkies who traded CD's like they were stocks. Both of them loved Bob Dylan and Jackson Brown, artists of that ilk. Barry was in for another season and, once again, after eliminating hundreds of potential candidates, we had our squad. We began teaching the fundamentals of the game.

There were a lot of bad habits to detach from each kid that they acquired on outdoor courts at pick-up games. Most of them carry the ball when they dribble, a violation. They'd take three steps when shooting when you are only allowed two. They've been indoctrinated by "street ball" to pass behind their backs, dribble between their legs all in the tradition of being a hot dog. When I caught one being fancy, I would put them all on the baseline for a suicide. Just before I blew the whistle for their sprint, I would utter the phrase, "Too much trick, not enough treat." It was a mantra they got used to hearing in my attempt to rid them of their quest to be prima-donnas.

It is worth noting a conversation that occurred between Barry and another student the last night of tryouts. Barry ambled over to a tall stocky, Cuban boy who had sprained his ankle the first day of tryouts. We never got to see what he could do on the court, but I did know that he was an outstanding pitcher on the baseball team who threw a couple of no-hitters. I could see on his face he wanted to play basketball as well. "Ryan," Barry said as the boy balanced on his crutches and winced. "I'm sorry you hurt your ankle because I really believe you would have made the team."

"Really," Ryan said, sounding surprised. "I didn't think I would. My shots not that great."

"Yeah, but you're an athlete," Barry said with passion and fervor. "There's more to basketball than shooting. Defense and rebounding are what wins games. You are strong like bull and with that strength you would be an asset. Don't give up. Try out next year!" Ryan smiled and I could see him being uplifted by this exchange. They began discussing *The Lord of the Rings*, an epic high-fantasy novel by J. R. R. Tolkien. Barry was Ryan's favorite teacher and was in his last class of the day, Period 6.

That night as I walked out of the gym, I reflected on the changes that occurred from 1990 when we migrated to the new school. That was a heady time for those of us who were working at Lake Worth Community Middle. To go from 800 to over 1,600 students was quite a transformation. A new school, L.C. Swain, in nearby Green Acres, was yet to be built and we were bursting at the seams with kids. The population doubling added with the influx of gangs made it challenging to say the least. Even though I shared with you the horror stories that abounded, I want you to know there were so many nice kids with hearts of gold. A young man named, Cory Neering, another former Warrior who had done well came back to Warrior Country for a visit. He played on my first team with Ishmael. He'd graduated with a Bachelor's of Arts in Sociology and a Master's in Science in Organizational Management and Leadership from Springfield College in Massachusetts. L-Dub was his launching pad and he made his rounds to former teachers. He and Peggy Cook had a bond. Today he is a West Palm Beach City Commissioner.

One of the cast of characters in our family was Rosie Richardson. She lived in the heart of Lake Worth and was everyone's mother in the hood. She was a teacher's aide and worked with the ESE kids assisting kids with disabilities. The neighborhood looked up to her. Rosie was a devout Christian who always asked me if I was going to church and let me know she was praying for me. She'd been working there for over thirty years. Lynn Collins, who is quite possibly the most committed Christian I know, came into my office and let me know that Rosie was sick. She suggested I should visit her. Frank and I decided to go to her house after school.

We decided not to go empty-handed so we went to a Publix Supermarket to get flowers. Inside the store the smell of fried chicken drew me like a magnet to steel. Flowers and a box of chicken would be a nice treat for Rosie. Frank was riding shot gun with the flowers in his hand and the chicken resting on his lap. I made the right off of Dixie and crossed over the railroad tracks. As I slowed down, I saw the huge red pickup. The owner of the truck, an old Black man with white curly hair, sold watermelons. I often grabbed one after dropping off players. They were gargantuan and mouth-watering.

"We should get Rosie a watermelon too," I said as I did a U-turn and pulled up on the grass and got the fruit. I made the turn where I thought Rosie's house was located. I didn't see her Chevy Nova in the driveway.

Just then I heard a scream, "Mascara!" Looking in my rearview mirror I saw no less than twenty of our students en route to the gym. Some were on bikes, but most were on foot as they ran to him. Once they got to the car, "O'Neal's with him." I really don't understand it, but all of my career kids called me "O'Neal." I didn't mind as the original man who came over from

Ireland in my family was named Thomas O'Neill. He broke off after the war and fought with the Indians. It was a scandal. Hence, the name change.

"Where's Ms. Richardson's house?" I asked.

"Her cribs right up the street; we'll show you," a boy said as he started to pedal his bike in front of my car waving for us to follow. All of the kids decided to run down the street on either side us. They were in stride keeping up as Frank looked out his window at the runners to his right. It was a moment as the sun was going down, accompanied by an entourage, on our way to our sick friend, Rosie's house.

"This is pretty crazy," Frank said, smiling and pointing at our striding escorts. "Do you realize we are bringing fried chicken and watermelon to a Black woman?" he asked.

"I didn't even think about that," I replied. We knocked on the door as the kids pulled away. The door was answered by a woman we didn't know.

"Y'all must work at the school," she said.

"Who is it?" I heard Rosie ask.

"I don't know, two White men with flowers and food.

"It's us Rosie. Neal and Frank," I said.

"Let them in," Rosie commanded. Her voice didn't have the usual fire and brimstone she used on the kids. She demanded their respect and they gave it to her. Rosie was the matriarch of this section of Lake Worth with generations of kids growing up seeing her as that voice of authority. I'm pretty sure she didn't have a college degree. What she may have lacked in academic knowledge, she more than made up with wisdom that she showered on her people. She liked Frank and I. When we entered the house, she sat up from the couch.

"Rosie, stay down and get your rest," Frank said.

"You don't tell me what to do. What is that? It smells good," she said, ignoring us by walking over.

"We got you some flowers and since we were at Publix we grabbed some chicken," I said.

"Mmm, thank you," Rosie said as she looked at the box.

"We got this for you," Frank said holding up the large round fruit.

"Where did you get that? It's a big one," said Rosie.

"From the guy up by the railroad tracks."

"That's Curtis," she said her voice gaining strength. "Go get a vase for these beautiful flowers," Rosie said to her sister. "Give me a hug," she said. Frank put the flowers down and they embraced. She then moved to me and put her arms around me. For a woman who looked frail and in her late seventies at the time, she had a strong, bear-hug squeeze.

"Put that watermelon in the fridge to get it cold," she said.

"Rosie, how do you feel?" Frank asked.

"The doctor said there isn't much I can do except rest. I want to get back to the kids, though," she said, sitting back down. "Are you behaving yourself?" she asked looking at me.

"Yes," I said.

"You know he's lying, Rosie," Frank said.

"I know that's right."

"Rosie, we hope you don't take offense that we brought chicken and watermelon," I mentioned.

"Why would I be upset?"

"You know the stereotype of chicken and watermelon," Frank replied sheepishly.

"Child please," she chided. "You two are a lot of things, but you aren't racists. Do you boys know how those stereotypes got to be?"

"No, tell us," I said genuinely curious.

"Back in the Jim Crow era that fruit symbolized Black self-sufficiency and freedom. Free Black people started to grow and sell it. Southern Whites, who were threatened by this, made the fruit out to be a symbol of our being lazy. We just were sittin' around eatin' fruit."

"How about the chicken thing?" Frank asked.

"The chicken thing started from a racist movie called, *Birth of a Nation* that showed Black people being shiftless. One of the Black characters has his feet up on a desk, eating chicken with his hands and being all nasty. It was the White man's way to try and make us look dirty and lazy."

"Wow!" Frank said. "I never knew this."

"Rosie can teach you a thing or two," she said, smiling.

"You didn't bring dessert," the sister added.

"Hush your mouth," said Rosie.

"We could have picked up a pie at Publix," Frank said.

"No, if you get a pie in Lake Worth you have to go to 'The Upper Crust,'" I added. "They're the best. I can go there tomorrow and get a pie. Their coconut cream is out of this world."

"Coconut cream," the sister scoffed. "We're Black people. Sweet-potato pie is what you need to get us."

"Don't you get pie, Jeff," Rosie said. "My sugar is way too high. That's part of my problem too."

We talked for a while longer, and Rosie lay back down. She waved and said, "I love you boys." We turned, in unison, saying, "We love you too, Rosie." A couple of weeks later she passed away at home. There were generations of students who had grown up in Lake Worth who came to pay their respects at the small church across from the gym. Rosie was the matriarch who touched them all with wisdom, maternal instinct, and Christian love. As the African proverb says, "It takes a village to raise a child." Rosie was a big part of that village and her years at Lake Worth Middle were a ministry.

CHAPTER THIRTY-THREE

"No Moon Pies or RC Cola"

There was a mammoth EH student named, Andre. He walked around the school like a zombie. Sharon was trying to get him another placement and it wasn't until he started to masturbate in class that the powers that be decided to make other arrangements for him to find a better setting. One day after one of his sessions stimulating his genitals Max and Q had enough. If he wasn't taken home, they were going to boycott teaching. Sharon asked me, the resident taxi-driver, to take him home. Andre lived with his grandmother in Delray. He attended our school because we were an EH cluster. Max was standing beside Andre who had his head down on the banister of a portable ramp.

"Andre, c'mon go with Mr. Neal," Max said. He didn't move a muscle. It was as if he was sleeping.

"Andre, I'm Mr. Neal. I just spoke to your grandmother. It's okay for me to bring you home. You want to go home early?" Nothing, it was as if I wasn't there. Max shook his head in disgust. When all else fails... "Andre, if you go with me, we'll stop at McDonald's," I said, trying to cultivate a rapport. Slowly, his head raised and he started walking toward the parking lot. Max shook his head and said, "Good luck."

It took him a couple of minutes to get the seat belt on as he struggled to wrap it around his giant body. We started on I-95 to Lantana Road where the closest McDonald's was located. About a half a mile from the off-ramp, Andre spied the Golden Arches and decided to grab the wheel. We were heading for the guard rail as the shoulder rumble strips vibrated underneath the tires. I yanked the wheel hard to the left and whacked his hand up in the air. We swerved back and forth.

"Don't touch my wheel!" I exclaimed. He started to reach again and I gave him my hardest hammer fist right in his upper chest. "Andre, if you touch my wheel again, I will stop this car and call the police, and we won't go to McDonald's." I'm not sure if it was the blow to his chest or the threat of no burgers, but Andre stopped grabbing the wheel. We exited off I-95 and in the parking lot I had to help him undo his seat belt. I told Andre to order what he wanted while I went to wash my hands. I walked to the counter. He had amassed a $34.57 bill. He had ordered the entire left side of the menu.

"Andre, what are you doing? You can't order all that food."

"Do you want me to cancel the order, sir?" a girl at the register asked. Andre turned to look at me. He seemed so sad. "No, go ahead and give him what he ordered," I said and got a Big Mac for myself. Part of me wanted to see if he could eat all of it. It took a good fifteen minutes for the food to be prepared. Three trays were needed to get all of it to the booth. I watched, in wonderment, as he methodically consumed everything in front of him. "Is everything tasting good?" I asked, trying to make some conversation. He said nothing. "Hey, Andre, can I have a couple of your chicken nuggets?" He slowly shook his head no. This guy had a future as a competitive eater if nothing else. Every morsel and crumb were consumed. He also had a large Coke and milkshake. I'd never seen anything like it in my life. We got back in the car and made the fifteen-mile trek to East Atlantic Avenue in

Delray. I had an idea where his street might be. I used to drive to away games at Carver Middle in the heart of the town. We pulled in front of a two-story house. Andre opened the door to get out. I followed him. He knocked and the door opened. His grandmother came out. She wore glasses with hands on her hips as she stood in the doorway and looked at her grandson. He was smiling at her.

"What did you do to get sent home?"

"He was walking around the school. It's hard for teachers to work with the other kids when he doesn't stay where he is supposed to be." I left out the masturbation part.

"I don't know what you're smiling about boy. Sit down on these stairs in the hot sun," she said in a no-nonsense tone. Andre complied and sat down with a heavy sigh.

"Sorry, for the trouble this boy gives you folks," she said wiping off her glasses on her dress. She shut the door leaving him on the steps. I heard the front door reopen. She yelled out something I'll never forget, "And you ain't going to sit up in here in the AC, eatin' moon pies and drinking RC cola either!" The door slammed.

Back at school I overheard Barry's voice. I needed some positivity and entered the classroom. He made literature come alive for his kids. You could see their wheels turning as he asked questions. There is a questioning technique called "wait time." This means when a teacher poses a question to the entire class you wait for someone to process the answer instead of calling on the first student with their hand up. Barry was a master of this method. I once asked him if he did this consciously or if it was his natural style. "Yeah, "wait time" is the equalizer," he said. "A lot of kids are smart, but they don't process as fast as some of their peers. I search the room to see who is percolating at a slower pace."

"Percolating?"

"I read this somewhere. The room is a bunch of coffee makers that are percolating. Some coffee makers boil and brew the grounds quickly and for others it takes a while to get the water through. It still coffee when it's done. If you only call on kids who have their hands up, the others never get that satisfaction of answering a question correctly." He also knew how to diffuse tense situations. The kids were in groups of three or four working on a project. Out of the blue a boy yells, "Knock it off you fucking, Guat!"

"Hey, hey, wait a minute. You can't use profanity in my classroom. Even worse you can't insult my people. I'm Guatemalan," said Barry.

"No, you're not," the boy answered.

"Yes, I am," he said. "Now apologize to all of the students for your profanity. Also, I want an apology to me and every other person who is Guatemalan in here. The boy waited for a second and then said, "Sorry for swearing and saying, Guat."

"Thank you. Now let's move on," Barry said. The Guatemalan boy looked visibly pleased from Barry's support. Instead of just writing a discipline referral he helped instill a little tolerance toward race. The bell rang and I approached Barry.

"That was pretty cool, saying you were Guatemalan."

"Yeah, well we're all connected, aren't we?"

Upon leaving I looked to my left and saw a man-child walking down the hallway. His name was Jeremey Lewis. This kid had to be 6'2" and he was thick. "Hey wait up," I said as I put a bounce in my step. "I have a hall pass," he said, waving the yellow sheet.

"What grade are you in?"

"Eighth," he said.

"How are your grades?"

"Good, Bs and Cs."

"Then why the hell aren't you playing basketball?

"I guess because I'm a football player," he replied. I want to play at the "U." He did end up playing for Miami and played pro ball in Canada That day he walked through the doors for his first practice. Watching his athleticism, I knew he would complete our pack. I picked up the "pack" reference from reading about the legendary NBA coach, Phil Jackson. He had a strong interest in American Indians. He would use an analogy to teach the team concept. "The strength of the wolf is the pack. The strength of the pack is the wolf." Once again, we were undefeated as the playoffs came around. JFK beat Roosevelt and we beat Barry's former school, Logger's Run, to be in the county championship. Peggy still was chiding me, "You are going to host the championship this year," she said. "You have home court advantage and you better win it this year. Get that monkey off your back."

"I hear you, Peggy."

It came down to the last practice. Joe shared his analysis of Kennedy as he had gone to watch them play. He lined-up the players on the baseline underneath the basket to share his wisdom. To watch the kids' faces as he talked with his country sayings was classic. He walked up to Jeremey and stood about two inches away from him staring up with his neck craned as the youngster dwarfed the short, stocky Kentuckian.

"Boy, you are finally going to face someone that's bigger than you. Do you know how big he is?"

"No sir," he said uncomfortable with Joe's close proximity.

"He's big enough to go bear huntin' with a switch!" Jeremey looked befuddled and with good reason. Joe moved down the line facing each of the players inches away yelling more outlandish colloquialisms. "Do you understand all I'm telling you?" He asked the entire team.

"Yes," they replied.

"Well, that just dills my pickle," Joe said finishing his tirade. Barry had a good suggestion and if I could go back in time, I would have followed his advice.

"Coach, I think it might be a good idea to not run 'em that hard today. After we go over how to break the press, why don't we just shoot some fouls and you know, rest up."

"Running them hard got us here and being undefeated. I don't think it's good to change their ritual. They're used to running suicides at the end of practice." I always knew when they were spent on energy when each one would grab the ends of their shorts and tug on them with their chests heaving for air. I lined 'em up and put them through the paces. As they were leaving a comment caught my attention.

"What time is the tryout tonight?" Sammy Lee asked.

"Shhh," Justin O'Neal said quickly.

"What tryout?" I asked, moving toward them.

"Uh, uhhh, there's a tryout tonight in the gym for an AAU travel team," Justin answered.

"We get to go to Epcot if we make the team, Coach," added Sammy Lee.

"I hope he doesn't run you. We need to be fresh tomorrow."

"We'll be okay," he answered. I looked at Barry and thought I should have listened to him. The thought of my players running into the night was not a pleasant one when they should be home eating and resting. It was March 16, 2000.

CHAPTER THIRTY-FOUR
"NOT DARK YET"

The following morning, I had my best red dress shirt on and a colorful tie. Checking my look in the mirror I thought I was representing my school well with my attire. The first bell rang and the kids were leaving the courtyard. A fight broke out. One of the combatants was named, Daniel. He was extremely strong and was punching with a precision that you don't always see in a school fight. The student who got him riled that day was having quite a time as he was just covering up. I grabbed Daniel under his arms. In a frenzy he squirmed out of my grasp and grabbed my shirt so hard it ripped the whole way to my waist. Daniel, however, upon seeing what he did to my shirt stopped. I drove home to change my favorite shirt ripped beyond repair. This was not how I envisioned the start of the day. JFK arrived in their bright green and yellow uniforms with Vikings emblazoned across the front of their jerseys. The gym was packed beyond capacity. Fans stood around the entire gym except underneath the baskets. We were breaking a fire code for sure. Barry took his place at the scorer's table. I went over to welcome the opposing coach. He was a strong looking guy in his forties. We shook hands and talked about some of the teams we faced that season. It was a short but friendly conversation as we both were there for the business of getting a championship for our schools.

There is a bond that happens with a team, and if the right environment is created you become a family. I felt like this as I watched the Warriors in their faded uniforms in pre-game warm ups. I called them in for a huddle. I quickly reviewed the offense we would use to try to get through that maze of a half-court press. Shortly, the buzzer rang and it was jump ball. The first time up the floor the ball was stolen. The Vikings went in for an uncontested lay-up. Kennedy brought a large contingency of fans and there was no love-loss between Riviera Beach and Lake Worth. You could feel the tension in the air. Sharon asked for three extra school policemen in case of violence. The first quarter ended up tied. Tito hit a long three and put us up by two points as the buzzer sounded signifying it was half-time.

"Sammy Lee what's wrong with you? You tired?" Ishmael asked. I looked at Sammy as he chugged a Gatorade, shaking his head no. I noticed that all of them were struggling with their wind. The AAU tryout entered my mind.

"Get hydrated," I said as I went to the chalkboard and reviewed some of the things that we weren't doing to attack their defense. Barry popped his head in and said," One minute coach. Don't give up guys." The noise was always loud in that locker room as the acoustics caused our voices to reverberate amongst the musty smell of sweat and Axe body spray. We started the second half in a 2–3 zone and it was working pretty well. The third quarter ended in a tie. In the fourth quarter the lead see-sawed back and forth. I wanted to save my time-outs in case we needed them down the stretch.

It came down to twelve seconds and we were trying to get the ball over half court. We managed to get through the traps that were set and one of their players knocked the ball out of bounce with seven seconds to go. We were down by one point. In the huddle I designed a play for Sammy Lee to get a shot in the corner with four seconds remaining. In case he missed we may have a chance for a rebound and a quick shot at the buzzer. The play went as designed and Sammy took the shot. It arched nicely with the proper backspin, but unfortunately careened off the rim. Jeremey grabbed the ball with his massive arms and backed into the players trying desperately to guard him. He went up strong for the shot. As he released the ball the buzzer sounded. It went in. The place went crazy! We finally got that championship.

Out of nowhere the referee waved the shot off. "Coach, he didn't get it off in time," he said. "I went by the clock, not the buzzer." Twenty years later people still say we got ripped off. My friend Chris Stevens even had a trophy made as he thought we were the true champions that year. In the locker room all heads were down and there wasn't a sound. Their pain was discernibly obvious. There was such a build up by the student body and community for them to dethrone the formidable Kennedy Middle School. All of them looked up at me for commentary. I was searching for something to say and then the door burst open.

"What a great season you guys had!" Barry exclaimed. "You guys all have bright futures in sports and there are going to be many more games to come." He went to each player and shook their hand and patted them on the back. Just as he did the year before he took a syringe of sunshine and injected it in their arms. They looked at him and nodded in agreement. Some of them even had a slight smile. This was the second time he came to an emotional rescue. I took Barry's lead and shook each of their hands. When I got to Sammy Lee, he stood up his eyes containing tears. "You're going to be a player, Sammy. Stay off the streets and keep working. The sky's the limit." Jarvis was already dressed. He shoved his jersey in the bag.

"Jarvis," I called to him. "You had a good season."

"Thanks," he said softly.

We worked as a team all season looking for that crowning achievement, but as the saying goes, "close but no cigar." It was St. Patrick's Day and Palm Beach County schools were on Spring Break. I went to downtown Lake Worth and went into a new establishment called, "Dave's Last Resort." Locals informed me that the restaurant's owner came from Aliquippa, Pennsylvania. I was introduced to Dave, the owner, and told him we grew up near each other. He was polite, but moved on to keep up with the Irish holiday's madness. Saturday rolled around and I met Barry and the Beatniks at the gym for our final game of the season. Gary, whom I beaned with a basketball, all those years earlier was on the other team. We guarded each other having a good time as that bond between player and coach endures. A foul was called and I bent over as my lungs were burning with a serious oxygen debt. "Coach, you trying to catch a heart attack," Gary said, punching my arm.

"I hope not," I said, standing and taking huge breaths. Barry, with his reddish-brown hair wet with sweat, was getting adulation from the students who surrounded him after the game. He was in his element, kids and basketball. The break passed and it was April. We were in the final nine-weeks grading period. The school year is very much like a marathon. In May it's hot and you feel like you are running in a stream of molasses. The last two weeks of school are always hectic. Final tests and grades are due. Concerts, Sports Banquets, and the eighth grade prom are all crammed in those final few days. The students take their eighth grade prom seriously. It is a formal event and they wear formal attire. The girls wear elegant dresses and the boys wear classic tuxedoes. They literally transform from ulcer breeding monsters to classy young ladies and gentlemen. The one thing I could never get over was the majority of them arrive in limousines. The faculty vs. student basketball game is held a day or two before the last day of school. Everyone has fun as the student body cheers against the teachers. Barry and I had a chemistry on the court. On one play we did a pick and roll and I delivered a bounce pass to him. Instead of shooting it he returned a perfect behind the back pass to me. I was startled as the ball arrived back in my hands as he could have easily made the lay-up.

"Hey," I yelled. "You had the shot."

"Good opportunity to show them what teamwork looks like," he said, smiling. After the game we were teasing the players that the old men beat them. They said we cheated. Barry mentioned he was going out to Mounts Botanical Garden for a plant sale and asked if I wanted to go. It is Palm Beach County's oldest and largest public garden. For some reason I declined his invitation. The second to the last day of school, I went over to see Barry and Brett. They were listening to a CD *Time Out of Mind* by one of their favorites, Bob Dylan. Brett liked the tune called "Cold Irons Bound" while Barry had picked "Not Dark Yet." It had a haunting sound with one of the lines, "It's not dark yet, but it's getting there." We didn't know just how dark it would be.

CHAPTER THIRTY-FIVE

"MURDER MOST FOUL"

The last day of school arrived, May 26, 2000. At the bus loop I saw the first egg launched in the air, arching high and splattering on the sidewalk, narrowly missing a young girl staring at her cell phone. More eggs made their flight. It was as if a catapult was launching these white, oval projectiles as one found its mark on an unsuspecting boy. He couldn't believe the deep orange slime coming over his head. The tradition of acting up on the last day of school was alive that morning. Bob and Larry Ludwig had done a nice job of cleaning house. There were at least twenty or thirty students starting their summer break early. It was nice knowing that kids prone to violence weren't there to create upheaval. Teachers had already submitted grades for the year so there was no need to allow the usual suspects a chance to cause havoc. The kids were happy this day arrived, and the teachers were even happier. Everyone was ready for some time off from the school house.

All hands were on deck for the four lunches as that is often a place where students plan a final day food-fight. I'll never forget witnessing this phenomenon at the old school. Tom Long was wearing a bright, white sports jacket that day. Suddenly all students stood up in unison and began firing food all over the place. After the food throwing frenzy Tom's white suit turned multi-colored. Those students may never know how close to danger they were. Students were taking up their trays and sitting back down just enjoying their last day together.

My task for the day was to pull my players, individually out of class, and give them one last motivational talk. I never had children and those basketball players may be as close as I get to parenthood. My words usually centered around staying off the streets as many had the opportunity to make a lot of money slinging drugs. I printed a copy of the legendary college hoops coach, John Wooden's "Pyramid of Success" for each player. He created an iconic triangular diagram offering a roadmap for excellence. I presented them with a laminated copy and read the building blocks to success with each of them. I particularly emphasized Wooden's definition of success. "Success is a peace of mind, which is a direct result of self-satisfaction in knowing you did your best to become the best you are capable of becoming."

Unbeknownst to me there was something that occurred during a class change. A group of seventh graders decided to have a water balloon fight. There were ten or twelve kids who engaged in this age-old practice. Kevin Hinds, first year guidance counselor, witnessed this as he was doing hall duty. He rounded up the kids who were throwing the latex rubber water bombs and marched them down to the office. At that time an administrator could call home and get parental permission from a parent and send them home for the day. They could be picked up or just walk home. One of the students who was involved in this ruckus was a seventh grader named, Nathaniel R. Brazill. A call was made to his mom and she gave permission for him to walk home. He joined the other balloon throwers who had their paperwork (discipline referrals) and exited the campus. The bell rang indicating the last period. I walked by Barry's room and he was laughing with the kids. The sun was shining on him. He saw me and waved. "There's the kid I've been telling you about," Barry said. He pointed to a muscular, light-skinned boy.

"Who's that?"

"That's Ant-Man's little brother, Marcus."

"I didn't know he had a little brother," I replied.

"The kid's an athlete. He could be a power forward for us."

"Ok, I'll talk to him," I said.

"Are you going to the cruise tomorrow?" Barry asked.

"I'm planning on it," I replied. It was the faculty end of the year celebration. Justin O'Neal was the last student who I called into my office. We'd gone over the pyramid and I was asking him about his plans for the summer. On this day busses typically arrive early. The drivers are as anxious for vacation as everyone else. I looked at the clock and it was 3:40. Five more minutes and it was dismissal. Summer vacation here we come. "Let's take the long way around," I said to Justin as we walked down the back hallway on the north side of the school.

We'd just passed the art room when all of the sudden students burst out of Barry's room. This was unusual. The strategy is to contain them and have them exit to the bus loop as orderly as possible. The whole class was out and they were sprinting. I thought they were all hysterically laughing. I smiled. That was until the three girls who were running toward Justin and I got closer. I knew immediately something was wrong as they had a look of absolute terror on their faces.

"Whoa, whoa, whoa," I said with my arms outstretched. Two of them bolted past me. I was able to stop one of them.

"They shot Mr. Grunow," I heard her say. Justin was frozen, wide-eyed, and staring at me. I thought about using the walkie, but that could start a panic. "Nobody shot Mr. Grunow," I told Justin, putting my hand on his shoulder. "Go to the main office and tell them what we heard, okay?" Justin nodded and darted off. I started walking toward Barry's room and the only thought running through my mind is that it was impossible for someone to shoot him. He would be the last teacher that could happen too, especially, with three minutes left in the school day. I stopped in my tracks in the middle of the hallway. The girl's words echoed in my mind. "They shot Mr. Grunow." Columbine had occurred a little over a year prior to this moment. Could there be roving gunmen on our campus? Just then I saw Bob Hatcher sprinting toward Barry's door. I headed back to the main office to make sure Justin had delivered the message. Coming through the door I saw Frieda Proctor on the red phone that is to be used only in case of emergencies.

"We have a teacher that's been shot," she reported.

Those words hit like a sledge hammer. Justin was sitting in one of the chairs in the Main Office studying me. "Stay here, Justin. Don't go anywhere."

"Ok," he said in a quiet voice. I jogged back to Barry's room and Karen Marchetto, Technology Supervisor, was white as a ghost having a look like every bit of energy was extracted from her being. "Oh, Jeff," was all she said as she pointed into his room. I gritted my teeth and entered. Across the vacant room at the other door, I saw it was propped open. Sharon's voice came over the PA system and announced a Code Red. As I looked through the doorway there was Brett holding Barry on his lap saying, "Hang in there!" Shelby Mann, a science teacher, was holding a paper towel over his forehead. Kenneth Long looked on from across the hall as he yelled to students who were trying to get a peek at what was happening. "Get back in that room," he said loud and authoritatively. The curious students went back to the sanctuary of the room. John James, a math teacher, looked on from two doors down. A Lake Worth Police officer came with an automated external defibrillator (AED). Bob Hatcher called me over.

"Jeff, we are still going to have to dismiss these kids."

"I know," I said. "Do you think he's going to make it?"

"I think he's already dead," Bob replied swallowing hard.

He won't die I thought. He could run all day on the basketball court, and is in better shape than anyone on the staff. Kenneth had gone back to his room to keep the kids in place as did Shelby Mann. Charlie Fowler, PE teacher and close friend of Barry's, had arrived. He began handing sponges to the paramedic who was trying to work on Barry. I found myself joining Brett in saying, "Hang in there." Our words futilely hung in the air as a pool of blood was growing wider as if a dam had broken loose. I remember thinking that it is unfathomable that we have that much blood within each of us. The paramedic looked up and said the words, "He's gone."

"No!" Brett said, standing. Charlie Fowler's eyes filled with tears. I just stood there looking at him not able to comprehend the reality that this good man was indeed gone. I remember vividly how still he was lying on that floor with his shirt open from the machine he was hooked up to in the attempt to revive him. His eyes were closed, arms outstretched on both sides, and his feet were crossed. For some reason, I reached down and gently uncrossed them. I walked through his room in a daze and went out into the hall and promptly kicked a large, gray garbage can spilling it all over.

Officer Baxter grabbed me with both hands and very calmly said, "Jeff, I know this sucks, but I need you to keep it together. We have a thousand kids on lockdown who know nothing about what happened. We need to get them home." I looked at him. His firm grip and calm voice brought me back to center. "Go to Building #200 and ask if anyone knew about any violence that was planned today," he said.

"You got it," I said and started down the hallway until I realized I didn't have my walkie. An officer from the Lake Worth Police department was already putting up the yellow crime scene tape in a crisscross on Barry's front door.

"Sorry," the officer said, putting his hand up and blocking my way into the room.

"I need my walkie, it's right there," I said, pointing to it.

"We have a little more important things to worry about than your walkie. This is a crime scene now." He went back to putting up the yellow tape. Fortunately, a school police officer who knew me handed me the device. Charlie Fowler was against the wall standing alone looking like a big, sad kid. I was about halfway down the hallway when Frieda Proctor walked up and said, "Jeff, I was looking for you. This is Bob Templeton, from our mobile crisis unit." He and I shook hands. "We need someone from the staff to accompany him to Barry's house to tell his wife that Barry is gone. Would you do it?" The words hit me with resounding effect. The realization that he was actually dead entered my being. I thought I could break the unfathomable news to his wife, but something in me hesitated. It seemed that someone more familiar to Pam should be the bearer of this horrific news. Pam and I had only said hello a couple of times.

Brett was the obvious choice, but his close proximity to the shooting had left him too traumatized in its wake. Charlie Fowler was still standing where I passed him, leaning against the wall. I knew that he and his wife had socialized with Barry and been to his house numerous times. "How about Charlie?" I asked. "He and his wife are closer to Pam than I am. If he doesn't want to go, I will." Frieda asked him and Charlie straightened up like a soldier and said, "I'm there." Every class room I entered in the #200 Building was the same. Kids sitting in silence with looks of bewilderment and fear. The teachers were being strong for them. Their eyes revealed what was quelling inside. I asked, "Did anyone know of any plans for violence today?" Each time there was silence and no one uttered a word. The last room for me to check was Alison Moe, an English teacher, a close friend of Barry's. After my query she followed me into the hallway.

"Jeff, what happened?"

"Alison, you can't say anything, but Barry's been shot."

"Barry Grunow! No one would shoot him! Is he dead?"

"He's hurt badly. To what extent I don't know," I lied.

"Ok, thank you Mr. Neal," she said as she opened the door to get back to her kids. She was calm on the outside as I watched her from the door window for a moment. I wandered out of the building and heard an officer outside by the bus loop say, "They got the perp in Lake Clarke Shores," he said referring to a neighborhood behind the school. "He got on his knees with his hands up when the police car came down the street and gave himself up." Overhearing this brought a small sense of relief as whomever did this was apprehended.

I opened the large, green door by the bus loop and hooked it to allow the river of children that would be exiting to flow. I breathed a deep breath and got my first look at a monster that had been born while we were all in the confines of the school. I couldn't believe my eyes. Hundreds of satellite dishes, television cameras, news vans, reporters, and thousands of people, many parents of the students in the lockdown, were pressing against the chain-link fence. The police were in a wall lined up to keep the anxious parents and hungry media at bay. How did they all get here so fast I wondered? I walked back to the main office and it was there that I first saw the interim Superintendent at the time named, Ben Marlin.

He was the epitome of calm as he listened to Sharon speak with the tip of his glasses that goes behind the ear in his mouth. When he spoke, he gesticulated with his eyewear only to return it to his pursed lips when listening. He gave off the vibe that he was calm and knew what he was doing. Bob Hatcher was with them as well. They decided to dismiss by buildings and we were told to be out front to supervise them getting on the busses. Sharon squeezed my hand her eyes fighting to explain how much this hurt. We had worked together for all these years and it dawned on me that this was her last day as Principal of Lake Worth Middle. She had accepted a position at the district office.

I got a water out of the vending machine and once outside I poured half of it over my head before chugging the other half. It was 90 degrees in the shade and the stress and adrenaline had me walking in a bowl of soup.

Frank was the first to give me one of the many hugs that were just beginning to start. When trauma hits hugs follow. The busses started their engines. The black diesel fuel was mixing in the hot air. The crowd clamoring at the fence looked as if they could break it down at any moment. It was the strangest thing to watch the kids file out silently to get on the busses. None of the joy and laughter of the last day of school was present. None of them knew what happened, but their faces told a story. They knew something bad had gone down. The gates opened. A few students waved to me from the bus windows. I watched them go off into the evening. It was now a full two hours after regular dismissal.

"Mr. Mascara and Mr. Neal please report to Student Services," Sharon's voice said over the walkie.

The first surge of tears started to well up in my eyes. I pushed it down not allowing the poison to be released. We were told that there were seven kids who were eyewitnesses. The Lake Worth Police Department had already interviewed them and they were in our Parent Resource Room waiting for their parents. Frank and I looked in seeing their stunned faces. Not one was speaking. "I need you to go in there and offer support," Sharon said to us. A Black gentleman from the Mobile Crisis Unit was sitting with them. Frank and I didn't realize that they hadn't been told what had happened. Each of them fled the scene after the shooting. As I pulled up a seat next to the crisis counselor, Ryan Otero, who had sprained his ankle in tryouts was there. He turned and looked at me, his eyes pleading for information. "How's Mr. Grunow, Coach Neal?" he asked. I was thinking of the right words to say as the counselor reached under the table and firmly grabbed my thigh. I turned and looked into his eyes. His grasp had stopped me from speaking. Slowly and imperceptibly to the children he shook his head no. I got his message.

"Mr. Grunow is hurt. That's all I know," I said as once again dancing around the truth seemed prudent. One by one parents arrived and Bob Templeton escorted them to an office away from the other kids. As the students were told Barry was dead the same screams and cries that reminded me of wounded animals caught in a trap filled the air. Later I learned that when someone witnesses a homicide, especially of someone they love, if they don't know the outcome you don't tell them until a support system arrives. In this case it was the parents of the students who were their support. The parents walked out with both arms around their children to shield them from the nightmare outside.

The media was embedded on the road leading into the school, Barnett Drive. The song by the Eagles called "Dirty Laundry" surfaced in my mind. I had this deep disdain for them as the cameras were flashing and filming. No wonder actors lose it on the paparazzi. The street leading to our school always lined with pot holes would become the home to these trucks and vans that were salivating over a teacher being murdered. One little girl, Dinora, was the last student left. Frank gave her a hug as we waited for her sister. The sister finally arrived and informed us that her car was down the street almost to Tenth Avenue a quarter of a mile away. Her look told me she didn't want to go back into that frenzy. I told the sister I would walk them out. Both of us held Dinora's arms. They were fragile and yet tense. The policeman seeing my school shirt and the student unlocked the gate.

"She's the one!" I heard one of the reporters yell. Dinora drew close to me as a mob of reporters with cameras and microphones descended on us like a pack of wolves. I put my arm around her and hugged her to my body as I pushed a camera back in the face of a reporter who flashed a picture that had me seeing blue spots.

"Did you know the shooter?"

"She has no comment at this time," I said, and eventually they parted like the red sea. On the way back it felt like a gauntlet as reporters kept asking me if I had any comment. Determined to get back inside the gate I said nothing. The entire staff was in the cafeteria. The superintendent, Jim Kelly, Chief of School Police, and Sharon stood in front of all teachers, counselors, cafeteria workers, custodians, and administrators. Everyone had an idea of what happened but Sharon wanted them to hear it from her. "Barry Grunow has been shot and killed today," she said. The gasps and cries came out that had been sitting inside everyone idling the entire time of the lockdown. Most people started to hug whomever was in the seat beside them. Strong embraces from everyone. I noticed that Max and Joe Owsley were sitting quietly their faces expressionless. It dawned on me that they were both veterans, and maybe they were desensitized? Later when Max and I got together he shared something that confirmed my suspicion. "I've had a lot of Barry Grunow's in my life," he said.

Sharon informed us that Crisis counselors would be on hand for the next few weeks for both staff and students. She encouraged all to come. Frank and I were asked by the Mobile Crisis Unit to be on hand as we had a rapport established with the students. We both agreed. Frank had been talking to a policeman while I had taken Dinora and her sister to their car. The identity of the shooter was revealed.

"Did you know a student named Nate Brazill?"

"Who?"

"Nate Brazill."

The name sounded familiar but it didn't bring up a face for me. Thinking back when the kids were running down the hall, it was possible I heard "They" when she actually said Nate. Everyone dispersed into the night. I saw Sharon and gave her a long hug. She is one tough woman and you could see her trying to be strong for everyone as a good leader does. I thought of Charlie and how he must have felt to knock on the door with Alison Moe and Frieda Proctor to tell a wife that her husband had been shot and killed at the end of the school day. That glorious finish line of the last day of school was forever changed for the Warrior Family.

CHAPTER THIRTY-SIX
"PRESS CONFERENCE WHILE IN SHOCK"

I was numb and thought a bath would give comfort. Just as I settled in the warm water the phone rang. I walked across the floor with water dripping on the tile. It was Sharon on the other end. "Jeff, I hate to ask this of you," she said with her strong voice now soft, "The school district has to make a formal statement about what happened today. Ben Marlin and Chief Kelly want a representative from our school. I can do it, but I really think that someone who knew Barry more than me should say something. I know you two coached together. You just have to talk about him. You know, what kind of person he was. Would you mind doing this?" I thought for a few moments. I'd already passed the buck once that day when I suggested Charlie Fowler be the one to break the news to Pam. "I'll do it, Sharon."

"Thank you, Jeff. You were a trooper today." As she hung up the phone the realization of facing a press conference became formidable. I drove back to the school that night to meet Ben Marlin who was out front by the flagpole talking to Chief Kelly. This would be my first conversation with him. He had a good reputation as a unifier and not a divider.

"You must be Jeff," he said walking over extending his hand. "Are you sure you're up to this?"

"I think so," I answered.

"You don't have to answer any questions about the shooting or Nate Brazil. Just say some nice things about Barry. I understand he was quite a teacher and a nice man."

"He really was," I answered, struck by the word was. The Lake Worth Police station was where the press conference was held. It was surrounded by a caravan of TV news vans, trucks, and satellite dishes. Looking out the window they seemed to move together like ants in a colony, each one busy with a separate task. We followed Chief Kelly and he led us to a side door into the station. The Lake Worth Chief of Police, William Smith met us in a conference room. Chief Kelly, Ben Marlin, and I sat around a table. Marlin's cell was ringing off the hook. I noticed a picture on the table. It was the gun the student used that day. It looked tiny, almost toy-like. It was a Saturday Night Special.

"Is this the weapon?" I asked.

"I'm sorry," Chief Smith said, "You don't need to see that."

Two officers entered to share updated information about the shooting. We got up. "If you have any problems," Ben said to me, "just let me know. I'll be right behind you." His soothing words brought some comfort, although, my heart was racing. I kept thinking I've got to pull it together. We walked into the lobby and hundreds of reporters were crammed in that small space. Chief Kelly stepped to the mic. The camera bulbs flashed, the bright lights above the television cameras burned, illuminating everything in the room. I was a few feet behind him and I saw those blue spots for the second time that day. I wanted to say something special about Barry and uttered a silent prayer for discernment of the right words. Chief Kelly fielded a lot of questions and then said, "Next, we have Jeff Neal, from Lake Worth Middle, who is going to make a statement." I looked at Ben who nodded, providing support. Looking back on it, I think he knew how truly nervous I was as I stepped front and center. Everyone in the room moved forward as I gripped the microphone. The flashing lights hurt my eyes.

"State your name and spell it, please," said a member of the press corp. "Jeff Neal. N-E-A-L." Then there was silence. When I started to speak, my voice sounded strange, like it didn't belong to me. I started out saying that he is a great teacher, and then I retracted that and said was a great teacher. The word "was" reared its head with a resounding effect again. I mentioned he was a dedicated husband and father. I said that he loved teaching and the city of Lake Worth. Then I got lost for a few moments. I wanted to vanish like a mist. As I stood there trying to regain my footing a reporter, Dana Palley, from Channel 29, looked at me and nodded slowly. He was trying to help me. I honestly don't know how much time passed as I stood there. I noticed a couple of female reporters had tears in their eyes. "Did you know the student Nate Brazille?" asked one.

"I'm here to talk about Barry."

"Do you feel safe being in education?" Palley asked.

"That is a deep question and I can't fully answer that right now. The one thing I know is that we lost someone special today."

"Is there anything else you want to add?"

I thought for a moment about Barry and said, "I think that Barry would want all of us to keep loving the kids." I stepped away from the microphone. "Good job," Ben said as he patted my shoulder and stepped to the mic. He seemed so calm, reassured, and collected. My thoughts were *I did anything but a good job.* In the parking lot a female reporter and a cameraman approached me. I turned and held up my hand, and when our eyes met, she saw I had enough and just wanted to go home. That night the phone rang and rang. Sometimes it was well meaning friends and other calls were reporters who somehow got my home number. I turned on the news to hear Tom Brokaw saying, "It's happened again, another school shooting in Florida." About midnight I turned the ringer off. I downed a glass of Jack Daniels but it brought neither comfort or sleep.

In the morning I made a cup of coffee and wandered into the backyard. Usually, that first day of summer vacation is a joyous one. I walked to the back corner of my tiny yard and sipped my coffee in the sunshine. The beginning of what they call survivor's guilt was scratching at the surface. Barry was such an evolved person; I know my shortcomings better than anyone and it begs the question of why did such a good man have to be taken?

In the following days I was about to understand what Barry Grunow really meant to his family, friends, and the students of Lake Worth Middle. I was naive enough to think there would be no more of the media the next day. They were camped outside of the school in legion. A Lake Worth Police Department officer waved me through the gate. Frank was already in his office talking to Bob Templeton. Bob had been the Manager of Psychological Services for the School District of Palm Beach County since 1994. He informed us that we would be doing a lot of the emotional work for kids, staff, and parents. The term was new to me. Bob gave us a crash course in grief counseling starting with the 7 stages of grief after death: shock or disbelief, denial, bargaining, guilt, anger, depression, and acceptance.

"Out of acceptance the best scenario is that a traumatized individual finds hope," Bob said. We learned that morning that denial would be present as a coping mechanism. Denying it gives one time to process the news. Anger would be a constant companion to the school community and would manifest itself in many forms: fury, resentment, bitterness, rage, and even hurting inanimate objects.

"What's the bargaining stage?" I asked.

"This is a way where individuals try to regain control," Frank chimed in. He had done some grief counseling as a young man in Ohio. "It is not uncommon for people, particularly religious people, to try to make a deal with God."

"What kind of a deal?" I asked.

"You make a promise to God in exchange for healing or relief," said Frank. I thought of Max's story in Vietnam.

"Bargaining is a line of defense against grief," Bob added.

"It's going to be a long road to acceptance for all of us," Frank said with sage-like wisdom.

Reading about trauma in a text is one thing, but applying it after a school community experiences a traumatic event is another. All of the college credits in the world don't prepare one for this. "Are you guys ready to counsel today?" Templeton asked. Frank and I agreed. We both had a perception that to help others would give us time to put off dealing with our inevitable journey in the grief process. Students and staff members along with parents started to arrive. Everyone kept going up to one another for the ever present "hugs." I hugged more people in those two weeks following Barry's death than I had in my entire life. We all did. The hugs were a powerful clinging like little children do when they are afraid. It took a murder for the societal message of "don't touch" to be stripped away.

Dinora walked through the door. She came to Frank and gave him one of those clinging hugs. She was crying profusely. They had built a rapport during the school year. Someone got the idea to get paper and markers and put them in the cafeteria for mourners to draw or write a note about Barry. There was a windfall of students who had shown up to write or draw. As these kids poured out their thoughts and emotions, I began to realize how deeply Barry touched their lives. They wrote long, lengthy texts on those papers exposing what a terrible loss they felt. Later, the kids wanted to put up their notes and drawings on the fence near the front gate as a memorial. Local stores and restaurants donated food and drink. The whole community was coming together to support us. Kevin Hinds was there as well, but there was something in his countenance that didn't look well. Later I was to find out the possible reasons for this.

I drove out of the parking lot and a U2 song "Pride" came over the airwaves. As Bono sang, "one more in the name of love," it took on a new meaning. When I got back home, I picked up the *Palm Beach Post* and decided to read how they covered the story. I couldn't believe my eyes. The story line read that I was the counselor who sent Brazill home. My phone started to ring from reporters wanting to know how I felt that he could have been coming to kill me. I called the Palm Beach Post and was able to get through to the writer. She told me that John James, the math teacher in Barry's hall, told her that I was the counselor who sent him home. In that moment I got a taste of what Kevin Hinds must have been going through. I called John James to ask what happened. He explained that he had confused Hinds with Neal and apologized. There was an awkward silence. I told him it was understandable as all White people look alike. He laughed and it broke up the tension. I wondered what emotional havoc was going on inside of Kevin. The sense that Nate was going back for him had to be alive in his mind. It must have been a weight to carry and a cross to bear.

CHAPTER THIRTY-SEVEN

"A WARRIOR SPIRIT"

The big question on everyone's mind was why? Night came and it was sleepless for me. Visions of Barry lying on the floor caused me to sit up most of the night. The next morning, probably due to the lack of sleep, everything seemed surreal like a dream. The media was part of the scenery. Pam was coming to find out what happened. We were still piecing it together ourselves. Sitting around the conference table were Ben Marlin and his wife, Chief Kelly, Sharon, Bob Hatcher, Larry Ludwig, Miriam Williams, Charlie Fowler, Frank, and I. Pam came in with a large sun hat accompanied by two friends. Her face was etched with pain, but there was a quiet strength to her. Pam informed us that she hadn't seen the news. She had no information except that Barry was killed. Chief Kelly had the job of answering her questions. We all were searching for something appropriate to say. Pam broke the silence by asking, "Can anyone tell me what happened?"

"First, I want to say how profoundly sorry we all are for your loss. To answer your question Barry was shot by one of his students," Chief Kelly said. She then asked who was with him when he died. Names surfaced although later I was to find out that many faculty members had been near Barry during his last moments. Pam ventured into the territory with the question that we still all ask to this day, "Why?"

"A motive hasn't been established," Chief Kelly answered.

Pam thanked everyone for their time. We all stood and then she asked something that pierced my heart. "Does the school have any videotapes of Barry? We didn't film things. I keep worrying that I'll forget how his voice sounds." Pam left with her friends. Ben Marlin's wife added some insight by saying that when her first husband died, she wanted anything to hold on to keep the memory alive. The whole discourse left me forlorn and empty. Later, I was leaving through the cafeteria. To my amazement, the place was packed with students. All were drawing and writing memories of Barry. The memorial, at the front gate, had grown exponentially with flowers, stories, poems, and drawings that stretched out further and further on the chain link fence. I hoped this memorial provided some comfort for Pam.

Before I knew it, I was turning on "O" street to drive past Barry's house. I just wanted to look at his trees and plants. Cars lined up on the street on both sides of his home. Brett Packard and Martin Pasquarello, a teacher at our school, were in a dialogue outside of the house that centered on how was this possible? "He was the last teacher that I would pick for this to happen to at our school," Martin said. It was true, Barry was the last one we all thought would go from a student's hands. Since Columbine I think most teachers were thinking that a school shooting could happen at any time.

Kurt, Barry's brother, pulled up. He saw us and I walked toward him. He didn't say anything and just grabbed me and held on as a hug says what we can't say. The Grunow family all had similar countenances, strong salt of the earth mid-western features. All faces carried pain. Barry's mom thanked me for speaking at the press conference. The next morning was Memorial Day. While I was thinking of Barry I sat down to write about the loss of this teacher, coach, husband, and father who left us in such a futile manner. The gnawing feeling that I fell short on speaking about Barry on TV drew me to the pen. Never had I written a letter to an editor. At the time a spectacular Reading Specialist, Tricia, read my rough draft. She wisely told me to write it again, but more about Barry and less about how I felt. I rewrote a second draft that hit closer to my aim. Here is what I wrote:

A WARRIOR SPIRIT

On Memorial Day, I was struck that it took the death of a friend and colleague, Barry Grunow, to fully comprehend the meaning of the holiday. Memorial Day commemorates those who gave their lives for their country. Although Barry was not a military man, he too gave his life while serving his country. His service made the world a better place for hundreds of children. It was an honor to call him my friend.

Barry was a humble man and a quiet hero. He put the needs of others before his own on a daily basis. He showed through example every day of his life what a person and teacher should be. I was asked to speak on behalf of the faculty to let people know what a wonderful human being Barry was, but I was too overcome by shock to do him justice. This commentary attempts to convey to everyone just what we lost at Lake Worth Middle School on May 26.

Family was foremost in Barry's life. He adored his wife, Pam. It was obvious to everyone that she was the love of his life and they were a perfect match. They were a throwback to a simpler time of peace and love. Barry loved his children and it was clear that his son, Sam, worshipped the ground his daddy walked on. I will never forget the picture of Sam sitting in the stands watching his father play basketball. His dad was his hero. I picture Barry at halftime lifting him to the basket so that he could make a shot. They always left the gym hand-in-hand. Barry's daughter Leigh Ann came into the world just a few months ago. I can still see Barry's proud smile as he told me, "I have a little girl!" How can we help her know her remarkable father?

As a teacher, Barry was in a class by himself. He was one of those rare individuals who was lucky enough to have a job that he loved to come to each day. He had an extraordinary smile that spread across his face and lit up any room he entered. I noticed that he had that rare quality of actually listening to people instead of just waiting his turn to speak. He had a sense of humor along with a sharp mind. These are two essential ingredients for a successful teacher. His laughter was wild and alive and I will miss hearing it. Barry loved Lake Worth and its children, and I believe he felt a calling to be here, where he was truly needed, as opposed to a more affluent area.

He was not just a wonderful teacher in the classroom. He also knew that some of the most important lessons are learned on the court or playing field. He was right by my side coaching a team that went 11 and 1this year. Our only loss was a heartbreaking one-point game in the county championship. After the game we watched fifteen boys enter the post-game locker room with heads down and eyes filled with tears. A lesser coach would have tried to console me by complaining about the referees or by giving the constant "if only..." Instead, Barry grabbed my hand and said, "What a great season! Just think of the life lesson our boys got today. The players heads raised up as they absorbed his energy. That was pure Barry Grunow right there. Always finding a positive in any situation.

Barry instilled a love of learning in all of his students. He realized that many of his students had never had anyone read to them. It was for this reason that his students heard classics of American literature from his lips while sitting in class. Where many an educator falls short of being a role model, Barry Grunow, a quiet, unknown legend in Lake Worth, never let any of us down. To honor him, our staff must live up to our name, The Warriors. We must come together as never before to fight the dark forces that visited our school on the last day of this year. Barry would have expected no less from all of us. We must strive together to follow his example every day, so that his spirit will live on at Lake Worth Community Middle.

Jeff Neal, Guidance Counselor

That day I mailed the above text to the Palm Beach Post. I felt better just having written the words. I was disheartened when an editor called to inform me that it was a nice piece, but too long. It stung because I wanted to share what a special man he was, and on some level, I wanted it to be a charge to our faculty. We were a lost ship without a captain. Sharon was leaving and there was no new principal at that time. Twenty some teachers were looking to transfer to another school. They developed "sanctuary trauma." This occurs when an individual suffers a severe stressor then encounters, in what should be a supportive and protective environment (the school) only more trauma. I sent the piece to the Sun-Sentinel, the main daily newspaper of Fort Lauderdale and southern Palm Beach County. They published it immediately and the editor gave it the title "A Warrior Spirit." Simultaneously, an article appeared in the Boca News that shared how, Logger's Run Middle School, Barry's former workplace, were in shock. Principal, Judy Klinek, remarked, "He was a wonderful teacher, and a kind, caring man." Another colleague a Social Studies teacher, Jane Fayash, said, "He was such a fun-loving person with such creative ideas for how to teach Language Arts. He was very devoted to the kids and staff."

of the many quotes from former students was from a girl named Lisa eed, "He was my favorite teacher. He was like a friend. I used to go back to visit him after I graduated. He had such a playful relationship with his students. He even let us call him "Shaggy" because he really did look like that character in the cartoon. Last time I saw him he was excited about getting married."

These comments mirrored what was being written by our students in our make-shift memorial. All that was created gave me more insight as to just how much he gave to his students. Frieda came to my office and handed me a wrinkled, dirty drawing that was brought to her by a woman. It was a picture that I believe a student drew that blew off the fence. Underneath what I surmised to be the Virgin Mary wearing a shroud with her hands folded in prayer was small boy underneath struggling to hold her up. I read the note that was attached. She had scrawled, "Found this on ground near fence of the Florida middle school where the teacher was shot and killed on the last day of school May, 2000. I thought the school should have it. In my Catholic faith we have a devotion to Our Blessed Lady, Our Lady of Sorrows."

CHAPTER THIRTY-EIGHT

"THE HEALING GAME"

The entire nation was focused on this event. There were several events planned to honor Barry's memory. One was a candlelight vigil in the sprawling 726-acre John Prince Park, located in west Lake Worth. It was a major outpouring of sympathy as the crowd, from all over, was a throng that spread out as far as the eye could see. A school committee had started a fund to benefit the Grunow family. The question of school safety, particularly, school shootings was foremost in everyone's mind. The candles glowing in the night moderately soothed me. After the vigil I went to "Dave's Last Resort." Barry's face flashed on the TV screen. Dave Palombo offered his condolences. He was making plans to put together a golf tournament at the Lake Worth Municipal Golf Course with all of the proceeds going to benefit Barry's family. I told him I'd do anything to help. "You have enough on your plate, just get some golfers," he said. "Each foursome is $300 and afterwards we'll have a barbecue and silent auction. The city has already given me permission to block off the street that day."

"This is going to be a lot of work on your part. Thanks for doing this," I added.

"I want Pam and her family to know the community is behind her. Hey, we're from Western Pennsylvania, that's what we do." Ben Marlin named Bob Hatcher to be the principal. This caused some ire in the county among those who were in line to be a principal. Bob hadn't been an Assistant Principal that long and candidates felt cheated. I spoke to Marlin at that time and his reasoning was that it would be better to hire from within as Bob was already part of the family. He also admired his cool head handling the crisis situation the day of the shooting. Bob's dad, a former principal in Palm Beach County, wanted to participate in the fundraiser. The father and son team along with Frank and I rounded off our foursome. It was Dave's Last Resort's first annual golf tournament.

It was a beautiful day and there were 260 golfers. Afterwards, we went to the barbecue. There was a tent set up with silent auction items. Some of those items included: Muhammad Ali's boxing shorts, golf clubs, all sorts of sports memorabilia, and raffle tickets. I remember distinctly a paramedic, named Billy Pirkle, spent $1,600 for the famous boxer's shorts. When I thanked him, he broke down in tears. One local character named, Joe May, a jolly giant who had served in Vietnam said, "Violence is terrible anywhere, but schools shouldn't have this. It's scared ground!" His voice cracked with emotion. The whole community was galvanized. When it was all said and done Dave had raised money for the family. I remember it was more than my salary in 2000. Dave and I took the check to Pam at her house a few days later. He did this quietly instead of calling the media to drum up some positive press for his restaurant. When Dave handed her the envelope he said, "This was all raised by our community and we are with you." His benevolent kindness will not be forgotten by me. A few other things were done in the community to help honor Barry's memory.

WRMF, an FM radio station, did a fundraising drive to raise money for the newly formed Barry Grunow Scholarship Fund. The idea was to start a fund in memory of Barry to provide scholarships to graduating Palm Beach County Seniors pursuing careers in education. Charlie Fowler, Brett Packard, Frank Mascara, and I went to the studio to be interviewed over the air to drum up support for the fundraiser. It was interesting to be on the air, but once again when the DJ's asked us to say something about Barry our words, to me, seemed inadequate. As we left the radio station, in the car, Frank and I tuned in to hear what they were saying after our brief time on air. What we heard was revealing.

"Did you see their faces?" remarked the radio announcer.

"Yeah, they all have that look," the other DJ replied. "Like it still hasn't sunk in yet." Frank and I looked at each other and we both knew they were right. We were grappling with this ugly surprise at the end of the school year. The entire staff, in his or her own way, was trying to regain footing. Our conversation turned to Bob Hatcher. Being a new principal is a tough assignment with a lot of responsibility. To take on the leadership role that had the fresh wound of a murder was a formidable challenge. We began to have informal gatherings at different staff's homes. It gave us a chance to be together as we all shared the unique experience of losing a staff member by violence. It was good that we had a chance to hug and debrief about our feelings. Many shared that they were seeing counselors. More than one mentioned their alcohol consumption went up in the aftermath of the tragedy. Insomnia was another side effect of dealing with the trauma that many of us were sharing.

Just before the summer ended there was a Jethro Tull concert in Fort Lauderdale. The lead singer of the band, Ian Anderson, got wind that a teacher was killed from across the pond in England. Somehow, he found out they were Barry's favorite band. Anderson, lead vocalist and master flautist, bestowed upon Pam and Barry's closest friends front row seats. After the show they were invited to go backstage. He spent almost an hour with them. During this time, I met many of Barry's childhood friends and got to know more about him. One of them remarked, "We used to call him the Gandhi of Lake Worth." After I thought about it, he did embody the essence of that spiritual and political leader.

Before I knew it, we were back at school. Bob and Assistant Principal, Miriam Williams had the foresight to hire an additional counselor which released Frank from grade level responsibility. He was able to take extra time to provide counseling to the kids who were in Barry's class. The extent of their post-traumatic stress that was triggered by witnessing their beloved teacher being shot and killed was not yet known. Studies have shown that when a human is taken at an early age that at least twenty or more people experience trauma on some level. This number is comprised of family and close friends. In Barry's case it was different because he had an extended family known as the Warrior Family. The number of traumatized kids was exponential. There were also seventy plus teachers that were dealing with their own wounds.

We didn't know how many people on our campus were in distress and to what extent. We were at ground zero. There were two schools of thought regarding this issue at that time. One was that we shouldn't address it and just start the year as normal. It happened last year; let's just sweep it under the rug. The other was to speak about it and clear the air. I thought we should address it with the kids because it was the elephant in the room. Parents were asking if their kids would be safe and many didn't want them coming to our school. All of the sudden when I would mention to someone that I worked at Lake Worth Middle their eyes would widen and they'd say, "Oh, I'm sorry."

Bob let parents know that their kids' safety was his first priority. Frank hit the ground running. He focused on the twenty-five kids who were in the room at the time of Barry's death. I chose to go into the English classes in the seventh grade. I decided to read aloud the essay I wrote, "A Warrior Spirit" and then lead a discussion. The English teachers agreed to ask the students to write an essay on how they feel. The purpose was to see who might reach out through their writing for help. Through teamwork we put our finger on the psychological pulse of the student body to assist those who were struggling. My first stop was in Barbara Myers's room who had been the brave soul to volunteer to teach where Barry was killed. Most students knew they were seated in a classroom where a homicide occurred a few feet away. Entering that room was tough. It was quite an experience to read the essays of those kids. They were amazingly respectful, and empathy exuded from them openly. Many of them asked how his wife and kids were doing. The ever present why did it happen was asked. Others asked what was going to happen to the student who shot Barry.

I shared that a trial was upcoming and steered the conversation toward their emotions. They were thoughtful and caring and seemed to have a strong resilience. Many lost a loved one to a shooting by violence before. I told them this was new territory for me, as a counselor, and that by writing their feelings it would help me understand how they were doing. Frank entered my office at the end of the day and looked like he had been dancing in a blender.

"Whooo!" he expelled as he sat down in my office.

"How'd it go?" I asked.

"Busy. Some kids are having a really hard time. I had to call several parents to pick up a couple having meltdowns. It's going to be busy. I'm already putting together names for Grief Groups."

"Do you need my help?" I asked.

"Not yet, but I will."

"The English teachers are on board with the essays," I replied. What came from the student's pens was astonishing. Their words were deep and gave me hope on a spiritual level. They fueled my mission that we would do all we could to get our school back on track and honor our fallen comrade. There are always detractors when you are attempting a positive endeavor. There was negative feedback from some teachers about Frank taking the kids out of class for the groups. They were missing precious instructional time and test scores were still at the forefront in their mindsets. I wanted to read to them some of the essays of the traumatic event that was still living inside of them. They should have been present with the dad who was reduced to tears in Frank's office as he sat with his daughter. He was a man's man still in his construction clothes from his workday. I was sitting in on the conference. Frank asked, "How can we help?"

"This is the problem," he said, holding a picture of Barry.

"Tell me what's going on?" Frank asked.

"She was there when it happened," the dad uttered.

"I'm sorry," Frank said.

"She's not adjusting. She's talking to him."

"What do you mean she's talking to him?" Frank asked.

"She just talks to him in our backyard like they're having a conversation. She says she sees him and he talks to her." Tears ran down his face. I was struck by how poised the daughter was as she just sat there listening. Frank added her to one of his groups and made a call to the Youth Service Bureau for additional counseling. This was just one example out of dozens of parents that approached us for help. The teachers who were concerned about the test scores over the emotional well-being of the kids, to me, were way out of touch. You don't have a beloved teacher shot before your eyes and tell the children who were eyewitnesses to just keep a stiff upper lip. Witnessing a murder of a loved one is a life-changing experience and if not dealt with, long lasting negative implications abound for all involved. Frank asked me to take on a grief group.

For the next eight weeks I worked with seven kids. Three were present at the scene. I promised confidentiality and I will honor that to this day. They were amazing kids who had the spirit and desire to keep their beloved teacher in their hearts. This was a big part of them beginning to win what I call, the "Healing Game." In that game we were looking for any ray of sunshine that provided hope. We all needed something to heal the unseen wounds we were carrying. One such thing was the Boys' Soccer team. Officer Baxter was the coach.

Most of his team were from Central or South America. They advanced to the playoffs and ended up in the county championship with the game being played at home. Usually, soccer at this level, doesn't draw a lot of fans. That day there were more students and parents than I'd ever seen in the bleachers by the track where I used to run Tyra. One of our players scored a goal that sealed the victory. Baxter's face was ecstatic with joy and Bob Hatcher, arms outstretched to the heavens, ran to the boys. The crowd poured onto the field and hoisted the Guatemalan boy who scored the goal on their shoulders. The whole school community rejoiced together in this victory. It was one of those rays of light we were looking for to bring about the recovery of our school spirit. Tryouts for basketball were coming up. It wouldn't be the same without Coach Grunow lending his expertise to the decision-making process.

CHAPTER THIRTY-NINE

"MUGGED IN HAITI AND A COVENANT"

The night before tryouts, I went to the beach and, while looking out on the water, I made the decision to dedicate the season to Barry and ask the team to do the same. Barry's last words to me were about Marcus Marshall, Ant Man's little brother. The first thing I did the next day was call him out of class. He was interested in playing. I kept waiting for Barry to appear in the gym apologizing for being late. One player who stood out was an eighth grader named, Matt Cornelius. He had size, strength, ball handling skills, and could shoot. I noticed my only returning starter, Jules, was missing. He appeared in Sports Illustrated for holding a sprinting record for thirteen-year-olds. Frank suggested that we call his AAU track coach. The news wasn't good. Jules went to Haiti to visit his parents over Christmas. While there he and his father were mugged and his wallet and passport were stolen. This left him in Haiti with no identification and no passport. I asked our Creole language facilitator to call the US Embassy in Port-au-Prince. It would be six months or more before he could return to the states.

It dawned on me, Frank's dad, was a Congressman from Pennsylvania. "Frank!" I yelled into the phone.

"Yeah, what is it?"

"Can we call your dad and see if he has any pull with the embassy in Haiti?"

"I didn't think to call him," Frank answered. "I will."

"Thanks," I said. You may remember Barry was encouraging Ryan Otero, who sprained his ankle to not give up. Ryan was standing behind Barry when he was shot. He was tall, strong and with a little work I thought he could be an effective big man under the boards. Greer Wright was another with potential. He had a decent outside shot and could handle the ball. Daniel Ross, who ripped my shirt the year before the day of last year's championship came out. David White and Marcus Blackmon were big men. Beranadette's son, Jeffrey, made the cut. Jarvis was in the mix as well. We had the 2000–2001 squad. The next day Frank's dad's was put through to the American Embassy in Haiti on a conference call. Jules would get a new passport and be on a flight to Miami International Airport in two days. Six months changed to two days with a five-minute call. It truly is who you know in this world. It was the third practice of the year when he walked into the gym, his face beaming. "Welcome home," I said.

"It's good to be here. Thanks for getting me back," he said.

"Don't thank me, thank Mr. Mascara over there. It was his dad's connection that opened the door for you." He was glad to be back in the States and we were glad to have him. I blew the whistle and pointed to the locker room. All fifteen players sat against the wall on a bench by the lockers amidst the musty smell that forever lingers there. Ishmael smacked one across the head who was talking and pointed at me front and center.

"This is where we gather during halftimes. The reason I brought you in here before practice is that I'd like to make a covenant with you. Does anyone know what a Covenant is?"

"It's in the Bible, ain't it" said Alphonso Razz, whose nickname was "Big Daddy."

"That's right, Big Daddy. The Bible does tell of an agreement between God and the ancient Israelites. A Covenant is a binding promise of far-reaching importance between groups. I'd like to make a Covenant with you today. If we choose to do it, we all have to agree." Ishmael had a look like he was wondering where I was going with this Covenant talk. "You all know there's someone missing from the room today." They stared intently now. "Today I would like for all of us to agree to dedicate the season to Coach Grunow."

"That would be cool," said Ryan Otero.

"Let's do it," said Jules. I was surprised that Jules, the quiet one, spoke up.

"Come with me," I said. We walked to center court and stopped at a wooden plaque on the wall that was put up by Joe Owsley. It was a commemoration to Barry that had words on the base of the wood that read, "In Memory of Coach Grunow." I put my hand on the tiny, carved basketball and invited all players to do the same. Frank and Ishmael placed their hands as well. "When you come out of the locker room during warm-ups each of you touch the ball as you run by," I added. We then stood and put our hands together in a circle as was our ritual. "One, two, three... "Warriors!" Our hands rose and came down and I felt chills down my arms and back. We gathered on the baseline for our first practice. We had eight days until our first game. Ironically, it was against Logger's Run, Barry's former school.

While this was getting underway an eighth-grade English teacher, Dorothy Ryan (now Schroader), was doing something else to remember Barry. Dorothy, who goes by Dot, was very close to Barry. She idolized him as a teacher and he was a mentor. She contacted a professional dance instructor from Caruso Dance Studio in Palm Beach to work with eighth grade students. Many were in the classroom the day of the shooting. Ryan

Otero was asked to be a participant. He shyly asked me if I would let him go to the dance practices that were being held once a week. When I knew that Dot was dedicating this in memory of Barry I couldn't refuse. Two more phenomenal ideas came forth from a committee that was formed to commemorate Barry. They were to dedicate the gym in his name and to create a butterfly garden. It was perfect basketball and plants, two things he loved. The gym is where Barry played and coached. He was what basketball aficionados call a "gym rat." Charlie McDaniel, Gardening and Horticulture teacher, was excavating the ground where the butterfly garden would be planted by students right outside of the gym by the courtyard.

I emphasized to the players characteristics of Barry. He was a team player who always gave that extra effort called hustle. Joe Owsley created the Barry Grunow Hustle Award that year. The one adjective that I think most described his game was selflessness. It was my goal to impart that to the kids. Basketball is an ego game and to get boys aged twelve through fourteen to rid themselves of street-ball mentality is never an easy journey. The day arrived for us to make the drive to Logger's Run Middle. The opposing coach was a gentleman as he offered his condolences for Barry's death. He emphasized how the staff of Logger's Run were blown away by his passing. It was obvious that Barry, just as he did at Lake Worth Middle, left his indelible mark. When it was the middle of the third quarter of the girls' game, we went into the locker room to change. I had a surprise.

The uniforms that we had were notorious for being old and faded. The "Warriors" logo was barely visible. Pam came up with the idea to buy brand new uniforms for both the boys and girls basketball teams. I think it was a way she could do something for our athletes as she knew how much Barry meant to them. They were beautifully done with "BG" in cursive letters in the upper left-hand side just above Lake Worth. When I started to pull the uniforms out of the box for the players it was like Christmas morning. Their eyes were wide as they bartered over numbers. Everyone wanted #23 for Michael Jordan, as that was when everyone wanted to "Be Like Mike."

The game began and I was impressed with the other team. They played well together. There was a sea of Logger's Run parents using camcorders in the stands that day. We were down by four at half-time. During the fourth quarter they started to relax and play ball. Jarvis was leading fast breaks with Matt and Marcus filling the lanes. We were in the lead in the fourth quarter. A few calls by the referee went in Logger's Run's way resulting in made free throws. Then the Warriors started to complain to each other about mistakes. As they argued I knew this was not going to end well. I sensed that they gave up and stopped giving 100%. We lost by five points. Accepting a loss is a part of sports, but I was disappointed with the attitude of the team. This was not something I was going to tolerate in a season dedicated to Barry. The next day at school, my frustration turned to anger, as I learned that two of my starters got into a fistfight in a pick-up game at the gym later that night. They were arguing over whose fault it was that we lost. As the players filed into the gym, I told them to meet me in Room #901, Joe's shop. As they sat down, I exploded.

I berated them for their street-ball mentality by bickering instead of encouraging each other. I lambasted them with a verbal skewer, laced with profanity, they'd never heard from me before. "Barry Grunow wouldn't have wanted to be represented by the team that took the floor last night." This caught their attention and I could tell it hit home. I continued, "If you're going to dedicate this season to Grunow, then do it! Honor the man!" Whatever I said worked. They were diving on the hardwood floor for loose balls. Their whole work ethic changed. It showed in our playing as we won five in a row. Congress is a school in the city of Boynton Beach just south of Lake Worth. It had a reputation, as did we, of being a tough school with a challenging population. Hester Taylor, who was the girl's coach at the old Lake Worth Junior High, now worked at Congress. She came over to say hello. We coached aside one another for years when we had no gym. We had a close bond.

"Neal, you got your hands full today," she said.

"We like a good challenge, Hester," I replied.

"You'll have one today," she warned. Hester wasn't kidding. They were big and they were deep. Their coach could put eight players on the floor and not lose a step. It was a battle right down to the final buzzer. Unfortunately, we came up short by two points. After the game I told them to hold their heads up as we leave the gym. They played hard and had nothing to be ashamed of. Sometimes it's not bad to lose a game. It can take the pressure off. It was time for the playoffs. We had to play Conniston Middle located in West Palm Beach. On Tuesday, two days before the quarter final, I got some disturbing news.

"Coach, Matt is having problems with his heart," David White said to me as practice ended.

"What!" I exclaimed. "Where is he?"

"He down there," David said, pointing. I saw Matt sitting at the end of the bleachers when he would normally be firing up jump shots. "Matt, what's up? You having problems with your heart?"

"Sometimes it beat real fast. Sometimes it slows and seems like it skips a beat," he said with his hand over his heart. I put my hand on his chest. The beat was rapid and irregular. Our eyes met after I removed my hand. "I can still play," he said with a sense of urgency in his voice. He was our leading scorer and had become a leader on the team.

"We need to get that checked out, Matt," I said. We walked to my office to call his mom, Marilyn. She agreed with me that we should have him examined by a cardiologist before we let him on the court again. The next day she took time off from her work at "Perkin's Pancake House" and took him to St. Mary's in West Palm Beach. I got a call from the doctor. He said that Matt would need further tests. Apparently, one of the pictures had a shadow over the area the doctor needed to see to make his decision. It would be next Monday before he could fit him in again for further tests. We couldn't take a chance on this as his life was literally on the line.

Thursday arrived and we were to face Conniston without our most potent offensive weapon.

I explained to the team, with Matt present, why he wasn't dressing and you could see the concern for their teammate on their faces. It was disheartening to watch him sitting on the bleachers before warm-ups with his chin resting on a basketball he clenched tightly atop his knees. His whole athletic body slumped, and his eyes told a story of deep sadness. I remember that feeling when I broke my arm in high school and couldn't play for half of my senior year. It tears at your heart because all you want to do is get on that floor. This game was a must win. One loss is immediate elimination.

The opposing coach had a look of glee when I pointed to Matt on the bench. He knew he was our top gun. The gym was standing room only. The cheerleaders led the cheer, "We, we tell the story, we tell the whole story, you're in Warrior territory!" The student body chanted along as the school spirit was contagious. As I suspected we were in a dogfight to the end. The dangerous thing is that when a team of lesser talent finds themselves in a close game in the fourth quarter, they start to believe that they just might win. Two of my players fouled out.

I put Greer Wright in the game. It was the first time he saw any action that season in a tight game. He had that deer in the headlight look when I told him to check in. It came down to :07 and we were trailing by one point. The whole season dedicated to Barry was on the line. Then Jarvis stole a pass and threw it to Marcus Marshall. "Take it to the hoop!" Ant Man yelled to his little brother from the stands. Marcus drove to the basket and leaped for his shot. A big player collapsed and was sky high ready to smack his shot out of bounds. Marcus had great leaping ability and he turned 180 degrees, and fired the ball back out to Greer.

He was standing outside of the three-point line 35 feet away. The clock ticked to :01 when Greer hoisted this rainbow-like shot that seemed to dust the beams on the ceiling. Everyone in the gym was silent. We waited. I remember thinking the Warriors needed a little blessing. The horn sounded. It hit nothing but net, and I actually heard the *swish*. It was pandemonium as the crowd rushed onto the floor. "Where'd you come from?" I asked, grabbing and shaking Greer by his shoulders. He had shock in his eyes. The crowd lifted him up on their shoulders. I felt so good for him.

Little did I know there was a family in the stands that was feeling happy that the Warriors won. Barry's mother and brother Kurt were present as was Pam and her kids. It was the first they were back in the gym where Barry had spent so much time. I told Pam that we all appreciated the new uniforms and she said she liked seeing Barry's initials on the jerseys. In addition to the nail biter win over Conniston we received good news from the cardiologist. He cleared Matt to play. It was the shot in the arm we needed. We would need to return to Congress and win to be able to return to the county championship for a second year in a row. Undefeated JFK was playing Roosevelt to decide if they would be at the big game as reigning champs.

CHAPTER FORTY

"ONE TWO THREE...GRUNOW!"

We were tied at Congress Middle with three minutes to go. Most players don't like to take a charge because you have to plant your feet and take a hit from the player in the air going to the basket. It can hurt to fall back on the hardwood floor. Ryan Otero, with reckless abandon, allowed opposing players to glide into him, drawing fouls and giving us the ball. It changed the game. Clutch baskets by Matt, who played like he was possessed, and some free throws by Jarvis put us ahead by seven at the final buzzer. We were on our way to the county for a second year in a row. My mind immediately turned to that half-court press that the Kennedy coach taught his players. His masterful defense made me think we were in a chess game with humans.

The most brilliant basketball mind I've known was my eighth-grade coach, John Dickson. He was from a well-to-do family and attended an exclusive independent preparatory school in Pittsburgh called, Shady Side Academy. Coach Dickson went on to Yale and graduated with a degree in Political Science. Being that he was among the best and the brightest in the nation the Central Intelligence Agency recruited him out of college to be an operative. This was at the height of the Cold War. He declined and became a history teacher at Knoch High School. He was a legend as a teacher and a coach. He designed most of the offenses that our high school used at the varsity level. His offense that attacks a 2-3 zone, called Yale, is the best I've seen on any level. If anyone had a way to attack this half-court press it was Coach Dickson. I called him. "Coach, I need your expertise in breaking a half-court press."

"How is it set up?" going right to the business at hand.

"They have three guys at the half court line and two in the back around the top of the key."

"They shift and block all your lanes?"

"Exactly," I answered.

"Let me look through my files, Jeff. I'm sure I can find something for you," he said in his distinct, no-nonsense manner. Two days later a USPS express manila envelope arrived. It was jam-packed with offenses that he designed himself to strike against the likes of Kennedy's fortification at half-court. I spread the offenses out across my desk and looked for one that would be our secret weapon.

"Damn, this boy isn't playing around!" Joe said as he sorted through the offenses. We decided on one and went over to the gym and put it into practice. It was a new chess game as I finally felt I had something to match what we would face. Unfortunately, the game was being played in their gym.

The night before the big game I remembered Barry's advice. I didn't run them hard.

"No tryouts or even going to the gym," I admonished. "Eat some food and get some sleep." The Warriors filed into the night. I knew there was not going to be much sleep for me. The following morning my shirt wasn't ripped to shreds. That afternoon Joe popped his head in my office shedding his blue apron covered with sawdust, for a shirt and tie, "You ready?"

"This day is dragging like all game days," I said.

"Yep, on game day the time goes like Molasses in January."

Frank pulled the activity bus up front. I went back to my office to grab our scorebook. All of the players were boarding the bus except one. Ryan Otero was staring into the glass-enclosed trophy case that housed last year's second place finish. I knew how deeply he was affected by Barry's passing. "You ready, Ryan?"

"I just told Mr. Grunow that we are going to replace that old trophy with a first place, one." We walked to the bus. As we pulled up to JFK, there were throngs of people walking along the chain-link fence on the way to the gym.

"Don't react to the fans today," I said, standing and addressing them on the bus. "Stay together and let's go into their house and bring a victory home." As the two teams were warming-up I saw Ant Man and Sammy Lee enter the gym. We smiled and shook hands. The whole neighborhood's going to be here today," said Ant Man. "We got your back if something jumps off."

"Thanks," I said and turned back to the court. Ishmael entered the gym. Just then I saw the coach of Kennedy. We met at half-court. The same firm handshake that had a steadfastness to it was present. Most coaches give the obligatory shake and move back to their bench to get ready for battle. He stood beside me. "So, we meet again," I said with a slight smile.

"As it should be," he answered. Here we were a year after he brought his Vikings to our gym and beat us by one. Now we are in his gym awaiting what was sure to be a barn burner. The buzzer sounded and we got in the huddle. Ryan's leg was pumping and I stopped his knee. I reminded them we would be in a 2-3 zone and reviewed quickly how we would be breaking that half-court press. I never coached a game like this one. Literally, we went basket for basket. I don't think either team was up by more than four or five points. Our new press breaker got us a couple of baskets that caused them to lose a little of that confidence that feeds momentum. At halftime we were tied. The kids slugged Gatorade as we made some adjustments defensively.

"Two minutes," said Frank, alerting us that the third quarter was about to begin. A couple of shots was all the time we had before the buzzer. I said to Ryan, "Hey, you haven't drawn any of those charges yet."

"I know Coach," he said. It was tied at the end of the third quarter. Jarvis and Greer started to gain confidence working Dickson's attack strategy like they'd been doing it all year. We got down to 2:00 minutes in the fourth quarter and their coach called a time-out. I had a leather folder that I'd been saving something for this moment. We were in a tight huddle. I reached into the folder and pulled out a picture of Barry. It was taken in his classroom, a couple days before his death. He had on a light denim shirt wearing that magnanimous smile. His fists were clenched and it captured his essence.

"Remember who we're playing for today," I said and passed the picture in front of the five players who were on the floor. Instinctively, they reached out and touched it without any prodding from me. Kennedy had the ball and I changed things up and put on a full court press. It worked and we scored and went up by two. They broke the press and Ryan planted himself and drew a charge. The kid made the bucket, and scored, but his foul put us in a one-on-one situation. They scored and it was tied. At 1:00 minute we had the ball and Kennedy knocked it out of bounds. During a time-out I told them to look to hit Matt for a jump shot. Before breaking into the huddle, we yelled, "Warriors!"

As they were returning to the floor Ryan stopped and said something to the other four players. Something happened that I didn't expect. Ryan Otero, Marcus Marshall, Matt Cornelius, Jarvis Jackson, and Jules Noel joined hands. The referee blew the whistle for them to join Kennedy on the court. Not before they counted in unison, "One, two, three…. Grunow!" I looked at Frank and he nodded. We were both filled with emotion. The ball was knocked out of bounds and we kept possession. The score was still tied. We were down to 00:16 on the clock and Matt fired a turnaround jump shot from deep in corner. It bounced around and went in. We were up by two.

We put on the press and they got it over half court and Marcus went for a steal. He hit the ball out of bounds and the time showed 00:05 remaining. Kennedy called a time out. For some unexplained reason the referees added two seconds to the clock. Kennedy had the ball out of bounds just past the hash mark in front of their bench. They had plenty of time to get the ball up and get off a shot and maybe a second if they played it right.

I knew their coach was coming up with something. Figuring the play he was going over was against our zone, I changed to a man-to-man defense. I told Jules to take #23, as he was their top scorer. This time the entire the team yelled, "Grunow!" We broke the huddle. 00:07 were remaining when they inbounded the ball. Sure enough the second pass went to #23, and he dribbled down the side of the court at top speed. He didn't know that the fastest sprinter in the county, Jules Noel, who would still be in Haiti if not for Frank's dad, was beside him. Jules cut the kid off and Ryan went over to help out. Jules was so tenacious the kid couldn't get off a shot. The player panicked, threw it across the court and it was tipped and bounced down the court as the buzzer sounded. The Warriors were the new County Champions.

The fans poured out of the stands and gathered together at half court in a circle dancing and hugging each other. Ryan Otero grabbed me and yelled over the ear-splitting noise of the crowd, "We can give that trophy to Grunow, now!" It's hard to explain the pride I felt in that group of boys that day who were well on their way to being young men. They dedicated that season to a man who ate, slept, and drank basketball.

I believe that Barry's spirit was with us that year as we played. It may not seem to be that monumental of an accomplishment, winning a middle school county basketball championship, but to our school community it offered another ray of sunshine we all craved. It was another step in the journey of our healing.

I remember reading how Columbine's varsity Football team won the state championship the year after their massacre. The principal, Frank

DeAngelis, commented on how it helped their healing. The next day a four-foot high first place trophy was on the counter in the main office. Bob Hatcher shook my hand and congratulated me on the team's victory saying, "You need to put that in the showcase."

"I have someone I'd like to place it there," I answered. I called for Ryan to come out of his first period class. He walked into my office and saw the grand trophy on the circular table. His eyes widened with a face shining with pure glee.

"I thought you might put this in the showcase," I said.

"Are you serious?"

"I can't think of anyone that Coach Grunow would have wanted more to put it in there to replace that second-place hardware." He grasped it carefully like it was a solid gold bar. The showcase was right outside of Student Services. I slid back the glass of the enclosed case and cleared a spot on the top shelf. Ryan placed it ever so carefully and said, "I told you we were going to put a trophy in there for you." Pam Grunow entered Student Services with a large bag.

"Congratulations to the team," she said. She reached in the bag and pulled out a large homemade card. There were fifteen little basketballs with a heart shape cut out in each one. She spent a lot of time to get them so perfectly configured. There was one for each player, and she asked me to tell them to keep Barry alive in their hearts. I gave out the little basketballs throughout the day. Each player treasured it. Now it was time for the performance of the students who had been working all year to learn the intricate moves of Rumba, Swing, and the Tango they learned from the instructor from the Caruso Dance Company.

The night of the dance recital they cleared out the cafeteria and decorated it as if it were a ball. A handful of teachers, administrators, parents, and students were on hand. Frank and I sat toward the back of the darkened cafeteria. The curtain went up and the students transformed from gawky adolescents to graceful dancers. Ryan Otero danced with Vonae

Ware to Chuck Berry's, "Johnny Be Good." We were yelling, "Go Ryan Go!" He was having the time of his life. Dinora Rosales looked like an angel as she did the challenging partner dance, the Tango, with Anthony Martinez. Edwin Bermudez and Lorena Castillo perfected the Rumba. After the event one of the parents told Dot, "This was great what you teachers did. A lot of those kids will be testifying in the upcoming trial. They needed a diversion like this." The parent who made the comment couldn't have been more prophetic.

One of the last photographs taken of Barry in his classroom. The Ghandi of Lake Worth.

1999-2000 Basketball Team. The last team that Barry Grunow coached.

The 2001-2002 County Champions team that dedicated their season to the memory of Barry Grunow.

CHAPTER FORTY-ONE

"COURT TV AND THE MEDIA CIRCUS, STUDENTS TESTIFY AND THE VERDICT"

The trial of Nathaniel Brazill was upon us. Assistant District Attorney, Marc Shiner, deposed the students who would be witnesses. Ones so young shouldn't have to be faced with the scrutiny and adversity of testifying in a murder case. To my surprise Jules Noel was on the list. Jules told me in his quiet voice, "I was sitting outside of the 300 Building when Nate pulled up his bicycle and walked into the building. I wished I'd never told the police what he said to me. Now they want me to testify." He put his head down. All of the students who were subpoenaed to testify were dealing with a lot of angst. The whole concept was a nightmare. Not only did they have to relive one of the most horrific moments of their lives, but they had to face their former classmate in the courtroom. Some of the witnesses had been his friend prior to the shooting. To add more pressure Court TV was going to film the trial.

Frank had quite a year with his grief groups. So much was on his plate and he absorbed a lot of pain. The stress was visible in his countenance.

He explained that he was having trouble sleeping. He kept getting awake at night with his heart racing with cold sweats. Finally, one day he came into my office. "We have this trial upcoming," he said. "Bob wants us to support the kids. I'm going to keep running the groups and will help to transport them to the courthouse, but I don't want to go in. I don't want to go into that circus."

"I get it, Frank. You've done so much this year. I'll be there," I said. Circus was a good description of the trial of a fourteen-year-old being tried for the murder of his teacher on national TV. First, there was the controversy regarding trying Nate as a juvenile. Florida had experienced another highly publicized trial when fourteen-year-old, Lionel Tate, in Miami was sentenced to life in prison without parole for the murder of a six-year-old girl. Governor Jeb Bush was asked for clemency for Tate, whose legal team included Johnnie Cochran. Troneal Magnum, from Conniston Middle, was convicted of first-degree murder of a fellow student. It happened in front of the school. He was 13 and tried as an adult. Jose Garcia was the Assistant Principal there at that time. These events festered into a major national controversy regarding trying youths as adults. Some said the nation was losing its soul.

Then there was the question of what charges should be filed. The jury had to consider six charges: First-degree murder with a firearm, Second degree murder with a firearm, Third-degree murder with a firearm, Manslaughter with a firearm, Aggravated battery with a firearm, and Aggravated assault with a firearm. Barry Krisher was the State Attorney and he was pushing for Nate to be tried as an adult. He was looking for a forty-year sentence and the local papers reported he was riding the "hang-em-high" bandwagon. Nate's defense attorney was named, Robert Udell, who reportedly charged a fee of $1.00 to Polly Powell, Nate's mother. The Prosecuting attorneys working under Krischer were Marc Shiner and Barbara Burns. Udell and his defense team chose not to depose anyone from school.

Bob Hatcher tried to get the trial to be closed door to protect the students to no avail. Presiding over the trial was Judge Richard Wennet. The nation tuned in daily to Court TV.

One of the bit-players who irked me more than anyone in this drama was a pastor from Riviera Beach. He seemed to accompany the Brazill family everywhere. Perhaps he was a supportive Christian preacher, but I saw a different side. He held daily press conferences outside of the Palm Beach County Courthouse. He had a gleam in his eye when the cameras came on and he was on center stage. I'm all for a man of God helping someone in a trying time. To me there was some self-aggrandizement. The first day of the trial I was walking behind Barry's family as they entered the courthouse. The media forest had sprouted up on the courthouse lawn overnight. I watched as Barry's mom, a petite classy woman, then seventy-three, and her daughter Kay Nichols, and brothers Kurt and Steve, walked right past the Reverend crowing about the miscarriage of justice of this young boy. The same youth who took their son and brother's life. I admired their self-control as they ignored him.

It was surreal to see Brazill being led into the courtroom. The twelve jurors sat stoically examining the youth for the first time. The TV cameras were capturing everything. There were no students testifying that day, and I felt a sense of dread for what these innocent, young fourteen-year-olds were going to face. Frank was back at the school preparing the kids for the crucible of a trial and the media gauntlet that seemed to swell almost jubilantly in the theatrics of it all. One person I believe deserved a lot of credit at this time was Bob Hatcher.

No one should underestimate the pressure of being a principal under these circumstances. He walked into a situation where an entire school, both staff and students, were traumatized. Where he really proved to be stalwart was in dealing with the press. They were literally camped out at the courthouse as well as being a constant presence at our school throughout the entire year. He took them on each day, balancing his feelings for the slain teacher while making sure his words were politically correct.

Now that the trial was beginning the courthouse was a jungle of cameras and all reporters were clamoring for the vestiges of the tragedy. The two prosecutors took an interesting strategy at the beginning of the trial. They started with the end. It must have been so hard for all loved ones to listen to vivid descriptions of the crime perpetrated. Shiner and Burns, after describing Barry's death, then laid out what they called a "storm brewing" inside Nathaniel. This entailed a "hit list" of people that he created, supposedly, that he would kill. The defense attorney, Robert Udell, took a different tack as he summoned a random collection of witnesses in an attempt to portray Nathaniel as a smart, good-looking boy as they flashed his school-portrait in a shirt and tie. The witnesses were acquaintances from his neighborhood who said nice things about him. The prosecution began calling their witnesses, that totaled thirty-eight in all. They began with students who days before had heard him remarking he was going to "fuck up the school." He had shown off the gun. One of the students was a girl who was suspended for throwing the water balloons that last day. Nate had told her, "Watch I'll be all over the news." Known to be a prankster she thought nothing of it. The prosecution's goal was to show that he was an angry kid who was fixated on the weapon.

Two of the witnesses that I felt so much empathy toward were Vonae Ware and Dinora Rosales. They were in Barry's room that fateful day. After Nathaniel got a ride from an Albanian pizza delivery man to his house, he went inside to retrieve his grandfather's gun. This is the same gun he was showing off to friends on a playground days before. He then hurriedly rode his bike back to the side of the school and hopped the fence. He entered Building #300, intent on talking to both Dinora and Vonae. We may never know why he wanted to see them. There was speculation that he was there to kill them. To me, that wasn't plausible as he was either in love or just friends with each of them. Some said he was angry with Kevin Hinds or

Bob Hatcher and was going to kill them and wanted to say goodbye to his close friends. Nate knocked on the door. Barry knew he shouldn't be on campus and when he asked to see the girls, Barry said, "Nate, you're suspended and you're not supposed to be here."

At that point he drew the gun up with both hands and pointed it at Barry's face. Then John James, the math teacher two doors down, came into the hallway. Nathaniel pointed the gun at him and told him to get back into the classroom. This was all recorded on the cameras in the hallway. The prosecution noted that Nathaniel held the gun for a full eleven seconds before shooting. Imagine being Dinora and Vonae whom he wanted to see and then being asked to testify on Court TV. The inner psychic battle of the students who testified had to be excruciating. There is a saying that from adversity comes strength. I witnessed that, first hand, as the students who were testifying found strength through each other. A trinket was passed back and forth that served as a pacifier to relieve the anxiety of going on the witness stand. They were unified and utilized humor and love to cope. To this day their resilience and love for each other left an indelible, perceptible trace on my heart. I believe Barry would have been proud of each one of them. After all thirty-seven witnesses were called, the prosecution concluded with the testimony of Jules Noel. After his testimony the state rested their case.

Robert Udell decided to let Nathaniel testify. Marc Shiner was relentless as he confronted the fourteen-year-old. He asked him whether he hit the "bull's eye" on Barry's face. When Brazill said Barry was laughing, Shiner asked if he was still laughing as he hit the ground. When Shiner pressed him at what I believe was the climax of his cross-examination he pressed Brazill to recall what Barry did after he was shot. "What do you think he did?" Nathaniel snapped coldly. The defense relied mainly on Nathaniel's testimony and that of ten friends and a former Lake Worth City Commissioner. They also called a firearm's expert who testified that the gun Nathaniel used had a history of firing easily. The Albanian pizza man, who required an interpreter, testified that Brazill seemed normal to him when he gave him a ride home right before he retrieved the gun. The defense rested their case after he made his statement under oath. The jury, comprised of nine women, many of whom had children, went into deliberations.

There was a lot of speculation as to what the verdict would be. Governor Jeb Bush weighed in saying he didn't believe that Florida's 10-20-Life gun law should apply to juveniles under sixteen years old. This law requires that courts impose a minimum sentence of 10, 20, or 25 years to life for certain felony convictions involving the use or attempted use of a firearm during the commission of a forcible felony. Bush also signed legislation, dedicated to Barry, that adds teachers to a "special risk" class of state workers. The Barry Grunow Act, sponsored by Rep. Jeff Atwater, R-North Palm Beach, increases insurance benefits for survivors following a job-related death.

After twelve hours of deliberation over three days the jury landed a verdict that was in between. It was second degree which may have spared Nathaniel a mandatory life sentence. This set up a dramatic sentencing date. Many people voiced their opinions about the verdict of this nationally televised trial. Paducah's shooting scratched the surface of the nation's psyche and Columbine shocked the nation out of its complacency. Our country was glued to this trial and heated debates about how to try a juvenile and his sentencing was on everyone's minds. Tom Ramiccio, then Mayor of Lake Worth, said, "Lake Worth lost a neighbor and a friend. No matter the verdict, it's a lose-lose situation. Both sides of town are hurting." When the verdict of second-degree murder was announced, Bob got on the announcements to inform the whole school. There were over thirty-eight psychologists on hand to offer services to anyone child or adult. There was a police presence on campus comprised of both School District and Lake Worth officers. There was a mixed reaction to the verdict. I was surprised when many of the students remarked that he should have gotten first degree murder. Some of course had a different view.

Personally, when I found out that he received twenty-seven years the number didn't seem to matter. He took a beautiful man's life and left a widow with two young children. The loss was exponential to the Grunow family, and to our school community. There were no winners. I understood family members and friends of Barry who thought he should have been punished more severely. Even if he didn't mean to shoot him, he came back to the school that day for something and it wasn't good. I often wonder what Barry's thoughts would be regarding the fate of Nathaniel. That is something we'll never know. My sense is that it would have involved forgiveness. He was the Ghandi of Lake Worth.

CHAPTER FORTY-TWO

"BARRY L. GRUNOW GYMNASIUM AND THE BUTTERFLY GARDEN"

The judicial proceedings were behind us and it was now time to dedicate the Gymnasium and Butterfly Garden. It was an absolutely gorgeous day. Family, friends, students, and teachers gathered under the live oaks in the courtyard between red brick walls to honor the life of Barry. This event was just what the doctor ordered. I invited Dave Palombo who had put forth that all proceeds from his next golf tournament would go to the Barry Grunow Scholarship Fund. The press was held at bay outside the gates until after the dedications.

The ceremony began with angelic choral songs sung by students and then went to rock and roll tunes. Brett Packard created a playlist that was chock full of songs from Jethro Tull. As the music played everyone walked the courtyard observing the cards, posters, and collages students created sharing favorite memories and stories of their beloved teacher. Particularly poignant was Dinora Rosales and Vonae Ware singing, "Everything I Do, I Do it For You." Filled with emotion they went hand in hand over to a white sheet on the gym's wall. Together they pulled away the banner revealing the words, "Barry L. Grunow Gymnasium." It was heartwarming to see his name on the wall of that gym where he spent so much time.

Dinora and Vonae spoke eloquently of the teacher they loved. Ryan Otero stepped up to the mic and shared how we dedicated the season to Barry, and how good it felt to put the first-place trophy in the showcase outside of Student Services. He proudly invited the guests to go see it for themselves.

Pam then spoke, "When you remember Barry and the fun and good times you had with him," she told his students, "He is with you. Keep that spirit alive. Carry on what you learned from him. Always hustle on the court and people are more important than things." She even joked about how his students called him "Shaggy." She looked around at all of us and said, "I think you made Barry smile today." Pam then faced the cameras and microphones. She spoke well, expressing herself clearly and powerfully, as she fielded a barrage of questions.

I didn't want to watch that and made my way over to Barry's name on the wall. Two children were playing by the Pentas and Lantana plants while butterflies fluttered around their heads. The ceremony was healing and cathartic. We all were given a brief respite from the trial and all the pain it had brought into our lives. It definitely put some wind in our sails as we all needed a little levity.

The year in the aftermath of our traumatic event was coming to a close. The staff had grown closer as we all shared the same grief over what had transpired on that final day of school on May 26, 2000. We were starting to learn to live in acceptance of our loss instead of in spite of it. There was something, though, that was fast approaching and there was no way to get around it. The last day of school. One of the things that is most difficult to traverse in the recovery process is the anniversary date. Those of us who were on campus on that day were forever changed. "School's Out for Summer" by Alice Cooper had lost its appeal. We were sailing to that final day of school with dread, and a hidden fear of please don't let this happen again.

An emotional moment for me was our annual Student/Faculty basketball game. Barry's smiling face was not present. More than one faculty member remarked that the kids might win this year without our ace in the hole. The journey we had, as a team, that season was remarkable. Jules being detained in Haiti and Matt's heart murmur were hurdles to traverse. The close games and finally winning the championship was an experience we all will remember. Dedicating their effort in memory of a lost friend gave us a powerful understanding of the true meaning of teamwork. The students actually won the game for the first time that I could remember. There was deep sadness within me as we shook hands after the game. The reality was that I wouldn't see too much of them after the year closed. I walked over to the plaque on the wall and put my hand on the basketball.

The final day arrived with many hugs occurring. We all had a look we gave each other. God forbid, I thought, that a crime would be committed near the school and we would have to go into a lockdown. This occurred earlier in the year and the cases of acute anxiety and panic attacks ran through our staff like a pandemic. Just hearing the words "We are in a lockdown" released the PTSD that was simmering in all of us. As the day came to a close, I saw that it was 3:45. I walked down to Barry's old room and had a moment of silence. This is a practice I continued every last day of school for the next nineteen years along the way to retirement.

A successful first day of school each student gets a schedule, finds their way to their classes, gets fed a lunch, and gets on a bus to go home. Sadly, a successful last day of school for many of the Warrior Family is that no one gets killed. The following week with no kids on campus I was in my office and was trying to come up with a list of who failed which class and who would need the PASS program. Joe walked in and sat down and put his foot up on the other chair. He had a way of molding himself into a seat and looking totally at ease. "You were on my mind last night," he began, "and I came up with a plan for you."

"What kind of a plan?" I asked.

"You need to be a principal."

"Joe, you had a bad dream. That's not me."

"Hear me out. I know from where I speak. You know I sat in that chair when I was principal of Heath High School, in the great state of Kentucky in Paducah."

"Where the school shooting occurred, right?"

"Yes. Back in my day all the principals were coaches. Do you know why?"

"I never really thought about it," I answered truthfully.

"To be a successful coach you have to build a team. The same principles that work in basketball work at a school. You get them to play as a team and that is why you win. If you get teachers to work together, they will teach to new heights. You can do this. Go for it, man." That night I went home and digested what Joe said. I thought about being an administrator. M. Wayne working tirelessly at his job. He brought professional development in the early 1970s to a school district that had none at the time. Just like when Tom Long suggested I should write a book, Joe planted a seed. Shortly thereafter, I met with Dr. Mel Coleman of Nova Southeastern University. He was formerly a Deputy Superintendent of the Palm Beach County School District. He was a sharp one and had a resume as long as I-95. He convinced me to go for a specialists as opposed to a master's. "If you go for a specialists," Coleman said, "if you ever decide to go for a doctorate, you will already have three credits toward the most advanced degree in education."

"I'm not planning on getting a doctorate," I said.

"Never say never," added Dr. Coleman.

The next thing I knew I was enrolled in an educational leadership program. Bob Hatcher got wind that I was taking leadership courses. He asked if I wanted to be a TOSA (Teacher On Special Assignment). This entails being a pseudo administrator and taking tasks that are the grunt work of administration. One was being over transportation. There are two jobs in education that employees should get hazardous duty pay, substitute teachers and bus drivers.

Imagine driving 80 middle school kids on a bus. Keep one eye on them and another on the road is challenging. They are capable of anything. As a TOSA each day started with no less than five bus referrals. The good news is that I was getting my exercise, walking 5 to 7 miles a day. Each time a teacher pushed a button to have a disruptive student removed someone had to put them in ATS (Alternative to Suspension). Sometimes there could be ten pick-ups in one fifty-minute period. The ATS teacher is another hero with a thankless job. The position pays what a substitute makes, and there are no benefits. So, you spend the day with no less than twenty students who should have been suspended and any students that were tossed out of class. It is an art to keep order in that environment. By far the best ATS teacher in all my years at Lake Worth Middle was John Marzlak. Musician by night and ATS Czar by day.

I was a TOSA for two years, just the amount of time that it took me to finish my Specialist's in Educational Leadership. The superintendent at the time was a man named Art Johnson. He moved principal's around like he was playing chess. Any principal, at any level, could get a call and be told where he or she would be moving the next day. Bob Hatcher got that call. He was placed at an Alternative High School in Boynton called Gateway High School. There was another man who got the same kind of call and was told he would now be the principal at Lake Worth Community Middle. This is when Jesus came into my life.

CHAPTER FORTY-THREE

"M. WAYNE'S PASSING AND THE COMING OF JESUS"

It was 2005 the same year Hurricane Katrina, the third strongest storm ever to make landfall, visited the southeastern coast. New Orleans was 80% under water. Little did I know that another hurricane was going on in August of that year with one of the most talented athletes that ever passed through Lake Worth Middle, Jarvis Jackson. A war that had its genesis when he was in seventh grade. Earlier I mentioned the friction that existed between the Haitians and Black Americans. It was at its worst in that summer. Top 6, the Haitian gang, had grown. Jarvis changed radically from seventh to eighth grade. He showed up for his eighth-grade year with gold teeth carrying a stack of Benjamins. The street had gotten to him. There are two proven tickets out of the hood, sports, or military. Kids don't always grasp that education is a vehicle. Jarvis could have had a scholarship for football or basketball. This is a kid who cut off his cast to play in a midget football championship. Instead, he took another road, actually a corner. One night watching the news I saw there was a shooting in Boynton at a Super 8. My ears perked up when some names were mentioned. One of the victims was Colby Jackson, Jarvis's brother, who played on my team. Two other boys were shot but Colby was the only fatality.

Top 6 had it out for the Jackson brothers, particularly, Jarvis. Not only was he not backing down, but one night at a Lake Worth High School football game Jarvis fought multiple gang members and got the best of them. He could have been a UFC warrior. After that incident he was attacked at his bus stop with machetes. The final straw occurred at the funeral of Colby. While at the service Top 6 drove by the cemetery and fired upon his family. That was when something snapped. A former player remarked, "When they shot at his family in the cemetery it was game on. He went apeshit." Jarvis became something of an urban legend. Everyone around him including girlfriends got shot multiple times. For whatever reason they kept missing him. Jarvis finally conducted his opus in vengeance for his brother's murder that had the connotations of a crime of passion. He and two other former Lake Worth Middle students gathered AK-47s and boldly drove to a house on "C" St. in the middle of the day. They snuck around the side of the house to the back yard patio and opened fire on a group of unsuspecting Haitian gang members playing dominoes. Three former Lake Worth Middle students lay dead riddled with bullets. It took a while for the police to investigate and close this case that landed Jarvis four consecutive 25 year terms. It was surreal to watch an episode of Gangland and see my former athletes faces on the screen.

Bob swung by my office to say goodbye. We had quite a journey together and for all intents and purposes he was the right man at the right time to deal with our critical incident. "I met your new principal," said Bob. "He's a good guy. You folks are going to be all right with him." Shortly, thereafter Jesus walked into my office. He was about my age, somewhat stocky, and looked like he could have been an athlete. "Hi, I'm Jesus Armas."

"Jesus, nice to meet you. I'm Jeff Neal."

"You wrote that essay about Barry Grunow? I saw it on the website last night when I was familiarizing myself with my new home."

"Yes, that was me," I said taken aback by his knowledge.

"You did a great job on that. It brought a tear to my eye."

When he walked out, I had a good feeling about him. I liked the way he said new "home." Jesus hired James Thomas who was coming from Jupiter High School. He was a smart, energetic sort who had been an English teacher. Wakisha Mawalli rounded off his administrative team. She was a former Warrior having been a computer teacher. For both it was their first year as an assistant principal. Being that LWCMS is a school with a high complexity level Jesus was allotted three AP's instead of the normal two. For better or worse Jesus gave me my first shot at being an administrator. In one of my leadership classes I had an assignment to give a speech as if I were a new principal speaking to a faculty for the first time. I remember wondering what Jesus would say to the Warrior Family at the first faculty meeting.

He was masterful in his delivery. The first thing he said was there are two things that are most important to him. I was ready for some core values of his educational philosophy in education. He hit his portable hand-held device, and a picture of his beautiful wife, Teresa and young son, Daniel appeared. All the woman on the staff said, "Ahhhh," in unison. There were many things that I learned in my leadership courses that I observed Jesus demonstrate. For instance, he called me into the office for our first conversation. He asked me two questions that let me know he was a deep thinker.

"I realize that it's been five years since the shooting, but I want to know how much it's still on the minds of the staff who were present that day?" I thought about that for a moment.

"It may not be on the forefront of our minds as it once was, say the year or two after, but it's still there simmering underneath, not far away," I replied.

"Ok, I have some ideas as to some things that I want to do that I'll discuss with you later. The other question is what are some of the traditions or practices that are part of the fabric of the school?"

"What do you mean?" I asked.

"The things that make Lake Worth Middle, traditions that we shouldn't do without," he replied.

"In sports, there are awards that are traditional."

"Like what?"

"There's the Bobby Bartz Award and the Coach Owen Academic Award, and the MaryAnne Hedrick Spirit Award."

"Give me a short breakdown of each of those," Jesus said.

"Coach Owen was a dean when I met him in 1985 at the old Lake Worth Junior High. He opened the school. He did it all. He coached baseball, football, basketball, and track and field for fifteen years. Bobby Bartz was a student in 1962," I continued. "He played for Coach Owen. He was this great kid who hustled and had a great attitude. He was a leader. The story goes that on the last day of school they were having a picnic and playing baseball in the park. Bobby went to get a foul ball in tall grass and was bitten by a rattlesnake. He died in the hospital that night. The MaryAnne Hedrick Spirit Award is dedicated to Mary Anne in honor of her resilience.

"She's the PE teacher in the wheel chair?"

"Yes, everyone thought the accident, that paralyzed her would end her career. It was when she got started. She worked hard to master her wheelchair and she does a great job teaching. Her extracurricular activities are amazing. You name a local charity and she is involved. She does marathons, hell, she was even asked to carry the torch in the Olympics. The one where Muhammad Ali lit the flame in Atlanta in 1996."

"Really, that's impressive."

"Yeah, she's a great role model and example for our kids. It also teaches them to look at someone with a disability differently." After talking we walked to the new state-of-the-art building in the back of the school. It still carried the smell of fresh construction. I could see his mind working as he went from room to room. On the east and west ends of the building are two large labs with adjoining classrooms. "Ok, Mr. Neal we are going to bring academies to Lake Worth Middle."

"Academies?"

"Yes, one is going to be Pre-Engineering and it will be billed as the Gateway to Technology. The other, and I think we'll get the best bang for our buck, is going to be a Pre-Medical Sciences Academy."

"I always think of academies as high school," I added.

"Academies are the wave of the future. There are twenty-one middle schools that already have them up and running. It's time for Lake Worth Middle to get on the map."

"How about a culinary academy?" I asked. "We used to have Home Economics and our kids enjoyed that immensely. Also, Florida's main industry is tourism."

"I agree but we're starting with Engineering and Medical. Gateway to Technology will be a cutting-edge program. The curriculum will be hands on and geared toward learning how technology is used in engineering to solve everyday problems through project-based learning. You will see many projects such as: compressed air rockets, water rockets, drafting bridges, mouse trap cars, and a Robotic competition that is county-wide."

"How about the medical curriculum?"

"Those kids will get a strong academic foundation in medical science. It's a challenging curriculum where they will study medical research, along with diseases and disorders such as childhood obesity, hypertension, and diabetes. They will get training on the medical skills necessary to be a certified healthcare provider."

"How do you advertise it?" I asked.

"The Showcase of Schools at the Fairgrounds." It's where the school district's 300 plus Choice and Career programs are put on display to advertise their schools. It's a one-stop shop for parents to see all of the options the district offers. It's competitive and we will have to show that we are offering a first-class education with a curriculum tailored to their kid's needs. It will be a long hard road because, I hate to say it, there's a stigma attached to our school."

I realized that Jesus was right in that we would have to overcome the adversity that having a shooting involving a homicide gives the reputation of a school. The night of the Showcase he met parents for five hours straight answering all questions and, like a good salesman, he got the customer to take a look at the product. The customers were the parents and the product were our two academies. James Thomas, who possesses a keen sense of humor said, "Jesus looks like a car salesman. Crazy Jesus, we've got a sale today! C'mon down!"

He was like the Energizer Bunny, rolling up his sleeves and digging in, creating relationships with parents. He had an attention to detail that rivaled one perfectionist I knew namely, M. Wayne Neal. Fortune would have it that Dad and Jesus would meet shortly after the Showcase of Schools. Seminole Ridge, Jesus' former school, was coming to Lake Worth High for a football game. Lynne McGee, his former principal, asked him to meet her in the press box to watch the game. Jesus asked, "I'm staying around tonight to watch Seminole Ridge vs. Lake Worth with Lynne. Do you know of a good place to get a bite to eat in Lake Worth?"

"Sure, I do. Come on over and I'll cook you a steak."

Mom prepared the side dishes and I manned the grill. Jesus knew that my dad was a principal and as we sat on the back porch they started to talk. Jesus asked Dad, "This is my first year as a principal. Do you have any advice for a novice like myself?"

"It sounds to me like you're doing very well," Dad answered. As I turned the steaks, I remember thinking that he could have said something more than that. He seemed quiet that night. Later that evening, after Jesus went to the game, I made a fire and Dad and I were enjoying the flames when he asked, "Jeff, did I embarrass you tonight?"

"Not at all," I replied. It made me wonder why he would say that. A few weeks later he fell and broke his hip just as he turned eighty. I was on a flight the next day. He was in the Butler Hospital. I sat by his bed. There was something different about him. His whole countenance had changed. He knew me and yet there was something different in his speech. He was a professorial man who always chose his words carefully. I went to a nurse and asked her what was going on with him.

"Does your dad have Dementia or Alzheimer's?"

"No, I don't think so," I answered.

"He's exhibiting behaviors that are consistent with someone with that disease." Her words struck with force. Here was the man who was known as "The Architect of Excellence" who transformed the Hampton Township School District. He was uncompromising with his integrity and lived a life that was above reproach. Now he was losing weight with desperation in his eyes. It broke my heart.

"Jeff, get me the hell out of here. You grab that wheelchair in the corner and help me into it and we go right out the door." This was coming from a man who was a stickler for following rules. Mom found something in Dad's desk that she stumbled upon that helped us solve the puzzle. Dad had been diagnosed as being in the early stages of dementia years before. One of the specialists explained the phenomenon to us. "Your husband was diagnosed with early dementia," the doctor said. "He never said anything to you?"

"Not a word," Mom answered.

"Did you see any signs?"

"Not really," answered Mom.

"I imagine your husband is a bright man."

"Very much so," answered Mom.

"Often times they will figure out coping strategies with everyday life and no one is the wiser."

"I think I know one," Mom said. "Sometimes we would be going to a restaurant and he would ask which way I thought was the closest route to get to a place we'd been a hundred times."

"That's a classic example," the doctor explained. "He was probably not sure and he needed your input."

"I never saw it," Mom said, looking down.

"Most people don't. They don't want their loved ones to worry. Your husband fell and was given anesthesia. If one has any form of dementia and anesthesia is introduced it causes whatever mental decline present to blossom. He could have gone from mild dementia to early Alzheimer's that fast."

I looked at Dad sleeping and I thought how scared he must have been to deal with that condition on his own. The next thing I knew he was being transferred to an Alzheimer's unit at Saint John's in Mars, Pennsylvania. The nurses and orderlies that work with those patients are angels. We had no idea how long Dad would be with us. One night he said, "Herman, let's get the hell out of here." Herman was his brother. We spent a couple of hours and whatever they were giving him must have been wonderful because he was in the best mood I'd seen him in since he came to Saint John's. It was getting close to the end of visiting hours.

"Dad, I'm going to have to go back to work."

"Do your best," he said.

"I will. I'll be back in a few weeks."

As he painfully got into his bed. I put my forehead against his for a moment. "That feels good," he said. I stood at the end of his bed. "Jeff, one more thing."

"What's that, Dad?"

"Put some good soil on the grass by my tombstone," he said and he made a raking motion with his hand. The man who kept his lawn manicured wanted his gravesite to look good. He turned his head on the pillow and closed his eyes. It was the last time I saw him. About a week later I got a call that he had passed. He finally got his wish and got the hell out of there. I was back on a plane and heading to Butler for Dad's funeral. Many teachers from the Warrior Family sent flowers and cards, but by far, the one gesture that really put a shot in my arm came in a short email from Jesus.

Date: August 9, 2008

Subject: Condolences to Mr. Neal

It is with heavy heart that I announce that Jeff Neal's father, Wayne, has passed away. The late Mr. Neal, was one of us a lifelong educator and former principal, and obviously instrumental in Jeff's outstanding career. Certainly. our prayers go out to Jeff and his family.

Jesus Armas, Principal

He sent this to the staff and the words comforted me. The day of the funeral one of the people who eulogized Dad was Walter Derkaz. Their friendship formed in West Chester, Pennsylvania, in the early sixties and was one of destiny. Walter and Dad both were born on the same day. Mom was a Home Economics teacher working for Walter at a middle school. Virginia, Walt's wife, was working for Dad as a second-grade teacher. Both men were avid skiers and dedicated principals. The wives hit it off and the friendship between these two couples would last over fifty years. Walter, aged 80 shared memories as he eulogized his friend. After the funeral we were back at the house and Walt suggested that we have a toast. We walked to the edge of the property that looks down at the red Ranch-style house sprinkled with friends and relatives. Walt poured a splash of scotch in both of our glasses. "To your dad and my friend, Wayne," Walt said. We drank the smokey peat liquor from Dad's ancestors in Scotland.

"Thanks for your kind words about Dad today."

"It was my pleasure. He was a gentleman and a scholar. I know there were times when your dad would be exasperated with my exuberance. It was an auspicious day on May 3, 1928 when we came into this world," Walt said whimsically. "I want to share something with you, Jeff."

"What's that?"

"The last conversation that I had with Wayne he said that he wished you would get your doctorate. You should go for it. It will open up doors for you. Your father and I both wished we had gone on for that advanced degree. I started the process, but I told them they could shove that dissertation up their asses." I laughed. We went back to join the wake. The next morning, I was seated in the kitchen having some eggs and leftover ham when Mom came out from her bedroom. She had just buried her husband of fifty-five years and looked drained. She poured herself a cup of coffee and motioned for me to follow her to the dining room. "I spoke with Walter about you going for your Doctorate."

"Yes..." I said with a mixture of curiosity and trepidation.

"That would have made your father very happy."

That was how it started. I was over fifty and it didn't make sense to begin the doctoral journey. What kind of doors could open I wondered? Another seed was planted.

CHAPTER FORTY-FOUR

"CADILLAC JACK AND PTG"

Jesus wanted to gain insight of the student body so the administration attended a gang conference in Orlando. The keynote speaker, a detective named Pic, reinforced things that I'd learned along the way regarding the gang phenomenon. Another professional development opportunity was a Ruby Payne Conference in El Paso, Texas. Payne is considered one of the seminal leaders in understanding poverty and how it relates to education. Jesus and I were the only staff members attending this seminar. At the Fort Lauderdale airport as we waited at the gate to board our flight Jesus noticed an Arab gentleman. He wore a turban on his head and was reading the Koran. "Don't worry, Jesus. I know Krav Maga."

"You know what?"

"I've been taking the Israeli Defense system, Krav Maga. I will subdue this radical if he gets out of his seat on the plane."

"I can't tell you how comforting that is," he replied taking his window seat. I was in the aisle. He was content to relax and look out the window. My nature craves conversation so I started to talk to a truck driver from

Pennsylvania. He had been going to El Paso for years. "There's a diner on the edge of town. Ask for Cadillac Jack," the driver suggested.

"What does that entail?" I asked.

"Cadillac Jack takes people over the border to Juarez for tours. He will give you the Gold, Silver, or Bronze tour."

"What do you recommend?" I asked. Jesus nudged me to stop talking to this stranger.

"The Gold tour is worth the money. A girl usually has sex with a donkey on that one."

"Do you want to go, Jesus. We should go meet Cadillac Jack," I said, smiling. Jesus didn't dignify my comment with a response. Payne's famous book entitled, "A Framework for Understanding Poverty" is for educators. The basic premise of the book is that the middle class don't understand the "hidden rules" of poverty. These rules are the unspoken habits of the lower economic class. It was time for lunch. As we pulled out of the parking lot, we were heading east on US 85 and saw a sign, Juarez 2 miles. Jesus looked over and said, "I won't go meet Cadillac Jack, but if you want to go get some lunch it's only two miles away."

"Sounds good to me," I answered, excited to go to Mexico. There was a huge pyramid and no check point to enter the country. When we followed the road on the right side of the pyramid we were greeted with a most unpleasant site. No less than twelve lines of traffic stretched out as far as the eye could see. Jesus looked as if he'd been bush-whacked. The phone rang.

"I'm in Mexico with Neal and we will be forever trying to get back across the border." I could hear James Thomas laughing on the other end. We pulled up to a traffic light and stopped. A young guy, wearing a wife-beater, rode up on a bicycle and knocked on the driver side window.

"I can get you anything you want," the man said with a thick accent. "Pills, weed, girls. The girls are clean."

"No thank you," Jesus said, putting the window up and pulling forward as the light turned green. He immediately pulled into a parking lot to a food truck. "We may as well get lunch. We'll be in that line forever. I can't believe we crossed the border," Jesus said, shaking his head as he ordered beef tacos and a hamburger. I noticed a guy getting into a Trans Am with Texas plates. He was wearing a sharp, white Stetson cowboy hat. I walked over.

"Excuse me," I said, "I see your Texas plate. How long will it take if we get in those lines to cross back over?"

"If you get in those lines," he said, pointing to the queue of vehicles that looked like a long parking lot. "It will take you a good five to seven hours."

"Five to seven hours!" I exclaimed.

"Or you could follow me through town and cross over. It will take you forty-five minutes that way."

"What's your name?" I asked.

"Pablo," he replied and we shook hands. Jesus walked over.

"Jesus meet my new friend, Pablo. He's going to show us a short-cut through town. I know how much you want to get back to the afternoon session." Pablo got into his car and Jesus, looking as irritated as he could be, shook his head. We followed Pablo while eating on the run. Jesus said, "If we follow this guy, your new friend Pablo, and we end up kidnapped, I'll kill you first before they get to us."

"Let's put on some Mexican music," I said turning on the radio. The man's voice over the airwaves was speaking Spanish. We were at a red light. "What's he saying, Jesus?"

"He just said that Juarez is the most dangerous city in the world. Cartels are killing thousands a year. Imagine that, we go for tacos and come to the city that has more murders per capita than anywhere in the world!"

"Glad we met Pablo," I said with a smile. We crossed over to El Paso on the same bridge where Josh Brolin threw the brief case of money in the movie *No Country for Old Men*. A successful excursion to Juarez. Sometimes when you go through a harrowing experience, like visiting the most dangerous city in the world, it galvanizes a friendship. Such was the case with Jesus and I. One of his take-aways from the conference was that it is critically important to create relationships with students from generational poverty. We brainstormed as to how we could do that with our student body. His idea was to have each teacher, counselor, and administrator become a mentor for a child. This was implemented and over eighty kids on our campus had an adult checking on how they were doing academically, socially, and on their home front. This practice made a big difference. The other idea was to help our staff understand the hidden rules of poverty. Jesus reasoned that if our teachers understood their rules, it may help bridge the gap between teacher and student. I shared how my job with Cities in Schools gave me insight into just what our kids deal with in their homes. Home visits became more prevalent amongst our staff.

Pursuing an EdD in Instructional Leadership was a new world to me. My first advisor was a former principal, James Williams, from Jacksonville. He was a Black man in his late sixties. We met at a conference in Orlando. He suggested I study a reading program and analyze how student achievement was affected by it. Many of the students in my cohort were doing just that as it was a process of analyzing quantitative data and reporting the results. I had another idea.

"Dr. Williams," I began, "I think I want to study something that happened at our school."

"What was that?"

"About seven years ago we had a shooting at our school and a teacher was killed."

"Oh, I see," he said. "What is it that you want to study?"

"I don't know exactly. I just know that we experienced something together as a school community and there is important information there. It just needs to be uncovered."

"Do you want to do a study on how to prevent a school shooting?"

WHAT A LONG STRANGE IT'S BEEN

"I would like to do a study on our recovery. We went through a lot and I think in some way we became stronger."

"It's called post-traumatic growth."

"What is that, Dr. Williams?"

"Post-traumatic growth (PTG) is a term I learned when I was a principal of a high school. It refers to practices that value life and bring about a positive change in one who has experienced a severe traumatic event. Finding the light or the positive growth after enduring a psychological struggle is the cornerstone of PTG."

"How did you know about that?"

"I was afraid you'd ask that," he said, looking down for a moment. His hand was shaking. "One morning when I was a principal at my high school, I saw a senior who hanged himself on the bleachers by the football field."

"Wow, that had to have been horrible."

"It was. He was a popular student athlete and a break-up led him to take his life. Everyone was devastated. A local psychologist contacted me and educated me about PTG. It gave me a playbook of practices that promote healing."

"I'd like to do a study on this," I added.

"You definitely have a phenomenon in that your school experienced a school shooting, but rolling out a case study has its challenges. You need a hypothesis and the vehicle to gather your information."

"Vehicle?"

"Surveys, interviews, or inventories. I think there is an inventory by two researchers, Tedeschi and Calhoun. Either way you have your work cut out for you. It would be much simpler, as I said earlier, to study a program and report the results."

"I understand that," I added.

"Well, good luck to you," he said, standing. I shook his hand that, once again, I noticed was trembling. That one conversation with a kind, bright man was the spark that let me discern what path I wanted to pursue with my study. He called me a few weeks later and informed me that his Parkinson's disease was advancing and he wouldn't be able to be my advisor anymore. Our brief encounter was fortuitous.

CHAPTER FORTY-FIVE

"RODNEY AND REGROW"

While I was narrowed the focus of my study Lake Worth Middle was chugging along with the winds of change. District meetings and trainings were now being held in Warrior Country on a regular basis. Each meeting was organized with extreme attention to detail. Jesus also set out to hire good people. The academies did attract high-level students and academic rigor in the new building was present. We still were losing electives due to the focus on testing. This phenomenon was countywide. However, due to a discipline practice of mine, Jesus actually created a new elective. It is the AP's job to deliver discipline. Sometimes, a really good kid would receive a referral. If this student was the recipient of their first referral from one of the teachers who writes them like traffic tickets, I would get a little creative. After an administrative reprimand their consequence was that they had to sing. One day a student named Fednike Nozistene came into my office. It was her first referral. Her wrinkled nose and lowered eyebrows indicated disgust.

"Fednike, I'll tell you what I'm going to do."

"Do I have to go to ATS?"

"No, not necessarily." She sat up in her chair. "No, if you will sing a song, I will let you off with a warning. Next time, I won't go so easy on you."

"What little song?" Fednike asked.

"Anyone you like?"

"I Will Always Love You by Whitney Houston?" she asked.

"That would be great," I said as I leaned back in my chair to listen. She stood up straight and put her hands down still at her sides. Her feet were slightly apart. Many students had sung in my office before. This one was different. I could have closed my eyes and thought Whitney was performing a private concert. Her voice was euphonious and melodic. Both secretaries got up to see who was generating this sound. This smiling Haitian girl could win "America's Got Talent" hands down.

"Where did you learn to sing like that?"

"I sing in my church," she said softly. "I've been singing as long as I can remember. My mom says she could hear me singing in her stomach."

"Come with me," I said and we walked to Jesus's office.

"Jesus."

"Yes?" he said, not looking up.

"I have a kid out there who—"

"I don't have time to play good cop/bad cop, Jeff."

"This is different," I said.

"Make it quick," he answered. I told Fednike that this was like an audition and I wanted her to sing for the principal.

"Jesus, this is Fednike. She would like to sing a song."

"Okay," Jesus answered. Fednike began and as she hit the second line, Jesus dropped his pen. He stared with a gaping mouth and absorbed attention. When finished she put her head down. "Very nice!" Jesus exclaimed, clapping. "We have a student with talent, Mr. Neal." He yelled, "Maria!" This was Ms. Suarez, his Confidential Secretary, and second Cuban mother. He often summoned her to his office. Jesus made a decision that day to create a new elective called, Advanced Chorus. At the end of her eighth-grade year Fednike passed an audition for the prestigious Dreyfoos School of the Arts in West Palm Beach. Today, she is a professional singer who has performed around the world. Sometimes a referral is not the worst thing to happen to a student.

Another music elective that was outstanding was Drum line. It was implemented by Bob Hatcher. Sam Rolle taught the class. Sam, a graduate of Florida A&M University (FAMU), was a member of that school's elite Drumline. He took the discipline he learned at FAMU and instilled it in his students. "Don't practice until you get it right. Practice until you can't get it wrong," was his motto. The students craved his discipline and were really amazing in their performances. The members kept their grades up and stayed out of trouble. Jesus noticed they needed new uniforms saying, "Sam could use some new attire for his drummers."

"Is money in the budget for that?" I asked.

"No, we are going to have a good old-fashioned fundraiser."

"How are we going to do that?" I asked.

"I'm leaving that up to you."

"Up to me?"

"You are Mr. Lake Worth and you have worked here for over twenty years and you know a lot of people."

"So, what are you asking?"

"I am asking you to contact your friends who may be business owners. Invite them to a demonstration of our drum line. Tell them there will be lunch and refreshments. We'll pass the hat after the exhibition." Karen McKinley and Russell Hibbard were the first to come to mind. They were the owners of the blues club, Bamboo Room. Next John Lang, Landscape architect, and a famous artist by the name of Dan Meyer were added to the list. Dave Palombo of "Dave's Last Resort," and his business partners Mark and Gretchen Szafaryn also received invitations. The newly elected Mayor of Lake Worth, Jeff Clemens, showed up even though the event was the day after he was elected. Jesus prepared the atmosphere, immaculately, with tables strewn purposefully on the basketball court with flowers. Lunch was ordered from C.R. Chicks, a local restaurant known for its rotisserie chicken cooked over flaming Brazilian Oak logs. The custodians waxed the gym floor to a shine that glistened.

Frank's Student Ambassadors, with their white shirts emblazoned with the Warrior design, led our guests to their tables. The drum line looked proud as they set up to perform. All drums were level as were the ensemble cymbals. They began their groove with syncopated ears and hands. Our guests were blown away by the precision and discipline that was evident in the exhibition. Russell Hibbard, an expert in music history, remarked, "This drum line is performing on a level I'd never imagine in a middle school ensemble." Our guests wrote checks in a generous manner and at the end of our exhibition the fundraiser allowed for new uniforms to be bought. John Lang said, "I grew up in Lake Worth and from what I heard this school was a war zone. What I saw today were polite kids who escorted us through a campus that is clean. Your drum line is extraordinarily talented. You should let the community know the good things that our going on at your school." He shook our hands and walked away.

"That's how we win hearts and minds, Mr. Neal." Lessons from Jesus. "You did a great job, Mr. Neal," Jesus said. "In fact, you did such a good job I'm going to put you in charge of our next fundraiser."

"What's that?" I asked, not what I was expecting to hear.

"Our first ever Lake Worth Middle Golf tournament."

"How are we to do that?"

"The same way you did this fundraiser. You know the community. Make it happen." Jodi Haugen, teacher and Lake Worth resident, and I teamed up. I got golfers and she was relentless in getting local businesses to sponsor holes. Dan Meyer did a sculpture of golf tees for the silent auction. Later Green Brier the prestigious golf resort in West Virginia commissioned him to do the tees in front of their clubhouse. We made over $7,000 dollars which is unheard of for a middle school fundraiser. During that summer I had a professor by the name of Dr. Jared Bucker. He found out I was studying recovery from a school shooting.

"Very pertinent topic. School shootings are a contagion." He remembered our incident and said, "Jeff, you have an expertise in this area as does everyone, sadly, that was at your school. The key search words are recovery and shootings. Then look for the seminal study." I took his advice to use those key words. A spate of scholarly articles appeared. I immersed myself in the literature. Many articles were written by Glen W. Muschert, PhD, a professor of Sociology at Miami University in Ohio. He was cited as being one of the leading experts on school shootings. I noticed a telephone number at the bottom of the title page of one of his studies. I called fully expecting that no one would answer.

"Hello, this is Glen Muschert," he answered cheerfully.

"Dr. Muschert?"

"Yes."

"My name is Jeff Neal and I am doing a case study of a school shooting that happened in Florida."

"How can I help you, Jeff?" I explained that I wanted to interview our staff regarding the recovery process. When I finished, he said, "There is someone you should contact. She is the only person I know whose has done a study like what you want to do."

"Who is that?" I asked excitedly.

"Johanna Nurmi of Tampere University in Finland." In minutes he read off the email address.

"Thank you so much for your time, Dr. Muschert."

"Make sure you tell Johanna I recommended you. Good luck to you, Jeff. I'm done studying the phenomenon of school shootings for now. It gets hard to ask people to tell me about the worst day of their life." We hung up and his words echoed in my mind. I would be probing the Warrior Family to tell me about a most abhorrent day in their lives. I emailed Johanna Nurmi and explained the intention of my study and asked if she would mind helping me. I dropped Muschert's name and gave my mobile number.

About this time Jesus offered to host a conference for all thirty-four middle school guidance coordinators in Palm Beach County. That morning at an administrative meeting Jesus said, "We have guests today. This is a good chance to have a first-class event. Let's have a presence in front of the media center. We don't need a lot of running and screaming and I really don't want any fights today. I'm going to encourage them to wrap up the meeting a little early so that they can get out of the parking lot before the parents arrive for pick-up." The library was transformed to the regal ambiance that was Jesus' trademark. I felt confident we were putting our best foot forward and our guests would see a campus that was secure and organized. Everything was going as planned.

That was until I got a call over the walkie from Q asking me to report to Portable 2. As I turned the corner I saw Max, Officer Cuellar, and his new replacement Officer Vargas. Cuellar was moving on to the Canine division to work with drug dogs. It was Max's last week as he was moving on with Bob Hatcher. I looked to my left and along the ramp were ten of our EH boys. They looked at me with glee as they were literally jumping with excitement. As I came to Q's side, I saw him. Rodney was the largest and strongest boy on our campus. He was bald and wore an ankle monitor indicating he was on parole. Somehow Rodney's pants, shirt, and shoes had disappeared. The only attire was a bright pair of Carolina blue boxers. I knew it was my turn to see if we could get the clothes back on him peacefully.

"Rodney, Rodney, Rodney... what are you doing?"

"Standing here," he said as if boxers only was okay.

"Butt naked!" Billie, a student, on the ramp yelled. This got the audience excited. This was not good because Rodney had to show up in front of them.

"Rodney, come on man put on your clothes," I said in a whisper, moving over closer and leaned forward slightly. "Rodney, I really don't want to call your probation officer."

"Go ahead and call the motherfucker."

"Put on your clothes. No one wants to see you naked."

Not my wisest comment of the day as at that moment he turned dropped his blue boxers around his ankles, grabbed his butt cheeks and bent over delivering a moon for the ages. The students went into hysterics, laughing, screaming, and jumping up and down. "Rodney's crack is so big you can swim in it," yelled Billie. The students convulsed with laughter once again. Q turned to Cuellar, Max, and Vargas and they went into a huddle. I listened.

"Get those students in the portable," Q said like a quarterback drawing up a play. "Max, you come with me and get his clothes. He's going to put them on one way or the other." I know when to say when and I turned to leave the scene. Coach Smith opened the door. Vargas had a quizzical look as if asking himself what he had gotten into at Lake Worth Middle. They got the students in the portable. Q and Max rushed toward naked Rodney. Walking back to my office I was confident that they diverted the situation and Rodney would have his clothes on. Our guests would be none the wiser.

Jesus called me to his office. He stated, "One of the area Superintendents paid a nice complement at how well everything went today. We need a calm dismissal." I walked to the front of the school. The parents who pick up their kids were already lined up along the sidewalk. The busses were idling in the loop. The huge flag of the United States was gently waving in the breeze. The sun shone brightly. It was beautiful day. Looking to my right some of the Guidance Coordinators were already making their way to the parking lot. Then, out of the corner of my eye, I saw him. Rodney was naked to the world running full speed. Q was right behind in hot pursuit yelling, "That's it, you did it this time!" Rodney had a look of determination as he was hauling ass, literally, while he passed the parents in their cars. The parents did a double-take as the unclothed man-child sprinted past them. One of the classrooms that faces the loop let out a mob scream as they observed the streaker. Rodney ran past the whiteboard where Max recorded the busses as they arrived. Q was gaining on him. The bus loop curves around in the shape of a horseshoe. As Rodney neared the turn Q caught him swiping his feet as they tumbled to the ground.

Miraculously, our guests didn't seem to notice the 300-pound naked student on the ground. Rodney was laughing and I was hoping Q would find some restraint regarding physical retaliation. I pondered my options. I asked the school nurse to bring a blanket to the bus loop. In moments Q wrapped it around him like a mummy and got him to his feet. We entered into a back door of one of the classrooms. Coach Smith arrived with his clothes. Q grabbed the clothes and handed them to him. Amazingly, Rodney put his pants and shirt on without comment. In moments we were heading to my office. Coach Smith already had Billie in my office as he was the instigator that dared Rodney to bare all and run in front of the parents at dismissal. Jesus came by and stood in my door for a moment. He was on his way to a meeting at the district office. "Things went well today, Mr. Neal," he said, taking a quick look at Rodney. "What's going on with these two?"

"You don't want to know," I answered.

"I'm sure you're right," he replied, heading off in his sport coat. As I picked up the phone and was about to dial Rodney's mother he reached over and tapped me on my shoulder and said, "Are you going to call my mom?"

"Yes, Rodney. You're being suspended and I have to let her know."

"You're going to mess up my football," he stated.

"No, Rodney you messed that up when you decided to take your clothes off and run naked in front of the school." I started to dial.

"I can help you grow your hair back," he said. I turned and looked at him. My curiosity piqued, I set the phone down.

"Just how are you going to help me grow my hair back?"

"Regrow," he said.

"Regrow?"

"Yeah, yeah you get it in the beauty shop. My stepdad uses it. You just pour it out," he said while demonstrating, "on your hand and pat it on the top of your head." He patted his head. "It will help you grow your hair back."

"He don't want no regrow from a negro!" Billie said with his cackling, carnival laugh. I didn't say anything as I dialed the phone and told his mother what happened. I always wondered about, Regrow, that came highly recommended by Rodney.

CHAPTER FORTY-SIX
"MEMORIAL CELEBRATION"

An email appeared from the researcher from Finland, Johanna Nurmi who left her mobile number on the communique. I called and it rang and rang. Just as I was about to hang up, she answered. As soon as I identified myself, she went right into discussing my study. She was encouraging and insightful. Her study centered around rampage shootings that occurred in two small towns in Finland, Jokela and Kauhajoki. She studied the reasons and dynamics of each shooting. More importantly, for me, she examined the recovery processes of both Finnish communities. "Jeff, these are important studies of this salient phenomenon and, unfortunately, shootings are showing no sign of decline, especially in your country. Prevention is important, but so is understanding what happens to the victims in the aftermath. My studies showed both communities as a whole were victims." She spoke rhapsodically. I heard terms that were unfamiliar such as: cultural trauma, moral panic, chaotic death, psycho-social support, gendered experience, memorialization, and solidarity. She cautioned me that to delve into this area of research you are asking people to relive something that may have been as traumatic as anything they've ever experienced in their lives. Dr. Muschert's comment on asking people to explain the worst day of their life came to mind. Then she mentioned she had to get up in four hours. I'd awakened her as Finland is seven hours ahead of the United States. Here was a leading voice in this field of systematic inquiry losing sleep giving me her time and guidance.

One day after testing Jesus said, "Mr. Neal, please swing by my office." When I got to his office, a young lady and gentleman were sitting in the two chairs across from him. He said, "Do these two look familiar to you?" It was Dinora. I hadn't seen her since her eighth-grade year and she had blossomed into a beautiful young lady. The boy I recognized as a former student, Christian. Both of them were Barry's students and had been present in the classroom the day of the shooting. I wondered the purpose of their visit. Jesus said, "Dinora, do you want to tell Mr. Neal what you're planning?"

"Yes, I do. We are coming up on the tenth anniversary of losing Mr. Grunow. We want to organize a celebration of his life and have it here at the school."

"That sounds great. What did you have in mind?"

"We want to have a 3-on-3 basketball tournament," she said her voice brimming with enthusiasm. "You know how much Mr. Grunow loved basketball. All proceeds will go to the Barry Grunow Scholarship Fund. We want do something to promote literacy. Mr. Grunow always encouraged us to read."

"We can do something with our school-wide novel," Jesus added. Dinora discussed the plans with passion and added that many former Warriors would be in attendance to honor their slain teacher. It was a testimony of how Barry's spirit was living on through his students. Jesus formed a committee and the wheels got in motion.

"Let's ask MaryAnne Hedrick to be in charge of the 3 on 3 tournament," Jesus said to me. "You can recruit players."

"Ok," I answered.

"Also, I'd like you to MC the kickoff of this project. This is going to be a two-day event."

"MC what?" I asked.

"I have an idea," Jesus said. His proposal was to have a private ceremony for Barry. This would be limited to close friends, family, staff, and selected former students who were present. Dinora and Christian put together a video with some great pictures of Barry at different stages of his life. Barry's childhood friends were contacted. The number of attendees grew exponentially. The reading coach, Sarah Barnes, lined up the author of the school-wide novel for a book signing. Things started to come together. "I have one more ingredient for this evening," Jesus said.

"What's that?" I asked.

"Patience, Mr. Neal," he said with a sly grin.

I knew he had something up his sleeve. The two-day event was going to entail a Memorial Celebration for family and friends on May 14th and the 3 on 3 tournament combined with a Literacy Fair on May 15th. It was Friday afternoon when Jesus handed me the program. It was in color and there was a great picture of Barry on the cover. The same one I had the players touch. The title of the program was, "Barry Grunow Memorial Celebration."

"Come with me. I want to show you something." I followed Jesus. It was the last period of the day and no one was in the gym. He unlocked the door and made a gesture that said after you. I walked in the door and looked across the gym. On the wall was a large mural that was an excellent painting of Barry, with a half of a basketball underneath his image. It hauntingly resembled him. The eyes and hair color were exact. Under this facsimile the school colors were present with the words, "Barry L. Grunow Gymnasium."

"Who painted this?" I asked in disbelief.

"Darius McCray," answered Jesus. "He's done murals at Sun Coast and Seminole Ridge High Schools." This mural added splendor to the gym. The night arrived. Vonae, Christian, and Dinora were dressed to the nines.

Pam and her kids arrived. I couldn't believe how big they had gotten. Pam had moved to Jupiter and it had been a long time since I'd seen her. Both her parents were there. Barry's mom looked as classy as ever. Kurt and many members of the Beatniks visited the mural of Barry and then sat on the bleachers that were full. Jesus made his way to the podium. A gifted orator he explained how Barry's three students were the inspiration for this special event.

"When I realized we were having this evening I thought who else, but Mr. Jeffrey Neal, should be the Master of Ceremonies," Jesus said. The pounding in my heart moved to my head as I took the mic from Jesus. I cleared my throat and looked at Sam and Lee Anne. Our eyes met. Lee Anne gave me a smile and for some reason my anxiety dissipated. I welcomed everyone and introduced the Lake Worth High School Color Guard for the Presentation of Colors. The United States Flag and the Florida State Flag coming in at a trail, they proceeded to the center of the gym and led us in the Pledge of Allegiance. The entire crowd was standing with their hands over their hearts as Fednike Nozistene began to sing the National Anthem. She easily hit the octave and a half range on the long "ee" of free like we were at an NFL game.

After making some remarks about Barry I introduced Bob Hatcher who spoke with emotion. Then teachers: Alison Moe, Dorothy Schroader (Dot) and Amy Colleran all shared heartfelt personal memories of Barry. The last two speakers of the evening were two of Barry's close friends, Mitch Krolic and Garth Rosenkrance. Mitch had the crowd laughing as he spoke of being the manager of a music store and Barry was his employee. I remember him saying that at sixteen Barry was wise beyond his years and was an old soul. A basketball game was played by teachers and former players. Jerseys made with one side being Team Barry and the other being Team Grunow. It did my heart good to see friends, teachers, and former Warrior athletes running up and down the hardwood floor playing the game that he loved.

The next day we couldn't have asked for better weather for the 3 on 3 tournament and the Literacy Fair. The sun was shining and the sky was blue. Even though it was May 15th, usually a scorcher in south Florida, the air had a breeze that made it uncommonly bearable. That was a good thing as many people were in attendance. It was nice to see many of the guys that were playing when Barry and I were coaching. They were in their early twenties now. Jeffrey Remmington, who was playing pro ball in Europe, thrilled the kids with some slam dunks that were reminiscent of Michael Jordan. Hoops wasn't the only attraction of the day.

There were school bands from Lake Worth Middle, Palm Springs Middle, and L.C. Swain that were taking turns performing in the courtyard. Frank informed me that the band director of Palm Springs was a recipient of the first Barry Grunow Scholarship Fund. Pam looked on listening intently. After the number she went over to the Band Director. The young lady let out a shriek and hugged Pam. She'd recognized her from the scholarship inception. This reunion touched my heart. The irony was that the scholarship helped that young girl go to college and she was performing at his memorial.

I looked over the courtyard and thought how happy Barry would be to see all of these kids having the time of their lives. The drum line performed as the smell of hamburgers and hotdogs blew in the wind. The Bounce House out by the track was filled with children jumping up and down while Star the Clown painted faces. The Literacy Fair was a big hit as Steve Allen, author of *Meg*, our school-wide novel, signed books. The science-fiction horror novel that followed the underwater adventures of a navy deep sea diver, Jonas Taylor, was immensely popular with the students. The author had no idea what he was getting into as at least four hundred kids lined up to get their books signed.

Perhaps the biggest hit of the day was LaRoi Wright, a solo musician playing Steelpan drums. He had a cult following as the kids paraded with him around the courtyard. He was in a bright white suit and his dreadlocks added to the sense that the kids were being swept away off to Trinidad. Jeffrey's team won the 3-on-3 tournament. Afterwards he pointed over to the mural, "Coach Grunow gets a front row seat to all of the games," he said with a smile. I could see Bernadette in his countenance. The event came to a close and all of the proceeds went to the scholarship fund. As the staff cleaned the debris of the day, there was restorative psychological relief and a satisfaction that we remembered Barry.

CHAPTER FORTY-SEVEN

"BOND...BILL BOND"

The last day of school wasn't holding the same trepidation that it had in other years for me. There was disappointment by both students and faculty as we just missed a B grade. We did however raise the scores of our lowest 25% which qualified us for money. The state offers a stipend because of this achievement and it is up to the school, through a vote, to decide who gets the money. Jesus gave me this as a task to conduct a faculty vote. Joe Owsley called me from Kentucky as he and Carolyn were visiting their grandchildren. "What are you up to, man?" Joe asked. "There is someone I think you should meet for your study."

"Who's that?

"His name's Bill Bond, former principal of Heath High. He was the principal when they had their shooting."

"Oh," I said.

"He's going to be speaking at a conference at some highfalutin' private school in Miami." I was interested in meeting Bill Bond and remember thinking what a cool last name for a principal; like the British Secret Service agent created by Ian Fleming. He was speaking at Miami Country Day School. This private institution, founded in 1938, is located in Hialeah. It is billed as one of the finest independent schools in the Southeast. As I drove in through the gates, I was impressed with the sprawling twenty-one-acre campus. Older buildings mixed with modern architecture gave the atmosphere a college preparatory energy. Well-tanned boys were practicing lacrosse.

On the agenda I saw Bill Bond, School Safety Expert, NASSP (National Association of Secondary School Principals). His session was in a room, set up like a studio, with big fluorescent lights. He was a tall gentleman. I sat in the back and took out my legal pad. "I was sitting in my office on December 1, 1997," Bond began with an unmistakable Kentucky twang, "and I could hear a faint sound outside like firecrackers. I smiled and thought these kids are starting early today as it was just past 7:30 in the morning. Then I heard pow! pow! pow! It was the unmistakable sound of gunfire. I ran to the door and saw Michael Carneal, a fourteen-year-old freshmen, holding his gun in a digital trance. I say this because Michael was addicted to playing video games. He fired, with no expression, while some people stood still and others ran. Those that ran got shot. I ran over and stood behind a brick pillar. On either side of me there were two girls who fled and were injured. Being a hunter, I knew the sound of his clip emptying and falling to the floor. I knew that it might take him some time to reload so I stepped from around the pillar, "I'm sorry, Mr. Bond," Michael said as he seemingly came out of his trance and handed me the .22 pistol."

"What happened next?" someone asked.

"After that I found out three girls, who were in a prayer circle, were killed in front of the school. Five more were injured. I hugged more kids that day than I did the in the other twenty-seven years of my career." As he said that I thought of how our school community hugged. Bond continued, "The healing process we had to go through at Heath High School began that day. I've spent the last fifteen years helping schools where people have died on campus from homicide. I flew to Columbine. A principal has so many decisions to make that day."

"Like what?" the same voice asked.

"Like how do we get 3,000 book bags that have been left behind in the aftermath back to the students. Logistical hurdles that one doesn't think of appear." Bond told the story of the young boy who did the shooting. He was a violence cocktail. Bullied, loved video games, and later was diagnosed as a paranoid-schizophrenic. Kids made fun of him as being gay. Unfortunately, he had access to weapons. Bond's experience and the fact that a non-profit organization flies him around the country to help schools after shootings was impressive. He concluded his session talking about the importance of speaking up. Apparently, Corneal told other students, "Something big is going to happen at school on Monday." No one reported his veiled threat. After the session I was in a queue to speak to Bond. Many of the principals seemed almost desperate to speak to him. I was last in line. "Hi, I'm Jeff Neal. Joe Owsley suggested that I speak to you," I said extending my hand.

"Joe, how do you know that good old boy?"

"We worked together," I said. "I'm doing a case study on the recovery of our school from a school shooting. Joe thought that I could learn some things from you. Maybe we could talk later?"

"So, your school had a shooting?"

"Yes."

"I have a couple more sessions and there is supposed to be a wine and cheese later. Let's talk then." I nodded. I was taken aback about the wine and cheese event. The only alcohol I knew on our campus might have been when Willie and Max were running the custodial night-shift. Just like that I was offered an opportunity to learn from a man that experienced as much involvement with the phenomenon of school shootings then, perhaps, anyone in the United States. It came time for the "social." In the center of the campus there was all the beer and wine you wanted. This was offered with a fancy catering company going around with trays of hors d'oeuvres. I was a long way from Lake Worth Middle. Bond waved from a chair and motioned for me to join him. He was sipping a beer. "Glad you're here," he said. "Tell me about your study?"

"We had a teacher who was shot and killed on the last day of school."

"I think I remember that. What was the teacher's name?"

"Grunow."

"That's right; I remember now. He was shot by a student?"

"Yes, on the last day of school."

"I remember the trial on TV. Brazille was the boy's name?"

"That's right," I answered, thinking Bond's mind was quick.

"My idea is to do a case study with our staff as to what helped us recover. I'm trying to tie it to Post-traumatic Growth."

"I know about PTG," he answered. "Go on."

I've talked to some people who have done studies like this."

"Who?" Bond asked.

"Johann Nurmi, from Finland and a guy name Glenn Muschert."

"I'm not familiar with Nurmi, but Muschert's a good man. His seminal studies have made him a leading expert in the field. This study is worth doing. Each school has to heal. Hell, the whole community has to heal. The ripple effects that reverberated through McCraken County where Heath High School is located were devastating."

"Any suggestions?"

"I imagine you'll have to come up with some open-ended questions to measure your participants experiences."

"Yes," I said.

"I know for us memorials were a big part of our healing. Right now, there are plans for a memorial where a statue is being built to symbolize the prayer circle of the students who were praying that morning. There are going to be five benches for the surviving victims who were shot that day."

"We just had a ten-year memorial celebration that I think helped people," I added.

"It's important. There is a test for PTG from some guys in one of the Carolinas," Bond said. "It's an inventory."

"Tedeschi and Calhoun," I said, remembering their names.

"There you go, those are the boys. You just have to do a little old-fashioned hard work to get this puppy started," Bond said as he finished his beer.

"Is there anything else that you think would help me?"

"I'll tell you what I tell principals around the country when I'm speaking," Bond said. "The hardest thing is communication with teachers, staff, and parents after a shooting. Parents want to know two things. Is my child okay? When am I going to get my child home? Information from students is far more important than a camera or a locked door. Most shooters give off clues and no one speaks up until it's too late. The way to help kids to speak up is to build trusting relationships with students and others in the community."

"This is good," I said as I began to write Bond's words.

"Jeff, I probably know the answer to this question, but I'm going to ask it anyway. Why do you want to do this study?"

"I guess the answer is that I think we did something, as a school community, that was remarkable. We came together and healed and actually thrived. We continued on in Barry's memory. If that makes sense?"

"It makes perfect sense. Part of me wanted to retire after our shooting. I stayed on 'til the freshmen class graduated. Then the shootings kept happening and I found myself going to help. Every time there's a shooting I instinctively go. My non-profit pays for it all. I understand the pain they're going through. Do you know what a bad day for a principal is?"

"What?"

"When there's more than twelve microphones in front of you. The study will help you continue healing. Finish your study. Finish it."

"Thanks, Mr. Bond." We shook hands and I watched the tall man walk away. I admired his kindness and courage. This brief exchange motivated me. If I could tease out the varying dimensions and information from our staff, perhaps, it could be a guide for schools experiencing the same unimaginable pain. As I drove north on I-95 I got a call on the way home.

"Jeff, I wanted you to hear it from me. I took a job at Santaluces High School," Wakisha Mawalli said.

"Congratulations Wakisha. That's going to mean some more money for you," I added.

"I know and I could use it to pay off these college loans. Jeff, I really enjoyed working with you and am going to miss you a lot."

"I'm going to miss you too."

Wakisha and I had a bond as I was a counselor when she was a computer teacher named Miss Davis. She was bright and I always thought she would make an excellent principal. Who would Jesus find as her replacement? Now he had three males on his administrative team. I called him. "Do you have any idea for a replacement?"

"I do. There's a girl in my Doctoral cohort that I think would be a good fit at Lake Worth Middle."

"Who is she?" I asked.

"Her name is Valarie Jones."

CHAPTER FORTY-EIGHT
"VALARIE JONES THE ONE AND ONLY"

Dr. Silvia Orta, professor of Educational Leadership had a rhythmic intonation in her words that I noticed were a Cuban dialect. Her first assignment was interesting. Each student was asked to do a presentation of the person who was their model for leadership. I chose M. Wayne. My PowerPoint put forth how he would be up until all hours recording things he was studying about reading programs. Like Barry, who would dress in togas for Greek Mythology, Dad would put on the attire of our Founding Fathers when one of his teachers was covering the American Revolution. After class Dr. Orta asked what topic I was considering for my study.

"Case study of a school that had a shooting. Although, I'm having some trouble getting started."

"Don't worry," she said with a comforting voice. "It's my job to help students. We'll work it out." I knew I had someone in my corner. My instincts were correct as her expertise proved invaluable. School was about to start.

"Jeffrey Wayne," Jesus said. "Meet Ms. Valarie Jones."

"Nice to meet you Jeffrey Wayne," she said.

"Nice to meet you, Valarie Jones," I said.

"Don't get it twisted, I'm Valarie Jones the one and only, if there's another one, she's a phony." Valarie hailed from a small town about twenty minutes west of Tallahassee called Quincy. Jesus reminded me I still had to determine, through a faculty vote, how to distribute the money for the gains of the lowest 25%. Word got out that a meeting was going to be on Friday. Everyone from cafeteria workers to custodians would be in attendance. The night before I wondered how to navigate this fiscal ordeal that pitted teachers against each other. Tying money to test scores is a slippery slope. Part of me thought it would be the best of all scenarios if we could agree to split the money between all stakeholders. Silvia Torres, the bookkeeper, did a quick calculation. The number was $387.00, if we divided it evenly. There wasn't a seat in the library where the meeting was being conducted. The cafeteria workers and custodians were in seats off to the side. Many were given headphones so that language facilitators could translate what was being said. Money was on the line and everyone had a vested interest. Jesus introduced the purpose of the meeting. He then turned it over to me.

"Good luck, Jeffrey," said Valarie discreetly.

"I need it," I answered, stepping to the podium.

"Good morning, people," I began "As you know our lowest 25% made gains in reading." Cheering ensued. "Yes, congratulations to everyone who concentrated on reading this year. "We are able to distribute the money anyway we want. Do we want to track what students were in the lowest 25% and give the money to those reading teachers who had them for intensive reading? Do we want to give some of the money to the Language Arts teachers? How about the Social Studies teachers who read passages all year long? Let's not forget that Mr. Armas trained our entire staff in Chriss." Chriss is a research-based program that provides reading strategies.

"Science classes had more Anchor charts than any subject in my observation. I'm hoping you're seeing the dilemma. This may not be a popular idea, but I am proposing that we agree we're all in this together. Those people you see on the seats over there," I said, pointing to the custodians and cafeteria workers. "They were a big part of what we did as well. Think about during testing and ask yourself who feeds our kids? Everyone knows that malnutrition affects how students do on tests. How about the day of testing when a student vomits in front of your door, and those folks arrive in moments to sprinkle those miracle granules that take up that odor that would disrupt your testing environment. We are a team here in Warrior Country, and my proposal is that we vote to divide the money evenly among all stakeholders in the room." There was some grumbling. There is no reason for me to disparage a teacher who was anticipating a bonus, an unheard of occurrence in education. Jesus called for a vote. Everyone dropped a ballot in the box as they exited the meeting. The votes were to be counted by CTA (Classroom Teachers Association) representatives. The next day Jesus called me into his office.

"Nice job. They voted to divide it evenly."

"Good," I answered.

"You are a man of the people," remarked James Thomas. "Your office will be the cleanest and your plate will be full in the cafeteria." At this time Jesus implemented the Warrior Way. The tenets of this were: Be Safe, Be Responsible, Be Respectful, and Be a Goal Setter. It became the school mission. Valarie and I were getting to know each other. She had some reservations about our student body. "Jeffrey, I've been told that your kids are "buck wild" and that I need to wear armor."

It's not that bad, you'll see."

"I don't want to deal with a bunch of heathens!" she said.

The first day of school arrived and Valarie was dressed for success. She wore a white pantsuit and her hair was straightened. She had high-heeled white shoes and her toes were painted bright white as were her fingernails. The students were wondering who this new Black woman was telling them to get in class. After the first class change, I went to my desk to check my emails. I looked up and saw two girls wailing on each other. Recognizing one of the girls, Lori, who fought regularly I got up from my seat. Valarie, in her white outfit, wielded her walkie like a magic wand was yelling, "Stop it! Stop it you heathens!" I ducked and went in low and grabbed Lori who had just landed a right cross. I thought I heard the girl's jaw break. She back pedaled and fell to the ground. I was on one knee and kept my hand on her back as she squirmed. Officer Vargas had rounded the corner and had the other girl. Lori stopped moving and was lying on her stomach. I kept my hand firmly in place as she could easily jump up and start the fray all over again. I went into de-escalation mode.

"Lori, are you okay?"

"I'm okay, but I fucked that bitch up!" she yelled so that the other girl heard her.

"Yes, you did," I whispered. Let's take a walk in the courtyard." She dusted herself off and we went around the corner. Lori had dark hair and a tattoo of a snake on her bicep. She wore a probation monitor on her ankle. Rumor had it that she hit a policewoman while being taken into custody. I used to tell her that I knew of a Snake Farm she could work at and she would reply she knew of a place for me to get black market Rogaine. She was bright but something in her energy caused her to be a rebel. Valarie, coming out of lunch duty, said, "I miss my old school. These kids are heathens."

"Valarie, they're going to grow on you," I said, smiling.

That was the first day and we hit the ground running. We had a reading coach, math coach, and Science coach. Our teachers had adopted a mantra that was county wide known as I Do, We Do, You Do. This means the teacher demonstrates a new concept on the board. Then the whole group performs the task at hand together. A lesson culminates with the student showing they have mastered the concept on their own. Learning Team Meetings, or LTM's, became a staple in our practice. The academic coaches were implementing strategies with each subject area. Everything was geared to improve student achievement.

Valarie had a small learning curb with the gang culture and street mentality of our students, but she brought a lot to the table. She was tough as nails and could raise her voice and deliver a verbal smackdown to a student who disrespected her. She had vast expertise on teaching reading and implemented Chriss Reading strategies, across all subject areas, to improve comprehension. Most importantly, she knew how to create relationships with students and teachers. They sensed she cared about them. Today she is a successful principal as is James Thomas. Jesus created an environment where administration was collaborating with teachers.

Targeted tutorials were held each Saturday and Q, the renaissance man, would grill burgers and hot dogs. This drew students to a tutoring session like bees to honey. The students would round the corner and smell the grill smoke coming across the courtyard and sprint to get in line for the food. They had a new energy and their desire to achieve was growing. To enhance math scores our students were able to participate in a global online event that allowed them to compete in random contests, against students from 240 other countries, solving mathematical problems. A big screen that showed a map of the world was set up on the stage in the cafeteria. In a matter of moments, a student was competing against a middle school student in Europe or India. Many of the voluntary participants were from our Engineering program. I used to keep my distance from them. They were too smart.

CHAPTER FORTY-NINE

"LIE DETECTOR AND THE HIDDEN CAMERA"

Todd, a frequent flyer, had a steady pattern of discipline referrals. Sitting in my office he put his head down, distraught. "Todd, are you okay?" I asked.

"No," he blurted out. He began to sob uncontrollably. Ms. Sites, Secretary in Student Services, closed my door so the myriad of students couldn't witness his meltdown.

"Todd, what's wrong?"

"It's my mom," he said, gasping for breath. "She died."

"Oh no," I said. "I'm so sorry."

"She just died. I don't want to talk about it."

"Okay," I said as I patted him on the back. "Do you want me to call someone, maybe your dad?"

"He said I should go to school."

"Are you able to stay in school right now?"

"I'll be okay, Mr. Neal. Can I go back to class?"

"Are you sure you're up to it?"

"Yes," he said as he regained his composure.

DR. JEFFREY W. NEAL

"Todd, don't worry about the referral. You're dealing with a lot. I'll explain to your teachers what's going on, okay?"

"Thanks, Mr. Neal," he said. He left Student Services. I emailed his teachers explaining that Todd lost his mother. I put a sticky note on Frank's desk. Deaths in the family get top priority in a counselor's never-ending to-do list. Dad's day time phone was right down the street at Wayne Aker's Ford. I called to offer condolences.

"He's on the floor right now. Let me check if he's with a customer. Just one moment please," the sanitized politeness coming through the receptionist's voice. "He'll be right with you, Mr. Neal."

"Thank you," I answered. Five minutes passed.

"Hello," answered the dad with an irritated voice.

"Hi, this is Jeff Neal from Lake Worth Middle and I—"

"What'd he do now?"

"Um, I was just calling to offer our sincere condolences for your loss, sir. If there's anything the school can do."

"What loss?"

"Todd told me of the passing of his mother."

"The passing of his mother, are you kidding me? Hell, she's not dead. He told you that she's dead! Unbelievable. I have to go!" The dial tone hit my ear.

"Ms. Sites, do you remember the boy crying in my office?"

"Yes, he sure was upset," Linda responded.

"His dad told me that he's lied about his mother's death."

"No," Linda said. "He sure looked like he was crying."

"Linda, please call him down for me?"

"My pleasure." In comes forlorn looking Todd.

"Todd, the school has a policy of sending flowers to the funeral home when parents pass away. What funeral home will your mom be seen for the viewing?" Todd shifted in his chair.

"Ah, she didn't want to be in a funeral home," he said just a trace of nervousness surfacing. "She's getting cremated."

"That's interesting I just talked to your dad." Todd's eyes bugged. "Todd, do you know what teachers used to tell me when I got caught in a lie?"

"No," he said, looking straight at the floor.

"The jig is up. That's what they told me. So, Todd, the jig is up. Your mom's not dead."

"No, she's not."

"Let's see here," I said, looking for the referral that brought him in my office. "You have one day of ATS for disrupting class and two additional days for Lying/Misrepresentation."

"Three Days!" Todd exclaimed.

"Todd," I said handing him his referral. "You should think about going into drama. I thought you were really crying. Get an audition for the School of the Arts." He smiled and left Student Services. Over the years I've heard "stories" from students that are miraculous. I've learned to try to stay ahead of them. Take for instance the case of Lori, the girl who was fighting on the first day of school. She was addicted to spraying the school with graffiti. One day she went overboard in the girl's rest room near the eighth-grade wing. Valarie was infuriated when she saw the walls covered. It looked like Jackson Pollock was in there. She marched down to Officer Vargas's office. "The girl's eighth-grade bathroom is covered with gang graffiti!" Valarie shrieked walking into the office.

"Let me check the camera," Vargas said. "It was probably done after the class change." Danny had quite a story working as a street cop in Boynton Beach and later with the DEA. After viewing the footage, he said, "Look, we have someone."

"That's Lori. We got her!" Valarie exclaimed. "It had to be her. Look how she ran out of the bathroom. I'm going to call her down and suspend her. You should arrest her."

"Easy," Danny said. "We have no proof she did it. It will be her word against ours. We'd have to get a confession out of her. She's from the streets and it will be a cold day in hell when she gives a confession."

"Are you serious Vargas," Valarie said. "She's guilty!"

"I could get her to confess," I interjected.

"Bull shit," said Danny. "That girl will never give herself up.

"Yeah Neal, Vargas is right," Valarie added resignedly.

"You two care to take a wager on this," I said.

"I like this action. What are we betting?" Danny said.

"Yeah, Neal what do you want to bet. There is no way Lori will confess," Valarie added.

"How about this. I will make it easy on you. When I get her to confess you two go halves on a bottle of twelve-year-old Scotch. If she doesn't confess, I will get you whatever you want."

"I'll have a twelve pack of Heineken," Danny said.

"You can get me The Hen," Valarie replied.

"The Hen?" I asked. "What's that?"

"Hennesy, Neal."

"All right, sit tight. I'm going to get a confession."

I retrieved Lori from her class. She didn't say anything and neither did I as we walked down the hallway. Finally, she yelled, "Where are we going?" I just waved for her to follow me and she stood her ground.

"I deserve to know where we're going?"

"Okay, Lori," I said, motioning for her to come closer as I hushed my voice. "I shouldn't be telling you this."

"Tell me what?"

"The sheriffs are on their way over," I said.

"The sheriffs! For what? I didn't do anything."

"If that's the case you'll be fine. Let's go to Vargas."

"Wait, what the fuck is going on?"

"Okay, I don't know why I'm telling you this," I said, looking around to see if anyone was listening. Lori drew closer. "Lori, they know you tagged the girl's bathroom."

"What! You got no proof!"

"That's why the sheriffs are coming."

"What do you mean?"

"Here's the deal. Ms. Jones checked the eighth-grade bathroom and the walls were clean. Then, someone went in and tagged all over the walls."

"You still have no proof," she added with a stiff upper lip.

"Vargas saw you on the cameras going into the bathroom during that period. So that gives him probable cause to investigate. He called the sheriffs and they are on their way over with a lie detector test. If you fail it you are going to get popped for criminal mischief and vandalism. Also, since you put up gang graffiti it will be coded gang related and that will be a mandatory ten-day suspension."

"Ahhh fuck!" Lori screamed at the top of her lungs. "I'm fucked. I'll be violated. Fuck, I was getting my fuckin' lojack off tomorrow."

"There is something you could do. Again, I don't know why I'm trying to help you."

"What?" she said a beseeching tone surfacing.

"There's one way to avoid the sheriff's lie detector."

"What!"

"If you confess to doing the graffiti then it becomes a school matter. I'll give you a couple of days at home and that will be it. You'll have to help the custodians clean the walls."

"Let me get this straight. I confess and there's no charges."

"Actually, you have to confess to Vargas."

"Fuck that. It's a done deal. C'mon," Lori said moving down the hall at a brisk pace. She was several yards ahead of me as she opened Danny's door. Valarie was still in the office.

"Hi Lori," Vargas said as he looked at me quizzically.

"I did it. I confess," Lori yelled. "I tagged the bathroom."

Valarie's jaw dropped and Danny smiled slightly. She stood there for a moment before saying, "So you can tell those sheriffs not to waste their time comin' for me 'cause I confessed."

"Sheriffs?" said Valarie.

"Okay," Danny said, getting my ruse. "No sheriffs, then."

"Yep," I confessed.

"C'mon Lori let's get your paperwork." I ushered Lori out quickly. It worked out nicely. She helped the custodians scrub the walls that she decorated. Valarie asked me how I got her to confess. I shared the lie detector technique.

"Lie detector, I'll be damned. That girl sure came in with a confession," Valarie said, shaking her head. This event got Vargas' mind going. All of those years on the street and working undercover he had a wheelhouse of experiences that he could mine to coerce confessions or return stolen items.

Cell phones are stolen every day. If a kid has a smartphone, he better look at it like he's bringing a gold bar to school. We were called to the Art room because a cell phone was taken out of a poor little guy's book bag. Danny motioned for me to step into the hallway.

"Give me a dollar," he said. He jotted down some numbers and handed the dollar back. "Follow my lead and keep that dollar handy," he said. We walked back into the classroom. "All right students I am going to give you fair warning." Danny said adjusting his holster. "There are two sets of cameras on our campus. There are those that are in the hallways and the ones you don't know about are in here. Every classroom has a camera." I could see the expressions of the class as they digested this information. "Right here," Danny said, pointing to a round object in the middle of the ceiling that was actually a fire protection system sprinkler. "I will be able to tell who took this young man's cell phone. If I have to go through this trouble, I will press charges on you. If the phone gets returned, you'll get off with a warning. Mr. Neal stay here and I will call you once the cameras are activated."

"You got it, Officer Vargas," I replied, enjoying this new technique. After a minute Danny's voice said, "Mr. Neal."

"Yes," I said into my walkie.

"Do you happen to have a dollar bill on you?"

"Why yes I do," I answered, removing it from my pocket.

"I just want the class to understand how accurate these cameras are that record everything. Hold up the bill and open it with the face of George Washington toward the camera." I opened the bill and held it up in the air. "Okay, I'm going to read the serial number to you. Ask a student to be a witness and look at the numbers to verify accuracy." I pointed to a girl who was more than happy to participate. Then he began to read the numbers slowly. He rattled off a letter and eight numbers and another letter. When he finished, he asked, "Young lady were those the letters and numbers on Mr. Neal's dollar bill that I read?"

"Yes, Officer Vargas," she said as the kids started to look around the room in amazement at the hidden technology. "Ok, class the camera is working. When I see who stole this phone you will be in handcuffs and transported to the juvenile detention center this afternoon. If I have to waste all my time you are going to take a ride. I will give you to the end of the day. If you give Mr. Neal or I the phone you'll get a warning."

Art teacher, Mr. Henson, called at the end of the period. He was with a boy who had his head down and handed Vargas the phone. The item was returned to the distraught boy. Danny spent the afternoon on the phone with the bandit's mother explaining how their son almost got arrested. He did get a warning and Vargas got him to agree to assist him with information. The hidden camera technique was another arrow in the quiver not to mention how to cultivate a Confidential Informant.

CHAPTER FIFTY

"LESSONS FROM NICKEL MINES"

As I was reading an article on Post-traumatic Growth by Richard Tedeschi, I sent a message email to him with my cell number. To my astonishment he called me no more than five minutes later. I presented the underpinnings of the research. He said, "I'll send you a copy of our inventory should you want to use it in your study." Johanna Nurmi emailed me questions she used in her case study. The words were in Finnish and fortunately, Ms. Niskanen, who was born and raised in Finland translated for me. Glenn Muschert, Johann Nurmi, and now Richard Tedeschi, took their time and effort to help an assistant principal on his quest to complete a dissertation.

Jesus had all stakeholders in boot camp mode as testing season had arrived. Twenty teachers were coming in on Saturdays to conduct tutorials in all tested subject areas: Reading, Math, Writing, Science, and Civics (Social Studies). Once again, a Q burger, bag of chips, and a soda of their choice were being served. High school students in the Teaching Magnet program from Lake Worth High were coming to tutor. Many were hoping to attain a Barry Grunow Scholarship to help with the exorbitant tuitions coming their way. Jesus was running a Parent University in the evenings. The ICAN after school program provided tutoring. Kids seemed more focused than they had been previously. There was a sense of urgency to achieve that wasn't present in other years. The Warrior Way had manifested itself on our campus. From March all the way through to April students tested and tested and tested. We had to wait until the summer for the results.

All administrators were in a conference at Forest Hill High School, run by Jeffrey Hernandez, Chief Academic Officer, when the district got the scores. At a break everyone got on the cell phones to find out how they did. Lake Worth Middle was a B! That may not seem like a big deal, but for years the Warrior Family was told that we were lucky to make a C. The raise in a letter grade was validation of everyone's hard work and that our kids were just as bright as students in other schools. Shortly thereafter Jesus found out that he was being placed at Royal Palm Beach High School. Ironically, my old friend Jose was exiting that school. One Cuban friend was handing over the reins to another Cuban friend.

I got a call from Jeff Eassa. He started his career at Lake Worth Junior High with me as a Social Studies teacher. Jeff moved up to be a principal at an elementary school. He got a call from the Superintendent informing him he would be coming back to good old Lake Worth Middle. I sang the theme song for Welcome Back Kotter to him. The names had changed since he'd been around. Someone asked me if I was upset that Jesus was leaving. I always think that if someone is pursuing a new goal it is to be celebrated. Jesus had vast high school experience and I knew he would take his voracious work-ethic to help transform Royal Palm Beach High.

That summer I decided to dive in and begin the arduous task of writing the dissertation. It was like all of the parts of a car were lying around on a garage floor and somehow you have to put them together. I reasoned if I could coin a title, it would help me get going. I came up with: "Post-traumatic Growth: A Case Study of Internal Stakeholders Who Experienced a School Shooting Involving Homicide." The problem under scrutiny was the need to uncover effective recovery strategies. Terms relevant to the study were to be defined. Acute Stress Disorder was a major component as those that experience a trauma show at least nine symptoms of this malady. A few of these are: (a) recurrent, involuntary, and intrusive distressing memories of the event, (b) distressing dreams, (c) dissociative reactions (flashbacks), and (d) negative mood and avoidance. Post-traumatic stress disorder (PTSD), of course, was addressed in the terminology. Depending on the size of the school, hundreds or even thousands, can be affected from a shooting. At the time I was writing the literature review in the summer of 2012, there were ninety school shootings since Paducah and Columbine. It always made me cringe when Lake Worth, Florida would appear in the list.

One evening at my mom's, I was reading studies. I'd read hundreds of accounts of shootings. However, the Amish shooting in Nickel Mines, Pennsylvania struck me as none other. A dairy truck driver in his twenties, entered a tiny, one-room school house. He ordered the fifteen boys to leave the school and then demanded that eleven little girls line up facing the blackboard. He tied them together and aimed his 9-millimeter semiautomatic at them and fired. He killed five of the girls, ages six to thirteen. Then, as is so often the case, he put a bullet in his head as the police stormed the schoolhouse. I put down the article and walked outside. The stars were out and the summer night air was cool. I couldn't stop thinking about those Amish girls in their dresses and bonnets and how afraid they must have been.

"Mom, how far is Nickel Mines from here?" I asked.

"I'd say a good four hours," she answered as she watered some hanging plants on the patio. When I awakened, I began the four-hour drive through the rolling hills of Pennsylvania. As a child I remember looking at the Amish men in their buggies. They always looked like they travelled through a time machine and were transported here. I hadn't been in

Lancaster in years. The countryside began to look familiar as stone houses, barns, and silos started to appear. The farms were always immaculate with green lawns, freshly painted white barns with everything in its place. A few buggies with the men in straw hats appeared complete with corn cob pipes jaunting from their mouths. I saw a sign for Nickel Mines. I asked an Amish woman, standing next to an antique shop, the location of the Nickel Mines Amish School. She pointed down the road. It didn't look like the small white school-house I'd seen in pictures. I walked up to a fence and could see Amish boys, at a baseball diamond, playing a fast-paced game. I looked over a cornfield and the beauty and simplicity of this small community breathed the agrarian lifestyle. The slight breeze brought a sound from chimes lofted from a nearby house. Then I heard a voice. "May I help you, sir?" I was startled as I turned to see a young, tall Amish man behind me.

"I was just, um, looking at the school."

"Ok," he said.

"My name is Jeff," I said extending my hand.

"I'm Abram," he said. I could feel his callouses made tough and thick from hard work.

"Abram, that's an interesting name."

"It's a contraction of Abraham, father of Issac."

"I see," I said knowing how faith is a big part of the Amish culture. Then I said, "I came here because of what happened six years ago."

"I thought maybe that is why you're standing here. We don't get a lot of visitors like we did right after it happened."

"I'm doing a study on recovery from a school shooting. I understand your community handled this tragedy really well."

"What do you mean a study?"

"I'm an educator in Florida and at my school we had a student shoot and kill a beloved teacher. I'm doing what is called a case study on how we recovered."

"Ah, I see," he said as I could feel his suspicion lessening. "I was here that day. In fact, I know the families that suffered the loss."

"Can you tell me about how you folks recovered?"

"A day of death of innocents," Abram continued with a heavy sigh, "Charles Roberts, was a milk truck driver, and he lived close to here. We found out later that he and his wife had a premature baby, their first child, named Amy. She died." He turned and looked at me as he talked. "Walk with me."

We headed up the street. "Charles blamed God for the loss of the child. It is believed that was why he committed the horrible act. He dismissed the boys and tied up the girls and had them face the blackboard." He took a deep breath as he continued, "Then he began shooting the girls. In all he shot ten, killing five."

"I can't imagine how horrific that was for the families of the girls," I said quietly.

"Yes, there was pain. We never forget Naomi, Marian, Anna May, Lena, and Mary Liz."

"How did the families of the victims cope?"

"They followed the guidance of scripture."

"Can you tell me about this?" I asked, immersed in what this kind gentleman in his straw hat was saying as we walked.

"There are many verses in the Bible that teach about forgiveness. I remember the one my father read the night of the shooting, "And when you stand praying, if you hold anything against anyone, forgive him, so that your Father in heaven may forgive your sins," Mark 11:25."

"So, the families coped through faith?"

"Yes, and we reached out to the killer's family with grace and forgiveness. No one hired lawyers. We went to the house of the family and let them know they were forgiven."

"That's amazing," I said. This culture was so different from the rest of the world.

"Also, there was much generosity from the outside."

"Like what?"

"The local community had barbecues to benefit the families of the victims. 3,000 motorcyclists did a ride that raised a lot of money. The whole country donated to a fund and eventually there was $4,000,000. One of the things we did with the money was raze the school and build the new one you were looking at today." Just then a chime sounded and I looked at the porch of the house we were passing.

"Those are beautiful chimes," I remarked.

"We put them up after the girls left us. As we hear the sound, we remember them." The long silver apparatus sent the gentle bell sound in harmony with the wind.

"Where are we going, Abram?"

"To my friend's house. I have a gift for you."

"A gift?" I asked perplexed.

"Here," he said, pointing to a small, white house. We walked up on the porch where a chime hung to the right of an old porch swing. The door was open and Abram spoke through the screen. "Caleb," Abram said.

"Caleb's not here," said a female voice. He's at the barn."

"Amity, this is Jeff."

"Hello," she said, looking through the screen. Amity wore a long dress and had her hair in a bonnet. There were several small children playing in the yard beside the house.

"I'm going to give Jeff a jug of the syrup," Abram said.

"Come in," Amity said as she pushed open the screen door. Stepping in the doorway the house was much like the yards and barns in the area, immaculate. There were no appliances that I could see. The place had a clean smell of lemons and vinegar. Abram led me back a small hallway on a wood floor to the kitchen. Once in the kitchen my eyes scanned the room. There was a gas stove, but I couldn't see a refrigerator. I noticed a wooden square piece of furniture, which looked like cherry, that was built into the wall.

"That's a beautiful piece," I said.

"That's the ice box," Abram said.

"Really? May I look at it?"

"Sure," he said opening up the insulated box that contained food items. Spread across on the table were various glass jugs of different sizes. They were all filled with syrup.

"Help yourself," he said.

I picked up the jug and studied the label. Pennsylvania Pure Maple Syrup with the Keystone shape of Pa. between two Maple leaves.

"Take it," said Abram. "It's my gift to you."

"I'd like to pay for it," I said reaching for my wallet.

"I insist," he said, stopping me from retrieving the bill fold. "My friend has a lumber farm near Shanksville on Route 30. He makes the syrup and we help him sell it."

"I came through there on the way here and saw where they have the Flight 93 Memorial," I added.

"Look for Stonebridge Woodworks just west of the memorial. Tell your friends about it. It's really delicious syrup. He boils the sap of the tree and adds water until the water leaves. All natural."

"Thank you so much," I said to this kind, Christ-like man.

"May God bless you on your quest to complete your study."

"Thank you for your kindness," I said walking out to the front yard. Amity was corralling kids into the house. I made my way back to my car, with the sound of the chimes growing fainter with each step. The Amish baseball game was still going on and a church bell sounded. It was hard to imagine in this peaceful, bucolic setting that such a horrific event occurred. Driving home after I passed the Flight 93 memorial, I saw the wooden sign. Turning left down a gravel driveway the friend came out of a barn where he custom makes kitchen cabinets, bookcases, and vanities. I told him about Abram's kindness and that I would tell my friends about his product. I bought a jug. He refused a picture with me. He explained that pictures can promote vanity and our forbidden. He did, however, give me a tiny package of maple sugar candy in the shape of the leaf. I dropped it in my coffee and it was the best sweetener I'd ever had.

The settings of the two shootings, Lake Worth Middle and Nickel Mines Amish School couldn't have been more different. The sound of the chimes still reverberating in my mind as I thought of the way they remember the five little girls. Summer was waning and another school year was coming.

CHAPTER FIFTY-ONE

"SANDY HOOK AND A GREEN LIGHT FROM PBCSD"

The year began with Jeff Eassa at the helm. Cooperative learning, inquiry-based instruction, differentiation, technology, and professional development were all being employed. Jeff had the common sense not to make a lot of changes. Coach Owen used to say a good administrator doesn't forget the shoes he was in while in the classroom. Jeff E. embodied this sentiment. On the doctoral front I had to slay this monster called a literature review. I searched for articles that correlated with my study. A term came forth that was the crux of what I was searching to understand, "organizational healing." The stages of healing that emerged from this phrase revealed many truths for me. Remodeling, Ceremonies and rituals, and Wound healing were all essential to recovery. A common thread to each study was that there was a before and after that divides their lives. It is in the after portion of that equation where everyone in the organization (school) needs to do their emotion work. A physiological and psychological war goes on for the entire school community that experiences a traumatic event.

Insights were gained from firsthand gut responses from leaders of schools that had homicides. Most felt they should sweep their emotions aside to help move the school forward. Each leader was aware that faculty and staff were taking their cues from them. Most of them emphasized that nothing in their background prepared them for the violence and shock after the shooting. Each leader had reflections that they never did enough and that without a crisis mentor their task would have been insurmountable. This brought to mind Bill Bond. Everything in my paper had to be in the writing style of the American Psychological Association (APA). Dr. Coleman suggested I hire an editor. I found Nancy Marble who lived in Pittsburgh. I saw it as a sign. There's something special about people from Western Pennsylvania. I sent off my introduction and literature review to her and kept my nose to the grindstone.

Basketball season had begun and James Smith was the coach. James is a serious Christian and an extraordinary mentor. Being a Black man who grew up in Belle Glade he saw a lot of the street while growing up. He offered players firsthand advice of the pitfalls of that life. One practice I admired is that he had the boys wear a shirt and tie on game days. I helped a few of them at the bus loop cross the wide end under the narrow end to begin the process of tying a tie for the first time. The boys stood out from the rest of the students and created a positive element to our student body. It was James who delivered some news to me on December 14 right before our Christmas break. Answering a discipline pickup, I saw him coming down the hallway. He was silent and I saw his eyes.

"Coach, what's wrong?" I asked.

"It happened again," he said as he stopped in his tracks.

"What happened?"

"A school shooting in Connecticut."

"At a high school?"

"No, little kids," he said as he took a deep breath. "He killed a bunch of them. It was a massacre. We got to pray for those poor people up there."

He walked away wiping his eyes with his shirt. I pictured little children torn apart from bullets and took two steps backward until my back hit the brick wall. Right away the horrific scene of the little Amish girls being lined up face first to a wall resurfaced in my mind. I knew that whatever happened that day was monstrously evil. Sure enough, as I learned what occurred, it was even more ghastly than I'd imagined.

Sandy Hook Elementary is located in Newtown, Connecticut. A small town with a rural New England charm. It was once billed as the safest place in America. It quickly became the new Columbine only worse due to the age of the children. As details emerged, I paid close attention. The gunman was a troubled soul named, Adam Lanza. He was a prototype of a shooter. That morning while the kids were in their classrooms, no one had any idea that Adam had just shot and killed his mother at their home. He destroyed the computer's hard drive to make gathering evidence difficult for what he planned to do on that fateful day.

His mother was an avid gun enthusiast and Adam gathered an AR-15, two semiautomatic pistols, and a shot gun before heading to the school. Once there he shot his way through a window that was next to the security door at Sandy Hook. The principal and a school psychologist confronted him and he promptly killed both women. The entire school was able to hear this encounter over the public address system. The school went into lockdown with kids being hidden and concealed in closets or bathrooms. Doors were barricaded with furniture and, in some cases, teacher's own bodies.

Lanza entered a first-grade classroom and killed fourteen six- and seven-year-old kids along with the teacher. He then went to another room where the teacher had hidden her students in a closet. The teacher positioned herself at the desk to portray an image that she was alone in her classroom. She heroically tried to misdirect the shooter by telling him that that her students were in the auditorium. Six of the kids panicked and made a run for safety and were immediately gunned down before Lanza murdered the teacher. The seven kids in the closet who didn't run survived.

Medical reports revealed that all of the victims were riddled with bullets being shot multiple times. Immediately proponents of gun control seized on the fact that Lanza was surrounded at home by an arsenal of weapons. He'd chosen the AR-15 and was able to burn through 30 rounds of ammunition in his magazines during the massacre. This allowed him to take out two classrooms in a matter of minutes.

The NRA said that the schools failed by not intervening in regard to Lanza's psychological problems. Like the shooters at Paducah and Columbine Lanza spent long hours playing video games. I remembered thinking of Bill Bond when he described the Paducah shooter as being in a "digital trance." Bond reported that those that didn't run in Paducah weren't shot, as was the case in Sandy Hook. Perhaps this is due to the shooters being used to moving targets in video games? The one thing that I kept thinking was how can the parents and community heal after that. Twenty first graders and six educators gone in mere minutes. The ensuing trauma inflicted that day was unimaginable to me. I wondered if Bond was going to fly there to assist the school.

The one thing we didn't have to deal with in the aftermath of our tragedy was hearing an American far-right radio show host, who is a conspiracy theorist, Alex Jones. At first, he put forth that the shooting was a false flag and didn't happen. Later he claimed that the government orchestrated the massacre as an elaborate plan to promote stricter gun laws. It is my understanding that the parents of the murdered children sued him and he had to pay for the damage he inflicted. The line should be drawn when your conspiracies involve people's children that were massacred. Sandy Hook gave me further conviction to carry on and finish my study. If there was anything that I could learn through my study that could help a school community to regains one's strength after living through a day like Sandy Hook then this was a worthwhile endeavor.

After the frenzied testing season, once again we were a "B." Dr. Coleman approved my proposal. On to Chapter 3, the Methodology section.

I contacted Dr. Orta. We spent a lot of time discussing the aim and purpose of the study. Eventually I came up with a formal purpose. She asked that I verbalize it. I said, "By examining the firsthand experiences of those in leadership at this school, a framework of protocols and practices that assisted in the recovery will be provided."

"Your next step are your research questions," Dr. Orta said. She was not unlike Yoda in the woods offering guidance to get this project off the ground. I set to work on my research questions. After some trial and error this is what came forth:

1.) What strategies and interventions were used for students and staff who were traumatized from experiencing a homicide on their school campus?

2.) What actions did those in leadership roles do that led to recovery and helped individuals to thrive and personally grow from the tragedy?

The participants in my study numbered forty individuals (36 teachers) with a four-member focus group. Administration with Bob Hatcher and Larry Ludwig was one group and Frank Mascara was the counseling component. Kevin Hinds didn't respond to my request to participate. Officer Baxter was the other participant. Eleven questions were put forth that centered around what practices helped to restore a sense of normalcy and healing to the school community. The final step before I could begin my study was to get approval from the Palm Beach County School District. Anyone who does research within the school district has to get approval from a certain department. I was sure that because there were no students involved in the research that it would be approved. However, nothing comes easy on the path to a doctorate. There were two and a half weeks left before the beginning of school. My phone buzzed and it was Jeff Eassa.

"Hi, Jeff," he said. "I've got some news today that was surprising. I was just informed that I would be the new principal of Woodlands Middle and their principal is coming to Lake Worth Middle."

"Who is the principal?"

"Her name is Tanya Daniel."

We talked a little longer and I told him that I enjoyed working with him and that I wished him well. Jesus, Jeff, and now Tanya means that our faculty would have three principals in three years. The teachers had to adjust to three different leadership styles. It took Sharon fourteen years to develop a sense of family in our school community. I met Tanya before school started and she asked me some interesting questions as to what my strengths were as well as weaknesses. She also gave Valarie, Jamie, and me a personality test that would indicate our leadership styles. She reminded me of M. Wayne in that she was very dedicated. She was the first one at school in the morning and the last one to leave. There were other changes on the horizon.

My old friend, Joe Owsley and his wife, Carolyn were moving back to Kentucky so she could be with her family. She had cancer. Joe called to let me know. "I'm sorry, Joe," I said, not knowing what else to say.

"Hell, we had a good run at Lake Worth Middle. I'm going to have to get used to the winter again."

"I'm going to miss you, Joe."

"We had some good times with those DOP kids, didn't we?"

"It was crazy," I added. "No one would believe those stories. Give Carolyn my best."

"I will, man," he said, his voice thick with emotion.

It was never the same without that stocky, old codger walking around with his coffee in the morning, telling every teacher he met, "It's gonna be all right." Jamie Thomas informed me that Jesus offered him an assistant principal position at Royal Palm Beach High. This was a good opportunity for him and the extra money wouldn't hurt being that he had two young daughters. His sense of humor would be missed as well as his keen knowledge of classroom instruction. As I waited on the district, I tweaked my questions for teachers and the focus groups. I couldn't begin the study without the district's green light. The first nine-weeks passed and still no word of approval.

Not only was I frustrated that I wasn't hearing from the district, there was a financial consideration. Each semester that passed, I had to pay an additional $1,600 just to be able to keep working on my study. I decided to reach out to someone whom I knew in the upper echelon. Mark Howard is the Chief of Performance Accountability for the Palm Beach County School District. Little did I know when I met him as he was teaching at Lake Worth High School and coaching soccer, in the mid-1980s, that a very astute mind lurked between his ears. I'd never expected that he'd have by all intents and purposes the most responsible position in the 11th largest school district in the nation. When I broke into the administrative world, I was amazed as he addressed thousands of administrators in a leadership summit about making data-informed decisions to drive achievement. His approach helped complicated pedagogical subject matters more accessible for academic coaches and APs. It had been many years since we'd spoken. When he answered, he had the same friendly persona I remembered. He understood my frustration. He said he'd make some calls. Once again, it is who you know in this world, and shortly thereafter, I received a letter granting me permission to conduct the study.

CHAPTER FIFTY-TWO

"Focus Groups"

Bob Hatcher was now the principal of Western Pines Middle. He asked Officer Baxter and I to join him to speak to his students in an assembly because a student brought a gun to school. Other students were aware and yet said nothing. This hit a little too close to home for Bob. We shared our experiences and he made sure the student body knew he wanted students to speak up when a weapon is present.

It felt surreal to interview Bob about what affected each of us in a profound way. He fielded my questions with great care. The importance of lockdowns and a Crisis Response Team was cited as was the superintendent's support during the event. The mobile crisis unit was mentioned as being imperative in the moment of crisis. As a new principal safety was his number one focus. Giving the staff opportunities to talk, in Bob's opinion, and letting the emotions pour out promoted healing. "Everyone needs to be heard," he said. Supporting the kids during the trial and the constant media presence was cited as the most challenging aspects of that time as a principal. He had to be ready to speak for the school community at every moment. He carries an awareness that tragedy can strike at any time. Interestingly, Bob stated that if he could go back, he would have stressed the academics less and been more focused on emotional support.

Next was former assistant principal, Larry Ludwig. Jesus once remarked that Larry is, "The nicest guy in the world." He left school the second year after the shooting and took a job at the district level where he ran the PNP program to prepare candidates for assistant principal positions. Mentoring potential administrators was a good fit, as he was an excellent one himself. I called him at his retirement home in Hilton Head Island, South Carolina. "Larry, how are you?" I asked.

"Jeff, it's good to hear your voice. I hear you're going for your doctorate."

"Yes, that's why I'm calling. Would you be willing to answer some open-ended questions?"

"Yes, I'd be glad to help. How about you send me the questions and I will write out my responses to you. That way I can think about them and, perhaps, give you more thoughtful responses." I sent him the questions via email. In three days, he sent back his responses. Larry mentioned the PTSD that was present for the entire school community. The coordinated effort between administration, guidance, and teachers was cited as necessary for recovery. He maintained that keeping a positive attitude was essential for one in a leadership role in order to be supportive of students and staff. He shared the same perspective as Bob, in hindsight, that he would have been more proactive with seeing people in need rather than concentrating on academics and discipline.

One of Larry's answers that I thought to be most insightful. He recalled, "This event took place when beepers were still present and cell phones were just coming onto the scene. The instant communication can be a great asset as well as a hindrance if not used properly. It is imperative to answer all questions from the media in a well-thought-out manner. Unfortunately, all too many times when students were asked questions by reporters located just outside school grounds the responses were often false, if fact-checked, and most assuredly they weren't qualified to give an accurate answer. Thirteen-year-old weeping victims were often ignorant theorizers when a reporter asked them to analyze the shooting at our school. This caused a lot of disinformation to be circulated about the events that occurred on May 26, 2000."

The guidance component was solely Frank. The morning I interviewed Frank, he was conducting another interview with Tanya to hire a new guidance counselor. The candidate chosen was a lady named, Cristelina Milan. "She was built for this place," Frank said excitedly," She speaks Spanish which is a plus but there is a wisdom to her. I want someone to fill my shoes as retirement is calling. To be honest I'm not looking forward to resurrecting those ghosts that have been lying dormant within me all these years." Frank's questions differed from the administrative query.

He was the grade-level counselor of the students who witnessed the shooting and became a prominent informal leader. He was tasked with counseling students who were the most traumatized and supporting students who had to testify in a nationally televised murder trial. This was the bulk of the "emotion work." When asked about the most therapeutic intervention Frank replied, "Probably the one thing, if I had to put my finger on it, was Art therapy. You remember when we passed out art supplies and the students made posters about Barry? Most of them who were in his class when he was killed wanted to send cards to his family. I believe this was very therapeutic. Posters lined the school gates and the fence became a makeshift memorial. This shower of love helped students and staff alike."

When asked if he'd change anything in retrospect Frank said, "I believe the students needed professional counseling. As guidance counselors we weren't trained to take on the conditions that manifested themselves in the kids. Under the time constraints there was no way to have the proper interaction between counselor and client. To get them to have the initial disclosure of what happened to them and explore that, was just impossible. To get to the other stages of counseling like getting them to commit to action, or provide an intervention, there was no way we could do it. We would have to have been relieved of all other duties. They needed in-depth counseling."

Two questions in their entirety:

Question 9: What was the most difficult part of the recovery process for yourself? Answer 9: The entire year I was drained physically, emotionally, and spiritually. It really took a toll on me taking on all of that pain that had manifested itself in the students and the staff. Support from the staff was an important factor in my recovery. I helped myself through helping others.

Question 11: What advice would you give to school counselors who are faced with the responsibility of counseling students who experienced a school shooting involving homicide? Answer 11: First, be ready to take on one of the main leadership roles in the aftermath. Seek counseling for yourself. You can't help others as effectively if you are wounded as well. Enlist professional mental health professionals, at the very least as consultants, to help navigate the world of pain that you are going to enter.

CHAPTER FIFTY-THREE

"OFFICER DUPREE"

Officer Dupree was my most potent technique to help students to acquiesce their disruptive behavior. Danny Vargas was monitoring who was active in the gangs, particularly, who was recruiting. One day after three Southside boys (a gang) exited his office he said, "I just wish we had something to hold over these kids. A suspension or detention doesn't cut it."

"I have a method that I've been working on for almost two decades. It's running to perfection right now," I said.

Danny said, "What's the method called?"

"Officer Dupree."

"What is Officer Dupree?" Danny asked.

Before I could answer a call came over the walkie. Two gang-oriented boys were caught skipping in the eighth-grade bathroom. There was the unmistakable smell of weed. Danny asked for me to search them while he looked in the rest room. It is legally more feasible for an AP to search a child for drugs or a weapon than a school policeman. Law enforcement needs probable cause where an administrator needs reasonable suspicion.

DR. JEFFREY W. NEAL

I always ask if there is anything in a pocket that will stab me. I had them take off their shoes as that was a common hiding place. I smelled their hands and the scent was there, but the bud was lost to the ages.

It was time to introduce Danny to Officer Dupree. I told the boys to follow us to my office. They sat down. I made a call from Frank's office to Max. He was working for Bob at Western Pines, as a library assistant of all things. He was available for our tactic. "I just talked with the principal," I said, looking at the boys seated across from my desk. One was leaning back reclining, the epitome of relaxation. The other was slouching both head and shoulders bent down looking bored and lazy. Neither made eye contact. "Ms. Daniel, approved you two for the new program. I need to call Officer Dupree."

"What program you talkin' 'bout," said the relaxed one with a tattoo of the smiling and crying faces that are popular in gang culture. For every smile there's a tear. I began the ruse.

"What's your name again?" I asked.

"Juan."

"Okay, Juan you see the school district is piloting a new program since we have a gang culture at our school."

"What new program, man?" his voice raised, showing agitation.

"This is a special school to help with our gang problem."

"You can't just put us in a school. You need our parents' permission. We have rights!" the boy with the tattoo said.

"That's not necessarily true," Danny said, sensing where we were going in this subterfuge. "You see if we can show that you are an active gang member, then you lose those rights due to the RICO statute."

"What's that?" the boy asked indignantly.

"Racketeer Influenced Corrupt Organization. RICO. It was created for gangsters, but in the 1980s, before you were born, it was expanded to help with gangs."

"It's why everybody gets locked up," said the other boy.

"That's right," added Danny. "It's a crime just to belong to a criminal organization."

"That's why we can just send you packin'," I verbalized. I dialed Max and put it on speaker phone.

"Good afternoon, this is Jeff Neal, Assistant Principal at Lake Worth Middle. I'm looking for Officer Dupree."

"This is Officer Dupree," Max answered. Danny's eyes widened as he recognized the voice. He'd met Max before.

"Yes, Officer Dupree we spoke the other day. I think we have some candidates for your school."

"Oh, good good. We need a few more. In fact, I am going to Lake Worth High right now to pick one up. I can swing by your school. Are they boys or girls?"

"Two boys," I replied.

"You can't just pick us up!" Juan protested.

"Who is that speaking while we're having this conversation," Max said his voice changing to a stern tone.

"That's one of the candidates for your program," Danny said, entering the deception we were perpetrating. "This is Officer Vargas."

"Officer Vargas, how are you?" Max said genuinely happy that he was present and participating. "It's been a long time. Mr. Neal, back to business, you only have two today? What were they doing to get in your office?"

"Skipping and smoking weed in the bathroom."

"You got no proof," the boy said.

"Boy, you're going to learn to keep that mouth shut when you're at my school," Max said voice rising.

"I'm not going to your school," he said defiantly.

"Here's a little information for you. I will speak in terms you understand. You don't run this. You are going to enter such a shit storm that it will make your head spin faster than your little stoned mind can

DR. JEFFREY W. NEAL

handle." The boy said nothing looking at the phone as Max asked, "What size are these boys?"

"Medium," I said.

"Good, because I have so many students in large uniforms."

"Uniforms, what uniforms?" the boy said his voice cracking.

"Is that that boy talking again? Let me tell you something, boy. You don't talk unless I tell you too. You have a uniform at our school, just like prison. You'll get used to it. Mr. Neal, did you tell them what type of school we run?"

"No, I was just getting to that when I called."

"Allow me to enlighten them. You are being placed in a residential alternative school. Do you know what that is?"

"No," the boys answered in unison.

"A residential school is one that you live on the premises. We take your cell phones. You wear a uniform every day. You take your classes and eat when we tell you to eat. Your grades must be up and your behavior perfect before we release you to your home school."

"You can't do that," the boy said his voice weakening.

"Welcome to the real world. Mr. Neal, I can be there in twenty minutes to pick them up." Both boys were sitting up straight and quiet.

"You know Officer Dupree, I've been thinking."

"There you go thinking again. Don't tell me you want to give these boys a chance?"

"Let me talk to them," I said. "I will call back."

"Don't be soft on them Mr. Neal. They need to come to my school. There are some big boys from high school that will keep them in line."

"You have high schoolers mixed with middle school kids? Danny asked.

"Yes, Officer Vargas we have seventh through twelfth grade."

"Wow, how does that go?"

"Not good for the little fishes in the big pond like those two sitting in front of you."

"I will call you back, Officer Dupree."

"Good, do it."

As I hung up the phone Danny knew exactly what we needed to do. It was a classic case of Good Cop/Bad Cop. Officer Dupree was the Bad Cop and we now were the Good Cops. They each had a stunned look as I began, "Both of you really aren't bad kids. You've made some bad choices getting in the gang and all, but I haven't heard one complaint from a teacher that you are disrupting their classes."

"I haven't either," Danny said.

"Let me check your grades, attendance, and discipline. Give me your student numbers." Each students had straight F's and were chronically truant. "Look," I continued, "it would be easy for me to let Officer Dupree pick you up and place you in his program. Two less students we have to worry about. But, if you two want to change a few things I will put you on double secret probation."

"What's that?" the quiet one asked.

"It means that as long as you do a few things differently, you can stay at Lake Worth Middle for now."

"Like what?" Juan asked.

"Like attending school. Like getting to class on time and not skipping."

"Like not smoking weed in the bathroom," Vargas said.

"Also, I'm going to ask you to have this filled out by your teachers every week," I said handing them a progress report where a teacher circles daily whether they were on time, not disrupting class, and doing their work.

"You two going to do this?" I asked.

"Ok," said the quiet boy.

"How about you, Juan?"

"Yeah, I'll do it."

"Officer Vargas you are a witness to this agreement. Let's shake hands on it." The boys stood and we all shook hands. "Sit down," I said. "You're both on double secret probation now." I dialed and Max answered on speaker phone again. "Officer Dupree we have a change of plans."

"Oh, don't tell me you are giving these two a pass. Let me take them. It's what they need!"

"They have both agreed to do a weekly progress report. If they don't do it, I will call you right away," I said.

"Okay, but you are wasting your time with those two. I predict I will have them in a uniform and a bed in under two weeks."

"I think they can do what they need to and stay at our school," I retorted.

"We'll see," Max said.

"Thank you for your time, Officer Dupree."

"Nos vemos luego," Max said as he hung up.

"What did that mean?" I asked.

"See you later," answered Danny as his dad was Puerto Rican and he speaks Spanish fluently. The boys walked to the glass door and entered the hallway. When the door closed Danny smiled and said, "That got their attention. What a great tool."

"Max and I have been doing this for years. There are a lot of kids on double secret probation walking around here."

"I had to work at not laughing when you said that. All I kept thinking about was Animal House. I have an idea that we can use to improve the Officer Dupree technique," Danny said enthusiastically.

"Let's hear it. There's always room for improvement."

Danny recorded his supervisor pulling up on the cameras in a school police car. We alerted Max that when we call him, he is to act as if he is out front about to come in for the wayward student. The student's eyes would widen as Danny showed them the screen as Max would say, "I just pulled up to the front." We would then offer the student double secret probation. Danny's idea of the camera footage took "Officer Dupree" to another level.

CHAPTER FIFTY-FOUR

"Emerging themes and an EdD"

The last participant of my focus group was the school policeman in 2000, Matt Baxter. If you remember, his team won the county championship in boys' soccer. Matt rose in rank to Lieutenant supervising multiple schools in northern Palm Beach County. Like Larry he opted for answering the questions in written form. Matt explained there was tremendous pressure on him to assure students, staff, and parents of students that safety was paramount. He always considered himself proactive in providing a secure campus, but he stepped up his efforts after the shooting. He described his actions as hyper vigilant. When asked about successful therapeutic interventions that contributed to the healing process, he mentioned the Barry Grunow Hustle Award as a great way to remember him. Matt testified in the trial and it bothered him having to watch those kids have to get up on the stand and relive the incident. He commented that testifying took away much of their innocence. He recalled the staff was very protective of them, particularly Bob Hatcher. He mentioned it helped to face the pain head on. He recalled debriefing with colleagues as being most helpful in the recovery process.

As a researcher in a qualitative study, I needed to look for emerging themes. The thirty-six teachers received their open-ended questions that were tailored to elicit their experiences in the recovery period. Most mentioned professional counseling should have been utilized more. The faculty becoming a family was emphasized as one of the factors that helped bring about solidarity. The participants highlighted that becoming a better person, empathetic, stronger, and resilient came about through the process of healing. The district being sensitive to our needs was mentioned. When a kid said something to a teacher like, "I'm going to be the next Nate Brazille," the next day he was transferred to another school. Being threatened by a student with death is a routine feature for teachers in classrooms today. Nothing was ever done about it before because it was so common. It helped deter threats when a student was immediately placed in another school or setting. Kids started to think about the consequences of what they were saying.

Without a doubt the media was perceived to be an obstacle by all participants. The reporters were like sharks circling with cameras to interview twelve-year-olds to make a comment. Many of the teacher's responses mirrored the focus group. I read all responses and coded them on index cards. Seven common themes emerged:

Theme I: Counselor's Role in Recovery for Both Students
and Faculty:

A consistent response from participants regarding the recovery process was the role of the counselor. Many teachers understood Frank's group work, or crisis work, was very instrumental in the student's recovery. He helped to reduce the psychological symptoms that manifested themselves in the kids. Also, the staff reported that counselors provided support for teachers in an informal manner. This is true as teachers often enter a counselor's office and let out the frustration of the moment. It is a natural environment to debrief.

Theme 2: Strategies that Created a Sense of Solidarity:
Participants reported that hiring a Greyhound bus to transport faculty to the funeral of Barry promoted a sense of solidarity. One respondent said, "This simple act of boarding a bus together to grieve galvanized the staff." Working with the committee to create memorials helped establish a sense of community, an essential coping mechanism in the wake of tragedy. Lynn Sands-Collins ran a prayer group and this created spiritual guidance, relief, and unanimity. The concept of being a family was emphasized.

Theme 3: Hiring a New Principal from Within Rather
Than an Outsider:
Many participants remarked that it was a comfort that Interim Superintendent, Ben Marlin, decided to promote Bob to be the principal as opposed to bringing in an outsider. It was wise of Marlin to make that call even though it was widely criticized, especially, by those hungry to land a principalship. Many responses mentioned the word relief in regard to this decision. As one respondent said, "An outsider would have been more to deal with in our heads. We were dealing with enough at that time." Having someone from the family, if you will, helps to restore a sense of normalcy.

Theme 4: Social Gatherings and Storytelling That Served
as Informal Group Counseling Sessions:
Almost a unanimous response from participants was the role that social gatherings had in the healing process. The administration set up a phone tree in order for us to have access to each other for support. What morphed out of that was that

social gatherings started to occur. These were not parties. We were too wounded to be jovial. It was sort of pot luck as far as food. Maybe someone would play some acoustic guitar by a fire in a back yard. Instead of the usual banter and playfulness, the staff would break off into pairs, or small groups and share. Sometimes it was a fond story or memory of Barry that would be the dialogue. One participant gave what I thought to be an excellent response, "The social gatherings allowed me to listen to others and myself, and through the exchanges we were able to come to grips with the abnormal circumstances we were faced with." Many respondents reported that given the chance to tell stories about Barry helped them to recover more quickly. The support among those who have a shared common experience cannot be underestimated. The social gatherings dramatically reduced our distress, increased our self-efficacy, and helped us to meet the challenge of going on after the unthinkable.

Theme 5: Memorialization as a Therapeutic Intervention: Without exception participants reported that memorials were therapeutic and cathartic in the healing process. The memorials that were named in their responses were: butterfly garden, gymnasium dedication, and the dance recital. The Barry Grunow Hustle Award was mentioned. The creation of the Barry Scholarship Fund was, perhaps, the most powerful of the memorials. One respondent remarked, "Knowing that young, aspiring educators are receiving scholarship money in Barry's name gave me a sense that he is being remembered and that his legacy will live on." Memorials are a historical touchstone that link the past to the present. When Pam hugged the band director, recipient of the scholarship fund, from Bear Lakes

Middle at the tenth-year memorial, it was poignant. That tool had gone full circle.

Theme 6: Safety Modifications

There was a need for a sense of safety amongst the staff as we all had Sanctuary Trauma. That event shouldn't have happened on our school ground a locus that was to be a place of refuge and safety. For many just walking on the campus brought symptoms of PTSD. Many respondents stated that the work done to upgrade our safety procedures greatly helped in the healing and coping processes. The addition of the police aide who checked each and every person coming and going on campus helped to reduce the anxiety of the staff. The cameras were updated which created a sense of security. One participant remarked, "All comfort and security were gone for us at our workplace. The extra attention to safety was paramount to our recovery as a school community."

Theme 7: Art Therapy

A majority of participants named art therapy as one of the most effective tools that were employed in the immediate wake of the tragedy to begin the healing process. Providing the space and encouragement to create drawings, posters, photo albums, and letters was immeasurably helpful to both students and staff. The makeshift memorial on the chain-link fence at the entrance of the school gave us a sense we were remembering Barry. I'm sure it was therapeutic to the students who created gifts for Pam using this mechanism for coping and healing, and may have helped her as well.

With the help of my editor and Dr. Orta's guidance, I took this information and finished Chapters 4 and 5. I submitted the dissertation. In a few weeks I received confirmation that the two letters before my name would change. No one was more surprised than me. It would have been nice if M. Wayne would have been able to see this accomplishment. I called his old friend, Walt. He still had a sharp mind and maintained that those two letters would open doors.

CHAPTER FIFTY-FIVE

"MARJORIE STONEHAM DOUGLAS"

Tanya moved on to the area office. She was a dedicated professional and her attention to detail was unequivocal.

One of the things that was one of her best practices, in my opinion, was she had each administrator write a positive personal comment about each employee. It was a lot of work, but many teachers appreciated the validation. I learned a lot from her. The next contestant as principal was Mike Williams, who previously was an Assistant Principal under Jesus Armas. It's a small world. This was 2018 and my 33rd year as a Warrior. Frank Mascara retired and left some big shoes to fill in the Counseling Department. He felt confident he was leaving the department in good hands with Ms. Milan and Ms. Dunkley. Vargas wanted a change and the new officer was Bryce Tai. He was a former student and a protege of Sam Rolle's drum line. He credited Mr. Rolle for being a role-model and instilling discipline during his time as a Warrior.

Walking on the cement all day, I developed Plantar fasciitis in both feet. I started to wear a pair of black Puma sneakers instead of dress shoes.

It was a move I should have made years ago. One morning supervising the courtyard I knew something was brewing. Three decades had afforded me a sixth sense that allowed me to see things before they occur. I thought of asking Mike Williams to ring the bell as that can be a remedy when trouble is on the horizon. "There's something going down this morning," I said to Brian Wilkinson, AVID Coordinator and Social Studies teacher. Sure enough, as I uttered these words a group of students started to move toward the front of the gym by the butterfly garden. Peter Drolet, a pro-active Assistant Principal, was moving that way. The sound started. It always starts out like a low rumble when two combatants are squaring off. The numbers grow as the kids usually know who is going to fight. Then came the roar. "Oh shit!" Brian said as we picked up our pace. A circle always forms around a fight and you have to be like a defensive lineman pushing blockers out of the way to get to the fray. Drolet and a PE teacher had one boy and Brian and I got the other. Drolet walked toward the Main Office and we headed across the courtyard in the opposite direction. Just when I thought we averted chaos another fight broke out across the yard.

"Keep him with you," I said to Brian who had the boy's arm. "Don't let go of him!" I yelled. It dawned on me that was what Coach Owen yelled to me in 1985. Not a whole lot had changed. Kids know that if fights are spread out it's harder for us to intercede. All said and done this continued until a total of four fights had erupted. Ten students were suspended that morning. I was still breathing hard as I stood in student services filling out the referrals with Pete Drolet and Yolanda Gregory, another Assistant Principal.

The fight originated from something posted on Instagram. Whenever I investigate the root cause of a clash between students it was something posted on one of these platforms. Particularly disturbing that day was an area administrator who happened to be on campus. He said, "The days of going hands on are over." It begs the question, how are you supposed to break up a fight? The other part of technology that concerned me as an educator is the use of cell phones. These allow 1,200 students to be amateur videographers recording live events at any moment of a school day. At any time when you are intervening in a fight or confronting a bully there are forty cell phones in the air with the little light on recording. Teaching at a college as an adjunct professor was starting to look pretty good. About a week after the fight in the courtyard the curse struck again. It was Valentine's Day. Mike's baritone voice summoned me to his office. He was on the phone and as he hung up his face was distraught. "I have some disturbing news," he said as he motioned for me to sit down. He began, "Today at a high school in Parkland Florida there was a shooting."

"Where? What school?" I asked my heart skipping a beat. My first thought was that I hoped it wasn't at an elementary school like Sandy Hook.

"Stoneham Douglas High."

"Casualties?"

"Yes, but they aren't releasing any details."

"You all right?" he asked in a caring tone. "I know this is a sensitive issue for you."

"I'm all right," I lied. "Thanks, Mike."

As I walked out of the Main Office the same gnawing sensation of anguish mixed with foreboding arrived. I digested the news. Valentine's Day of all days was when an expelled and very disturbed youth named Nikolas Cruz decided to visit Marjory Stoneman Douglas High School and open fire in the Freshmen building with his legally purchased AR-15 rifle. As he loaded his gun in the stairwell, he warned fifteen-year-old student, Chris McKenna, "You better get out of here. Things are going to get messy."

On the first floor Cruz opened fire shattering windows and shooting through doors murdering eleven people and injuring thirteen others. Moving to the second floor he fired but hit no one. He ascended to the third floor where he killed his last six victims. He went to the faculty lounge where he set up a bipod, and began firing sniper-like at the fleeing students outside. Thankfully there was hurricane glass or there would have been more fatalities. He then blended in with the students who were leaving in masses and was later apprehended at a McDonald's. Parkland, once billed as the "safest city in the state" was devastated.

That night I couldn't sleep. I knew the immeasurable pain that was going on with the student body and community that was thirty minutes away. The next morning, I went to my office early and began writing to the principal of Stoneman Douglas. I told him that I'd done my dissertation on best practices in recovery from a school shooting. I went into great detail and offered to come down to speak to their faculty. Just as the last day of school was forever changed for us at Lake Worth Middle, Valentine's Day will never be the same for those who were at Stoneman Douglas that fateful day. As I read over what I'd written to the principal, I decided to take a leap and send it to our then Superintendent, Dr. Robert Avossa. My thought was that maybe he would be able to open the door for my attempt at aiding their school community. I fully expected to not get a reply from the man who was running a school district with 21,000 employees.

To my surprise the next day he emailed me and said he would send my communique to Robert Runcie, the Superintendent of Broward County Schools. I never heard from Runcie. This didn't surprise me. After a school shooting all stakeholders are in a whirlwind. Something interesting did arise from the havoc and loss at Parkland. The student survivors took to the streets in the same spirit as those in the late sixties did protesting the Vietnam War. At one of the candlelight vigils the students started to chant, "No More Guns!" Many of the survivors from Stoneman Douglas took to social media to make their anger known at the ease at which a disturbed kid like Cruz could purchase an AR-15. One student named, David Hogg, who was a newspaper reporter at the school became somewhat of an overnight celebrity. In a CNN interview he articulately begged lawmakers, "Please take action." Using Twitter, Instagram, Facebook, and Snapchat he and his fellow crusaders created a student-led demonstration called March for Our Lives (MFOL). Some 200,000 people marched that day along with 880 sibling events around the United States and the world. Many schools in Palm Beach County had walk-outs led by students. The youth believed this could be a tipping point for gun control legislation.

There was some action taken by then Governor Rick Scott. So much pressure was on him to do something that he, even with his A rating by the NRA, signed the Senate Bill 7026 that imposed a 21-year-old legal age requirement for gun purchases and a three-day waiting period. This made sense to me. I have been standing in front of our campus with hundreds of students walking to the cafeteria in the morning from their busses. It would take one drive-by with an automatic weapon to cause carnage and devastation that I don't want to imagine. The controversial part of the bill was that teachers can carry weapons to school. I'm not sure if that is a good idea. The mantra could change from someone going "postal" to one going "educational." Florida passed a $67 million "school marshal" program that stipulates arming teachers in classrooms.

There's so much tied to this topic. Listen, I'm from Western Pennsylvania where the men are men and the sheep are nervous. Most of my friends hunt and have weapons. Often, it's a family affair. They respect the animal they hunt. There's a rifle in my house in Pa. We have that right. Is the slippery slope that slippery that we can't have some red tape to possess weapons that are designed for war? No country in the world has the mass shootings we do in the U.S.A. The NRA stipulates that schools need to do a better job of recognizing students with psychological issues who are potential shooters. This is true. There were warning signs with Nikolas Cruz, but when you have thousands of students on a campus the idea of identifying the next shooter is like finding a needle in a hay stack. The Columbine shooters didn't stand out to their peers or parents, let alone the school. The 2018 school year wound down three months after this sad chapter from Parkland. Along with Marjory Stoneman Douglas there were twelve other school shootings with more than thirty people killed. This contagion was not going away.

CHAPTER FIFTY-SIX

"END WITH FOND FAREWELL TO THE WARRIOR FAMILY"

My thirty-fourth year in Warrior Country had arrived. Officer Mitchell came aboard and he would be the last school policeman that I would work beside. He is a veteran and a former Rivera Beach Police officer. From the old school he could say things to young Black youth that they need to hear that would have been impossible for me to utter. The thought of making my exit stage right into retirement started to wedge its way into my thinking. It was strange as I began to think what it would be like not to have a school year. After some calculation I was deeply disturbed to discover that students from my first year of teaching would be forty-seven years old. I began to look for discernment as to the path I should take. I was looking for a sign.

It came in the form of a childhood friend by the name of Bill Zadernak. Big "Z" was his nickname. He was a big man and a remarkable athlete. After college he moved to Georgia with his high school sweetheart and began his teaching career. "Big Z" taught for several years and then slid into an Assistant Principal slot, eventually becoming a principal. After thirty years he decided it was time to leave education. Six months into his retirement he called me to let me know he had leukemia. It didn't seem possible. He had a time-share in Riviera Beach. "Jeff, it's the Z-man. I'm in town. Let's get some lunch?" I drove to Riviera Beach to his Marriot time-share. "The doctor tells me inside I'm like a seventy-year-old man," he said with his strong voice being the one familiar thing about my old friend. "You know, Jeff, I see things differently now. I knew everything about good instruction. Going into classrooms for observations I knew what to look for to see if kids were engaged. I knew curriculum front and back and could put together a master-schedule with the best of them. I had a real passion for being a principal. I was good at it. The sad thing is, I didn't get one good year where I could fish, golf, and do some of the projects around the house that I wanted to do for years. Now it's done. I don't have too long left on this earth."

"Bill, you don't know..."

"I do know Jeff," he said cutting me off. "Let me tell you something. When you can retire, go! Spending time with family and friends is more important than working. A few extra coins in your bank account doesn't mean anything when you're staring death in the eye." We finished our lunch. I talked with Bonnie, his wife, for a while and she thanked me for coming. Bill passed shortly thereafter. I got in touch with the district to find out the protocol for retiring.

I watched with more sentimentality as students filed off the busses each morning or laughed and talked while eating their chicken nuggets during lunch. When Ms. Peres and Ms. Flower, who were in Student Services my last year, were being extra patient with irate parents I called them angels. They started referring to me as "Charlie." Occasionally, I would go out when I heard a parent raise their voice and see if I still had the chops to de-escalate their anger. It is an art to take a parent with a full head of steam, red-faced angry and cool the fire.

A technique is to let them say everything they needed to say as if they were climbing a mountain. When they said all they had to there is a silence. I knew they were at the top of the mountain. Then it was up to me to speak softly and bring them slowly back down to where we could discuss the issue.

During this year an event was held that gave me the sense that my career had gone full-circle. Mike Williams had decided to implement an AVID (Advancement Via Individual Determination) program at our school. It places average students in advanced classes. It targets students whose parents haven't gone to college. It attempts to level the playing field for minority, rural, and low-income students. Mike put Brian Wilson, Social Studies teacher, at the forefront of this program as the AVID Coordinator. He was having guest speakers come in to motivate students. I told him that I knew some former students who would fit the bill. I called Cory Neering and Kelsey C. Burke. My thinking is that it would be powerful for our students to hear from someone who once was a student in Warrior Country. Cory was the first speaker that morning in the library. All of the students in the program, wearing their bright, red AVID shirts, were listening intently and taking notes. He explained how he went off to college with all of his worldly possessions in the back of his car. I believe he said he was the first in his family attending college. I smiled when he pointed at me and remarked how hard I ran him when he was a Warrior back in 1986. He showed footage of him doing his work as a West Palm Beach City Commissioner. He expressed the importance of them setting their goals and studying. Also, he conveyed the hard work he put in to earn a Bachelor's of Arts in Sociology and a Master's in Organizational Management from Springfield College in Massachusetts. This pillar of the community ended his talk by saying, "I was sitting in the same seat as a Warrior years ago. Set your goals and through hard work you can be anything you want." It was a soulful moment as through their eyes I could see he ignited their passion.

Next up was Kelsey C. Burke, Attorney at Law. She had come a long way since that conflict resolution her first few weeks in the United States as a young Warrior. She recalled her harrowing journey that began in Honduras, at the age of ten that landed her in Lake Worth. As Cory did, she recalled her start at Lake Worth Middle and the hard work and dedication it took for her to take Advance Placement classes at Lake Worth High School in their Criminal Justice Program. The students took notes as she told them that she put herself through college as she wasn't illegible for student loans. She was undocumented. Setting goals and perseverance were the two points she hammered home to the students. After Cory and Kelsey's articulation, they took pictures with the kids like they were rock stars. I left that library that morning with a deep satisfaction that an educator can experience when they see, firsthand, the fruition of many educators' hard work in two outstanding members of the community.

Day by day I attempted to extract myself from this organism that I was attached to for over three decades. Gradually, I cleaned out my desk. Looking at yearbooks brought back memories from the old junior high. Pictures of young Ant Man and Sammy Lee and the different teams I coached made me smile. All of the reminiscence delivered strong waves of emotion. The four nine-weeks rolled by and the days wound down to ten. As usual the last week was filled with banquets, concerts, academic awards, proms, and finally the 8th Grade Moving On Ceremony that was created by Mike Williams. It was held at the high school.

As I was the eighth-grade Assistant Principal, I was charged with being the Master of Ceremonies. It was interesting to look at this last class that I would supervise, looking very much like young ladies and gentlemen dressed in their suits and dresses. I gave out the Coach Owen Academic Award to the two athletes with the highest grade-point average and the Bobby Bartz Award started by Coach in memory of one of his student athletes who died from a snake bite. The female who received the Bobbie Bartz award was a girl named Ruth. She helped me in the bus loop each morning. I would give her a new vocabulary word each day. She liked "ambiguous." There is something special about her and I believe she will do something important in her life, much like Kelsey Burke. It felt good to mention Coach and hopefully pass along the traditions started by that kind man. The last award was the Mary Anne Hedrick Spirit Award that I presented to two eighth graders. Mary Anne was in the back of the auditorium watching from her wheel chair as the two students received the award inspired by her. Unbeknownst to me she was already planning a surprise retirement party for me. Sadly, a couple of weeks after my celebration she died unexpectedly. Her death coincided with the beginning of the quarantine lockdown. The Warrior Family lost a special soul with her passing.

The last day of school arrived. Around 3:40 I made my way down to Barry's old class room and had a moment of silence outside of his door. It was a shame that he couldn't continue his journey at our school. I believe he would have stayed in Warrior Country for the long run. The final bell rang and the kids filed out one last time and boarded the busses. As the last one went through the gate to Detroit Street, I performed a ritual where I kick the dirt as NFL football player Joey Porter would do after a tackle. Mike knew I didn't want a party and insisted that I couldn't just leave. He suggested we make a video. "I can come over to your condo and we'll go by the water and you can say your good-byes. I will play it at the first faculty meeting when school is starting."

"That I'll do," I answered. We made the video and it was fun wearing my straw hat and favorite Tommy Bahama shirt while drinking coffee on my beach chair. I tried to leave some tidbits of wisdom and express my heartfelt gratitude for my years as a Warrior. The many friendships that were born there were so much a part of the journey. At the end of the video, Mike panned away and had, "Dr. Neal, Lifetime Warrior" on the screen. I thought that was pretty cool. Ironically, my retirement date coincided with my birthday, July 22, 2019. That was my last day. A true two for one. It was summer and for the first time in my life I didn't have a deadline to another first day of school. I felt like an indentured servant that had been set free.

It was 1985 and this was Lake Worth Junior High School. Jeffrey Neal started his teaching career as an English teacher, which is what we now call Language Arts. This was his first job out of college and he was hired by Coach Owen who told him "if you can stick it out here it will feel like family".

Dr Neal says that students have stayed the same over the years and have been both challenging and rewarding.

The best thing here has been the relationships that he has made with students and staff and the feeling of family that has developed over the years.

Dr Neal is looking forward to traveling to the Caribbean and visiting family and friends. He will be spending time enjoying the beach, biking and golfing. Eventually he hopes to teach education at the college level.

He leaves Lake Worth Middle School students with the following advice: " follow your heart, and don't let anyone tell you you can't achieve your dreams".

Thanks for everything Dr. Neal! You will be missed.

We say goodbye to DR. JEFFREY NEAL

Goodbye

This was a page out of a Lake Worth Community Middle Yearbook as I was retiring.

EPILOGUE

MaryAnne Hedrick organized the party at Dave's Last Resort. Walking into the establishment no less than two hundred people yelled, "Surprise!" at the top of their lungs. It was so nice that all of them showed up for my bon voyage. They were taking decade pictures with representatives from 1985 all the way through to 2020. This was unexpected and my heart was touched. Three decades had passed and it had been an odyssey. There is a movie that I thoroughly enjoy by the Cohen brothers called, "Burn After Reading." At the end of the movie J.K. Simon's (Farmer's Insurance pitchman) character, who is a CIA. supervisor, asks the question, "What have we learned here, Palmer?" That is the question.

Coach Owen asked in my initial interview, "Do you have a sense of humor?" He was wise as it is essential to one's survival as an educator. Middle school is a most crucial phase of education, a period that can make or break a child. To take a child's hand and help them traverse the rough seas of middle school is truly an art. It is the last chance for a lot of them. Once in high school the die is cast and there is no turning back. You can still reach them in middle school. The master teachers I worked with never lowered their expectations for their students based on race or household income.

As I grew to understand my Black students, I noticed how sharp and quick they were with their wits. If you question this watch them "roast" each other. Students gather in a circle. My assumption was a fight was going to occur. There was a fight going on, but it wasn't physical. It was verbal combat. The weapons were language arts skills, particularly rhyming. Once an insult was delivered with a deftness that was like an arrow to the other combatant the crowd would yell with glee. Usually, the insults involved a mother. "Your mother's armpits are so hairy she looks like she has Buckwheat in a headlock." One of the students seeing that I was an interested spectator said, "Don't worry, O'Neal, we do this to avoid fights." One hurdle to help Black students it to help them understand that it is okay to be a good student. I've heard the statement to bright students who are excelling, "you're acting White." Often kids are more impressed with how well they fight or how many girlfriends, and not what type of grades they are earning.

Latin students need to hear about great Hispanic mathematicians such as Alberto Pedro Caleron and Run Luis Gomes. I always showed the movie *Stand and Deliver* that highlighted Jaime Escalante teaching his Hispanic students to pass an advanced placement Calculus exam. He taught them that math was in their blood. The state assumed they cheated when they all passed the exam. Escalante fought for his students and they passed a second time. I could see the pride in my students' eyes as they watched the film. The other thing you must become as a teacher is a detective.

The split-brain theory purports that you must discern whether they are Left-brain or Right-brain learners. It took me quite some time before I could observe a student and see if they had traits that were left or right in their thinking. Howard Gardner had a model that is, perhaps, the most succinct regarding learning styles. He had eight ways of learning: linguistic, logical-mathematical, spatial, bodily-kinesthetic, musical, interpersonal, intra-personal, and naturalist. It is a teacher's task to find out how each student learns and create lesson plans geared toward their learning style. Teach students the way they learn. Kids that have ADD need to move. Group work helps them. Any time I had an errand I would ask the hyperactive kid to go for me. It was like they were a horse being untethered.

Reading is paramount for each student to succeed in whatever their endeavors might be. It is not enough just to have a child to decode. Kids need to understand over 90% of the words in a text passage to understand a test question. I always use an example from E.D. Hirsch who Tom Long recommended for me to read in 1986. If a child gets a test question about hiking in the Himalayas and doesn't know the meaning of hiking or what the Himalayas are, then their chance of answering the question is nullified. Students must gain information of the world if they are to have a chance on tests of reading comprehension. Background knowledge is essential and one of the biggest challenges if you are working with students coming from generational poverty.

My experience afforded me the opportunity to be a teacher, coach, counselor, and an administrator. To become an administrator and truly do the job well you must realize that it is a time commitment. High School administrators put in ten- to twelve-hour days on a regular basis. They go to school when it's dark and return at night with the same lack of light. Principals are held accountable for the smooth functioning of the school house. They set the tone and their impact is significant. A measuring stick for an administrator is how many principals did you help groom. Sharon Walker had many of her proteges at the helm of a school. Jose Garcia, Marilu Garcia, Terry Costa, Ian Saltzman, Nicole Patterson, Jeff Eassa, Miriam Williams, Michael Berg and Bob Hatcher to name a few.

Guidance counselors, I like to refer to as my people. They are an indispensable part of the school community. To take on that job you have to have a heart as big as Texas. A middle school counselor has to guide students to navigate the quagmire of bullying, divorce, sexual abuse in the home, pressure to have sex, being pregnant, eating disorders, and cutting. Those are to name a few and not the big ones like suicide or maybe the student is a potential shooter. They also must support them in their academic pursuits. Counselors are key allies for kids and sometimes the only advocates a child lost in the wilderness of middle school knows. Counselors are the heart of the school community. They help assure that everyone belongs, matters, and is deserving of compassion and respect.

Teachers are my heroes and arguably are the most important members of our society. Good ones give kids purpose and set students up for success as citizens of the world. They are not just a helping hand or a mentor they inspire kids to work hard and push themselves. They help under-achievers to rise up and over-achievers to get grounded. Administrators, counselors, and teachers who create relationships are responsible for the survival of one of the "cornerstones of our democracy, public education." Thank you, Dr. Art Johnson for that quote.

Writing about my journey as a Warrior allowed me to remember being the eager young English teacher driving to Florida in my Green 1977 Mercury Monarch to inhabit the dilapidated classroom at the old Lake Worth Junior High. Coach Owen was bailing me out when I was throwing erasers at kids. The move to the new school with the school population nearly doubling was an incredible experience. Losing Barry and our recovery as a school community was tragic and extraordinary. I believe he would have been proud of how we carried on and remembered his legacy. M. Wayne cautioned me about going into middle school and dealing with those "ulcer breeding monsters." Some days I knew he was right. In the end I wouldn't have changed it. Lake Worth Community Middle School was a great place to be in the company of great teachers who "perform miracles every day." Mrs. Crandall, ELL teacher, coined that phrase.

Even though I'm not on campus anymore I know what's going to happen. So as you teachers put your date and learning objective on the board and ready your lesson plan, and the guidance counselors are tweaking schedules and thinking about the fifteen students that they have to help navigate through the minefield of the day, and administrators are looking at the stack of discipline referrals and thinking of all the evaluations that need to be finished, and the school policeman is thinking about the kid he needs to search to make sure the school is safe, and the custodians and cafeteria workers keep a clean school and feed everyone, all are working together as a team. In the best of all worlds, they are family. I was proud to be a part of the Warrior Family.

AFTERWORD

If you purchased and read this work please know that portions of all sales will be going to the Barry Grunow Memorial Scholarship Fund. The average cost for tuition in the United States is over $30,000. Since Barry's death hundreds of students, who are aspiring educators, have received partial scholarships for their Bachelor's Degree in Education. When the pandemic arrived the scholarship fund took a devastating hit. There were no more golf tournaments or fundraisers. To put it simply the coffers are low. We are just starting to see the consequences that the pandemic had on student achievement and performance. The growth percentiles for students fell in all subject areas nationwide. Now it should be obvious of the vital role teachers play in our society. Also, as mentioned earlier teacher retention is a huge problem in education today. If you would care to make a donation for a senior in Palm Beach County Florida who desires to be a teacher the address is below. It's tax deductible and is a great way to honor the memory of a great teacher, Barry Grunow. Thank you.

Lake Worth Dollars for Scholars

Lake Worth Dollars for Scholars
PO Box 1166
Lake Worth Beach, FL 33460

(Notation on check should read: Grunow Memorial Scholarship)

CPSIA information can be obtained
at www.ICGtesting.com
Printed in the USA
LVHW041404150123
737212LV00014B/490